Literary Lives

Founding Editor: Richard Dutton, Professor of English, Lancaster University

This series offers stimulating accounts of the literary careers of the most admired and influential English-language authors. Volumes follow the outline of the writers' working lives, not in the spirit of traditional biography, but aiming to trace the professional, publishing and social contexts which shaped their writing.

W. David Kaye
BEN JONSON

Phillip Mallett
RUDYARD KIPLING

John Worthen
D. H. LAWRENCE

William Gray
ROBERT LOUIS STEVENSON

Angela Smith
KATHERINE MANSFIELD

Lisa Hopkins
CHRISTOPHER MARLOWE

Cedric C. Brown
JOHN MILTON

Peter Davison
GEORGE ORWELL

Linda Wagner-Martin
SYLVIA PLATH

Felicity Rosslyn
ALEXANDER POPE

Ira B. Nadel
EZRA POUND

Richard Dutton
WILLIAM SHAKESPEARE

John Williams
MARY SHELLEY

Michael O'Neill
PERCY BYSSHE SHELLEY

Gary Waller
EDMUND SPENSER

Tony Sharpe
WALLACE STEVENS

Lisa Hopkins
BRAM STOKER

Joseph McMinn
JONATHAN SWIFT

William Christie
SAMUEL TAYLOR COLERIDGE

Leonée Ormond
ALFRED TENNYSON

Peter Shillingsburg
WILLIAM MAKEPEACE THACKERAY

David Wykes
EVELYN WAUGH

Caroline Franklin
MARY WOLLSTONECRAFT

John Mepham
VIRGINIA WOOLF

John Williams
WILLIAM WORDSWORTH

Alasdair D. F. Macrae
W. B. YEATS

Literary Lives
Series Standing Order ISBN 0-333-71486-5 hardcover
Series Standing Order ISBN 0-333-80334-5 paperback
(*outside North America only*)

You can receive future titles in this series as they are published by placing a standing order. Please contact your bookseller or, in case of difficulty, write to us at the address below with your name and address, the title of the series and one of the ISBNs quoted above.

Customer Services Department, Macmillan Distribution Ltd, Houndmills, Basingstoke, Hampshire RG21 6XS, England

---

William Faulkner

A Literary Life

David Rampton

palgrave
macmillan

First published 2008 by
PALGRAVE MACMILLAN
Houndmills, Basingstoke, Hampshire RG21 6XS and
175 Fifth Avenue, New York, N.Y. 10010
Companies and representatives throughout the world

PALGRAVE MACMILLAN is the global academic imprint of the Palgrave Macmillan division of St. Martin's Press, LLC and of Palgrave Macmillan Ltd. Macmillan® is a registered trademark in the United States, United Kingdom and other countries. Palgrave is a registered trademark in the European Union and other countries.

ISBN-13: 978-1-4039-4680-5   hardback
ISBN-10: 1-4039-4680-9   hardback

This book is printed on paper suitable for recycling and made from fully managed and sustained forest sources. Logging, pulping and manufacturing processes are expected to conform to the environmental regulations of the country of origin.

A catalogue record for this book is available from the British Library.

Library of Congress Cataloging-in-Publication Data

Rampton, David, 1950–
  William Faulkner: a literary life / David Rampton.
      p. cm. — (Literary lives)
  Includes bibliographical references and index.
  ISBN 1-4039-4680-9 (alk. paper)
    1. Faulkner, William, 1897–1962. 2. Authors, American—20th century—
      Biography. I. Title.
PS3511.A86Z946935 2008
  813'.52—dc22
  [B]   2008000155

10   9   8   7   6   5   4   3   2   1
17   16   15   14   13   12   11   10   09   08

Printed and bound in Great Britain by
CPI Antony Rowe, Chippenham and Eastbourne

For Elizabeth

Contents

Preface and Acknowledgements

With so many excellent biographies of Faulkner available, the emphasis in this literary life had to be on the adjective rather than the noun. That choice resolved one problem only to create another, namely how to justify adding to what has already been said in all the books and articles devoted to Faulkner's fiction. One of the critics in Frederic Crews's parody of academic criticism, *The Pooh Perplex,* remarks that 'our ideal in English studies is to amass as much commentary as possible upon the literary work, so as to let the world know how deeply we respect it.' By this criterion, Faulkner is probably the most deeply respected American writer who ever lived. If those who read him, for the intense pleasure of the experience or with a combined sense of intrigue and bafflement, find something of interest here, I shall feel at least partly vindicated. The references in my notes acknowledge only a small fraction of my indebtedness to Faulkner scholars and critics. They are an extraordinarily large and diverse group with a formidable amount of expertise in a range of areas, and I have greatly benefitted from their engagement with his fiction. My colleagues in the Department of English at the University of Ottawa deserve special mention as well for being so supportive and for setting such high standards with their own work. I also want to extend my most heartfelt gratitude to the departmental support staff there for making my administrative tasks so pleasant during the period I was working on this book. At Palgrave Macmillan, Richard Dutton helped from the outset by outlining the directions the project might take and was always encouraging. Thanks are also due to Palgrave's readers for their helpful suggestions, to Paula Kennedy for her enthusiastic support and her seemingly limitless patience, to Christabel Scaife for her resourcefulness and encouragement, and to the staff of Macmillan India Ltd for copy-editing and guiding the typescript through the final stages.

Finally I would like to thank my family for their forbearance during all those nights when 'sharing the computer' meant watching me work on it. This book is dedicated to my wife Elizabeth, to whom my gratitude for so many things is not the less heartfelt for being so inadequately expressed.

Grateful acknowledgement is made to the following for permission to reprint previously published material:

William Faulkner, for the following excerpts:
From *Soldiers' Pay*: reprinted with the permission of Liveright Publishing Corporation and Chatto & Windus/The Random House Group, Ltd.; from *Mosquitoes*: reprinted with the permission of Liveright Publishing Corporation and Chatto & Windus/The Random House Group, Ltd.; from *Flags in the Dust*: reprinted with the permission of Random House, Inc. and Chatto & Windus/The Random House Group, Ltd.; from *The Sound and the Fury*: reprinted with the permission of Random House, Inc. and Curtis Brown, Ltd.; from *As I Lay Dying*: reprinted with the permission of Random House, Inc.; from *Sanctuary*: reprinted with the permission of Random House, Inc. and Chatto & Windus/The Random House Group, Ltd.; from *Light in August*: reprinted with the permission of Random House, Inc. and Curtis Brown, Ltd.; from *Pylon*: reprinted with the permission of Random House, Inc.; from *Absalom, Absalom!*: reprinted with the permission of Random House, Inc. and Curtis Brown, Ltd.; from *The Unvanquished*: reprinted with the permission of Random House, Inc.; from *The Wild Palms* [*If I Forget Thee, Jerusalem*]: reprinted with the permission of Random House, Inc.; from *The Hamlet*: reprinted with the permission of Random House, Inc.; from *Go Down, Moses*: reprinted with the permission of Random House, Inc.; from *Intruder in the Dust*: reprinted with the permission of Random House, Inc.; from *Requiem for a Nun*: reprinted with the permission of Random House, Inc. and Chatto & Windus/The Random House Group, Ltd.; from *A Fable*: reprinted with the permission of Random House, Inc. and Chatto & Windus/The Random House Group, Ltd.; from *The Town*: reprinted with the permission of Random House, Inc. and W.W. Norton & Company, Inc.; from *The Mansion*: reprinted with the permission of Random House, Inc. and Chatto & Windus/The Random House Group, Ltd.; and from *The Reivers*: reprinted with the permission of Random House, Inc. and Chatto & Windus/The Random House Group, Ltd.

1
Introduction

There are great artists who simply unfold, like Mozart, and those who give the impression of being in a state of constant evolution, like Picasso.[1] William Faulkner (1897–1962) is a splendid example of a writer who managed to do both. Even as he worked out the continuities of his regional world, creating and populating the imaginary county he called Yoknapatawpha, he was responsible for some of the twentieth century's most startlingly original work. He insisted he had only one subject ('I am telling the same story over and over, which is myself and the world'[2]) even as he explored an impressive array of different ones. Although he was constantly compared to other novelists, his books helped redefine the genre. His style was distinctive from the beginning, but he put it to the most varied uses imaginable. All this makes Faulkner's career particularly intriguing for the challenges it offers those interested in defining its contours. Its development is so striking, its stages so marked, its output so varied, and its longevity so impressive, that it invites us to think of serial Faulkners, each one worth studying for its own sake and as part of a composite portrait.

Faulkner began as a poet and fiction writer in search of a style and subject matter, trying to imitate voices he admired and sometimes having his own drowned out by them. Few aspiring young authors can have lived more intensely in books or for books. He wanted to imitate his great-grandfather, who had been, among other things, a hugely successful popular writer. Influenced by the Decadents, Faulkner began his literary life in thrall to aestheticism. As a special student at the University of Mississippi – he had dropped out of high school and sometimes referred to himself as a 'veteran sixth-grader'[3] – he began publishing in his early 20s in the literary magazines, at a time of great ferment in the arts. He gave bound books of his poems to young women

1

he admired. His work created so much controversy that his request for membership in a literary society was turned down. While managing to find gainful employment, he also spent a lot of his early adulthood doing what Whitman, another American autodidact, described as creative loafing. But however uncommitted he was to the menial tasks he performed at places like the University Post Office in Oxford, Mississippi – like Whitman he was eventually fired from his job – Faulkner quickly developed an astonishing capacity for hard work, and he came to savour the solitude necessary for doing it. In New Orleans and back in Oxford, eventually on trips to New York and abroad, Faulkner started to live the literary life he had dreamed of for so long. Between 1925 and 1928, he wrote sketches and stories and published three novels, having more or less abandoned poetry for prose.

The next incarnation began in earnest when he went from being an interesting young writer to a literary innovator intent on producing his own stunningly original creations. As the author of a series of novels published between 1929 and 1942 – *The Sound and the Fury*, *As I Lay Dying*, *Light in August*, and *Absalom, Absalom!* among others – Faulkner was responsible for a body of work that was to make him the single most important twentieth-century American novelist. Most of these books sold poorly, and even *Sanctuary*, a *succès de scandale* that came out in 1932, did not make him as much money as it should have, given the number of copies sold. Still, the 1930s was an extremely productive decade for Faulkner, during which he wrote almost all of the fiction for which he is remembered today. Selling short stories to national magazines and working for long stretches as a scriptwriter in Hollywood during this time proved quite lucrative, but he was constantly beset by money worries, and, like Hawthorne and Melville before him, he resented having to compromise his artistic ideals in order to make a living.

Reviewers and critics were interested in Faulkner from the beginning. Some of his first published poems were parodied. His early novels attracted positive and astute notices along with the negative ones. The series of great novels he produced, starting with *The Sound and the Fury*, were enthusiastically reviewed by a number of thoughtful commentators, yet the same books were also harshly criticized for their wilful obscurity, obsession with cruelty and violence, and lack of social relevance. Faulkner was the subject of discussion at a conference devoted to Southern literature as early as 1931, a much sought after writer of short stories throughout the decade, and made the cover of *Time* in 1939. Although critical interest in his novels flourished, by the time

The Portable Faulkner appeared in 1946 almost all his books were out of print. Its success and the popularity of reprinted novels from the 1930s helped Faulkner win the 1949 Nobel Prize for Literature (awarded in 1950). In the next decade he went on to become something of a venerable spokesman in American letters, 'articulate in the national voice',[4] as he put it in a letter. The success made him the subject of a debate that sought to redefine exactly what his strengths as a novelist were: the Faulkner industry proper was born. Its development over the last 50 years has been astonishing, even when compared to the relentless appropriation of other modernist writers by an academic audience. In this sense at least one can say of him, as Auden did of Yeats, that on his death in 1962 'he became his admirers'.[5]

Part of Faulkner's appeal for readers and critics can be explained by how acutely he seems to have anticipated his own posterity. His fiction has an uncanny ability to adapt itself to his readership's changing tastes and interests, as implausible as that sounds. His work is also extremely varied and, once he had finished learning by imitation, he never sounded like anyone but himself. When one adds to the lives already discussed those assigned him by his professional readers in academia, Faulkner's evolution is that much more striking. Whatever one makes of the claim that Faulkner the Great American Novelist of the 1950s was in part a creation of American intellectuals and the politics of the Cold War,[6] he has been recreated posthumously, not once but a number of times, as successive schools of criticism find things in his multifaceted work that enable them to make him their own. There is of course more continuity and overlap in this series of lives than such a breakdown implies, and I shall be emphasizing that as well in considering them, but the accent in what follows will be on the multiplicity of the literary incarnations that can be discerned in the course of Faulkner's career, and on the way his varied output has affected his reputation.

Though he courted fame for a time and enjoyed some of the trappings of it, Faulkner insisted that he wanted to be remembered only for what he had written, 'abolished and voided from history': 'It is my aim and every effort bent, that the sum and history of my life, which in the same sentence is my obit and epitaph too, shall be them both: He wrote the books and he died.'[7] Posterity was unlikely to be satisfied with such an epitaph for a writer who drew extensively on his own experiences, shocked sensibilities, frustrated expectations, puzzled would-be admirers, counselled the citizenry on national questions, represented his country on cultural missions abroad, and generally put the stamp of his personality on the work at every stage. 'If I had not existed', he said in the *Paris Review* interview, 'someone else would have written me.' That, we can say with some assurance, is manifestly not true, but it does speak eloquently of Faulkner's desire for privacy and of his conviction that in this sense 'the artist is of no importance.'[8] Like Frost and Hemingway, he was one of the few twentieth-century American writers of his generation to achieve national celebrity status. Because he occupied such a privileged position on the fault-lines of so many questions concerning race, class, and gender, reading his fiction for what it says about all manner of political and social issues has been a matter of intense interest for more than half a century. Yet even when he had acquired considerable fame, he often sought to deprecate the importance of the literary side of his life, zealously guarding his privacy from prying journalists and would-be interviewers.

He was semi-successful while he was alive, but ultimately of course it did not work. At last count there have been more than a dozen thick descriptions of Faulkner's life, and many important shorter accounts devoted to specific aspects of it. In fact, there have been so many books and articles, written by so many diligent and insightful researchers and critics, that we know more about William Faulkner – his background and family, his reading and struggles to get published, his triumphs and personal tragedies, the history and culture of the region he came to be identified with in the public mind, the things that happened to and around him during the almost 65 years he lived, and the complex links between his life and work – than we do about any other American writer. Half-remembered lines from his work stay in the mind: 'The past is never dead. It's not even past'; 'Between grief and nothing, I will take grief'; 'I believe that man will not merely endure: he will prevail.' There has been a much-publicized faux Faulkner contest every year since 1989, in which the best Faulkner parody is awarded a prize, a sure sign of an enduring popularity. Allusions to him crop up in films directed by Robert Altman and the Coen brothers. As far as twentieth-century American writers are concerned, Faulkner is as big as they get. Sales of his fiction were given a boost recently when Oprah Winfrey chose *The Sound and the Fury*, *As I Lay Dying*, and *Light in August* for her book club in the summer of 2005. Even this remarkable appearance, replete with excellent lectures and support offered by some of America's most distinguished Faulknerians, led to a spirited debate about his work: who should read it, what its status was, and how it should be used, including a great deal of speculation about whether 'Our Lady of Self-Help' would try to dragoon Faulkner's fiction into service for whatever advice to dysfunctional families or solutions for those suffering from low self-esteem she was pushing. Oprah did nothing of the sort, and the members of the biggest book club in the world enjoyed this foray into new territory and learned a lot from it. Another literary life had been created.

As I suggested above, Faulkner was the most dedicated of craftsmen, and spent an enormous amount of time reworking his material, obsessed with the idea of getting it right, yet he answered one interviewer's question about his profession by saying that he was not a writer but a farmer who likes to tell stories, and he often described himself as a failed poet. He shunned gatherings in which writing people congregated and always felt more comfortable with those who knew the land, preferably his land, people who liked hunting and fishing and farming.[9] This is just one of the many contradictions that make his career such an intriguing one. In what follows, then, I have focussed on a range of questions linked to his complex responses to the literary lives he lived. I consider Faulkner's motives for writing and how they changed as his career developed; how committed to experimentation he was and how this links him to a more comprehensive modernist tradition than is sometimes recognized; how keen he was to keep the reader off balance while he worked through his own ways of making his material new, and how this desire characterizes his major fiction and is a significant part of his lesser works, early and late; how skilfully he represents his characters' desires to impose meanings on their experience and how arbitrary those attempts often are; how aware he is of the limits of language and how keen he is, by virtue of his interest in innovation, to have a go at saying it anyway; how influenced by the fable form he was, not just in a later phase, but right through his career; how confused he originally was about how to use the vaguely autobiographical material that so intrigued him and how he managed to make great art and strange hybrids out of that confusion; how painstakingly he acquired his knowledge of Southern society and its history and how comprehensive and coherent his view of its glories and its failings was; how marked he was by a curious blend of contempt for humanity ('human beings are terrible', 'man stinks the same stink no matter where in time') and respect for its capacity to 'endure' and 'prevail'; and how closely related he considered comedy and tragedy to be, with tragedy 'walking a tightrope ... between the bizarre and the terrible'.[10]

The subjects that I have been outlining are also inevitably bound up with matters stylistic, and it has been suggested that 'The best part of a writer's biography is not the record of his adventures but the story of his style.'[11] Faulkner's story is particularly instructive in this regard. He could be unapologetic when quizzed on why his novels were so difficult to read. There is the following famous exchange in the *Paris Review* interview: '"[Interviewer] Some people say they can't understand your writing, even after they read it two or three times. What approach would you suggest for them?" "[Faulkner] Read it four times."'[12] But he could also be quite self-deprecating about the way his novels were written. He wrote to Cowley, while *The Portable Faulkner* was being prepared: 'The style, as you divine, is a result of the solitude, and granted a bad one. It was further complicated by an inherited regional or geographical (Hawthorne would say, racial) curse. You might say, studbook style: "by Southern Rhetoric out of Solitude" or "Oratory out of Solitude."'[13] Especially when the tricky business of representing mental processes is concerned, sentences can veer off in strange directions, sometimes go on for pages, or seem to break down before their point has been clearly made; figures of speech shift in unusual ways, the lexical register varies widely, and syntax is obscured. Sorting out how much of this is a 'regional curse' and how much an attempt to be faithful to those processes of thought that he was interested in conveying is part of my project as well. Faulkner may have been the most uneven great writer who ever lived, but a summary judgement like that begs all kinds of questions that are still worth asking.

It is interesting to think about why, despite all that has been written about him, there are still so many fundamental contradictions in the way he is perceived, why all the competing claims that characterized the early reception of his work are a permanent fixture of the commentary it has generated since. Was Faulkner so involved in a world of masks, so remote in his personal and public dealings, that he is fated to remain an enigma (Donald Kartiganer, Joel Williamson), or are his character traits and the contours of his psychological makeup and relationships clear (Frederick Karl)? Does he resemble his great nineteenth-century forebears – Balzac, Dickens – in his desire to create figures on one large stage whose activities are governed by the same set of cultural norms (Edmund Wilson), or does his distrust of grand narratives make the comparison with these creators of worlds misleading (Philip Weinstein)? Why has he been criticized for his blatant misogyny ('in no other writer in the world do pejorative stereotypes of women appear with greater frequency and on more levels'[14] [Leslie Fiedler]) and praised as a feminist who celebrates womanhood in its infinite variety (Linda Wagner)? Why has he been called a profoundly Christian writer (Randall Stewart), even though many feel that God is absent from his works (Marcel Aymé)? How can Faulkner be a puritan moralist (Roger Asselineau) on the one hand, and a writer who sees the individual as the victim of chance desires, neuroses, phobias, and conditioned reflexes (Henry Steele Commager) on the other? Was he uninterested in the intellectual tradition of his time (Lionel Trilling) or profoundly indebted to it (Daniel Singal)? Why do critics like F.R. Leavis dismiss as shamelessly self-indulgent and overwritten passages in Faulkner's novels that others – Alfred Kazin, John Longley – commend as memorable representations of an exalted symbolic power worthy of Joyce? Is there a clear line to be drawn between writing to please a public and writing to please himself? For example, did Hollywood have a negative effect on him as a novelist (David Minter) or a beneficial one (Toni Morrison)?

Other questions that may have no definitive answers follow hard upon these. How did Faulkner's Janus-like attitude to his own profession affect his fiction? Is it significant that a novelist who so resisted the idea of being an 'Author' became such an inspiration to innumerable writers, very different from him and from each other? How does Faulkner's use of historical material relate to the activities of his characters, who are themselves preoccupied by trying to make sense of their own history, by reimagining it, assessing it, and resisting its attempt to master them? Are some of the questions associated with his work simply the inevitable consequence of critics' endless search for originality, or is there something in the very nature of Faulkner's fiction that compels such singular and diverse responses? Perhaps the search for definitive answers to such an imposing list is as doomed to failure as his characters' efforts to exorcize their respective demons, but just lining them all up like that will help give some sense of just how much is still at issue insofar as this particular writer is concerned. Someone determined to add to the material already written on Faulkner has a lot to answer for; a literary life appropriate to this moment in the history of his reception has a lot to find answers for.

This diversity of views may help explain why, despite the colossal amount of secondary material that his work has generated, Faulkner's commentators still tend to emphasize how much remains to be done on him. A collection of essays by the group of distinguished Faulknerians who gathered in 1997 to mark the centennial celebration of his birth is a case in point. In that volume, Lothar Hönnighausen argues that Faulkner's masks should be analysed, not for the moralistic or clinical conclusions that might be drawn from them, but as shifting patterns in his life and work; for Thomas McHaney, the problem is the lack of attention paid to Faulkner's intellectual development; for André Bleikasten, the paucity of serious study devoted to Faulkner and time, Faulkner and sensations/perceptions, and Faulkner's brooding on suffering and death. Although all of these topics have been the subject of extensive sorts of scrutiny, these critics want more, so impressed are they by Faulkner's uniqueness, so moved by the experience of reading him, so committed to dig deeper and understand better, and so determined to continue the impassioned discussion of his work that began more than 75 years ago.

These various takes on what remains to be done dovetail nicely with other meditations on the somewhat amorphous subject I propose to focus on in what follows. In a brilliant essay, first given as a paper at the 1998 Faulkner and Yoknapatawpha conference, Joseph Urgo suggested that all the attention paid to what Faulkner represents in his novels, 'the Southern qualities, ... race, sex, gender, and class issues', has prevented us from acquiring 'an adequate understanding of [Faulkner's] mind'. Urgo notes that 'Faulkner the intellectual remains enigmatic', and says that the one thing needful in Faulkner criticism is more thoughts on thinking, the thing that his novels are mainly about, which he defines by quoting this definition from *A Fable*: 'To think: not that dreamy hoping and wishing and believing (but mainly just waiting) that we would think is thinking, but some fierce and rigid concentration that at any time – tomorrow, today, next moment, this one – will change the shape of the earth.'[15] At the end of his splendid study of Faulkner, *The Ink of Melancholy*, Bleikasten strikes a similar note, suggesting that 'little has been said so far about [Faulkner's] thought as it actually moves in his fiction'.[16] Defining what one means by 'Faulkner the intellectual' is as tricky as explaining how his thought 'actually moves', how he works at representing how the mind receives and processes impressions, how he uses different kinds of narrative voice to work through ideas, or what effects the emotions have on his characters' attempts at ratiocination, although all these things are linked. What follows is among other things an extensive look at different examples of 'fierce and rigid concentration' in Faulkner's fiction, a process often driven by emotions such as fear, despair, hatred, and outrage, at how his interest in representing this process develops over his career, and at how often this 'fierce and rigid concentration' manifests itself in fierce and rigid conversations that men have with each other and themselves. There are other, equally interesting ways of thinking about his literary life. Ultimately, the justification for bringing together this set of issues as part of an attempt to plot the shape of a career that spanned more than 40 years, during which Faulkner wrote 19 novels and a clutch of immortal short stories, is that these questions intrigued him, and continue to interest his readers.

Modernist writers often portray the mental isolation of solitary thinkers and the mixed success of their attempts to make connection with the world: Lawrence does it with a figure like Birkin in *Women in Love*, Woolf with Bernard in *The Waves*, Mann with Hans Castorp in

The Magic Mountain, and and all those furious debates between Naphta and Settembrini that he listens to in his mountain retreat. The ideas generated by such portrayals constitute an important contribution to twentieth-century thought. Faulkner's characters are, for the most part, not speculative thinkers. For every Horace Benbow or Gavin Stevens there are a dozen inarticulate or semi-articulate types who have trouble finding the words for the questions that interest or the problems that afflict them. Yet the way Faulkner represents their thinking, in the broad sense of that term, makes him relevant here. His characters are often intensely interested in the past or obsessed by some slight real or imagined, some notion of personal or family honour, some conviction strongly held, and this makes them characters in search of explanations and justifications. His fiction tells the story of that search and its often tragic consequences. The characters in Faulkner who engage so avidly with uncertainty, ponder their origins so fiercely, size up so intently the forces arrayed against them, and so often end up being complicit with those forces in acting against their own best interests, these figures and their interactions make his fiction relevant to the twentieth century's intellectual concerns. The discursive role assigned the narrative voice, as it summarizes and interprets, digresses and explains, is important in this regard as well.

Many of the great modernists are also avid theoreticians of their own profession. Proust wrote an important introduction to his translation of Ruskin's aesthetic treatise *The Bible of Amiens;* Hermann Broch analysed the breakdown of values at the end of the nineteenth century in his study of von Hofmannsthal; Andrei Bely discussed the ways violent social upheaval affected art in his essay 'Revolution and Culture'; Virginia Woolf argued in 'Mr Bennett and Mrs Brown' that new aesthetic assumptions were needed because the old world had died in 1910. These figures were keen to stake out positions, to take part in an argument, and to describe what they saw as a profound change in the way human beings had come to perceive the world and how literature was to reflect that. American novelists were interested in all of these issues, but in the United States during the first half of the century, the poets tended to be the ones with theoretical things to say: Pound, Eliot, Stevens, even the antitheoretical E.E. Cummings and William Carlos Williams, as different as they all are, resemble each other in this respect. But there was no sustained attempt in America to articulate a poetics of the novel during this period, unless one includes the working out of a set of progressive ideas held by some of the naturalists and novelists such as Lewis, Caldwell, and Steinbeck. Whatever his relation to modernism, Faulkner clearly had no desire to make a contribution to it in the expository, conceptual sense. He wrote no artistic manifestos, nor did he pen prefaces or afterwords to his novels in which he took up the aesthetic questions they posed. Instead, he contented himself with pronouncing occasional *obiter dicta* ('The people to me come first, the symbolism comes second'[17]) and answering questions about his work posed by students and professors on university campuses or at seminars where his fiction was the subject. Although his comments in such forums are always of interest, especially when he is not feeling embattled, Faulkner is one of those writers who gives the impression that he would prefer to let his published work do the talking. He sometimes seems fearful of being exposed by intellectuals as not knowing what a writer is supposed to know. Yet the emphasis on thinking as fierce concentration in his fiction, including questions such as how adequately language can represent reality and how our desire to make narratives of our lives affects them, arguably constitutes a contribution at one remove to the debates that modernism helped create. The exchanges in the literary salons that Faulkner avoided by staying away or drinking quietly by himself, he participates in by charting the contours of the minds he created.

The next chapter is an account of Faulkner's early poetry and fiction, an interesting combination of experimentation and imitation. He had an unusually long period of apprenticeship for a writer: in effect Faulkner was a young man, at least in the aesthetic sense, for almost half of his 65 years. The leisurely pace at which he learned his trade between 1919 and 1928 and the variety of the fictional experiments he engaged in before writing his great novels make this a particularly important period in his literary life. It manifests itself in all kinds of ways in his later work. Critics have pointed out the quasi-Keatsian 'negative capability' that Faulkner possessed at this early stage, as he assumes various guises. Yet one of the chief traits mentioned in the letter in which Keats defines that capacity is an ability to obliterate the self and identify completely with whatever creature or object has attracted one's attention. The Narcissus-like figures in his early verse that serve as stand-ins for the author – the Marble Faun, Pierrot – systematically represent a solipsistic being quite different from Keats's chameleon poet. When the characters in Faulkner's poetry and early novels reflect on what they experience, their speculations are often couched in a sort of double language, one inspired by a combination of an erotic and an aesthetic sensibility. Studying this language is crucial for understanding one of the aspects of Faulkner's thought, especially when it tries to deal with the swirling emotions that bedevil all these youthful attempts to reason with desire and make sense of the larger world.

Chapter 3 takes up *The Sound and the Fury* and *As I Lay Dying*, and interrogates them with a view to finding answers to similar questions concerning aesthetic choices and the representation of mental processes in Faulkner's work. With these novels Faulkner started to make himself a reputation as one of the most interesting and challenging writers of his generation. They eventually helped define what innovative fiction meant in the American context, and the way he wrote them, in reaction to publishers' rejections and public indifference, listening to no voice but his own, is important for anyone interested in understanding what this breakthrough meant for Faulkner's career. I go on to deal in Chapter 4 with other fiction written between 1930 and 1935: *Sanctuary*, *Light in August*, and some of Faulkner's best-known short stories belong to this period. *Sanctuary* we know he wrote to appeal to a new readership. The version we have represents a complete rewriting of the original, which the author dismissed as a 'cheap idea'. The radically altered style and the different approach to representing what goes through the minds of a new set of characters make it of particular interest here. *Light in August* weaves three stories together in ways that show how keen Faulkner is to go on experimenting in structural terms. The experimental prose and the play with different voices found in his early fiction take on new life and raise new questions in this novel. Finally, the short stories from the early 1930s give us a Faulkner who is very much a product of this era, reacting in yet another way to market forces – his stories became quite popular and earned him considerable sums – and organizing in powerful and evocative fashion the material that he had begun to make a part of the Yoknapatawpha world.

Chapters 5 and 6 are devoted to works from the second half of this extraordinarily productive period in Faulkner's career. Here he continues to pursue his double purpose, experimenting with formal innovation in some very different novels, and filling in the history of his imaginary county. Having examined in previous chapters some of the ways that Faulkner represents the movement of thought and the circumstances that can both occasion and inhibit it, here I want to study what happens when this subject takes centre stage. The uncertainty into which reflection plunges so many of his characters often helps create pivotal moments in their lives. Their attempts to reflect on their situation by inventing stories that will help them make sense of those moments are also of great interest in the fiction from this period. In *Pylon*, a book he published in 1934, he pares down the human, eschewing the sorts of characters he has occupied himself with to this point, and focussing on the mysterious forces that are reshaping humanity in the midst of a technological revolution. *Absalom, Absalom!* is *Pylon*'s complement, a novel in which Faulkner gives in to the impulse to produce a novel which contains practically nothing but fierce speculation, a novel whose subject is meditation, uncertainty, the way thinking about the past involves the attempt to create a self and a history that will be more than idiosyncratic fantasies. In Chapter 6, I consider three novels published between 1938 and 1942. In *The Unvanquished*, Faulkner revisits Southern history, and here the emphasis is not so much on what happened in the nineteenth century when the nation almost tore itself apart, but on how those divisions affect those who, in reflecting on them, try to understand their ancestry and the consequences of being born and raised in the South. *If I Forget Thee, Jerusalem* organizes itself around another sort of fierce reflection. The protagonists' meditations on time, death, emotion, and thinking itself help frame one story that makes up the novel; the narrator's ruminations on equally large questions shape the other. Like both these novels, *Go Down, Moses* is another strikingly uneven book, despite its thematic unity. Again, Faulkner's interest in having his characters think about their past and America's origins is responsible for the most successful parts of it.

In Chapter 7, I look at works dealing with the Snopes family, 'Barn Burning', *The Hamlet*, *The Town*, and *The Mansion*. This fiction occupies the very centre of the regional world he worked so hard to create, and Faulkner deliberately arranged the novels to form a trilogy even though they were written over a period of some 20 years. During most of his writing life, this imaginary county meant far more to him than it did to his readers. He started working on it in the mid-1920s, in a story called 'Father Abraham' that made him realize that he had discovered his own 'little postage stamp of native soil was worth writing about', that he would 'never live long enough to exhaust it', and that it would enable him to create 'a cosmos' of his own.[18] As early as 1931, he acknowledged the need to think about maintaining consistency when recycling characters and events from this world. But few contemporary readers and reviewers knew or cared about this. The first version of his third novel, *Flags in the Dust*, splendidly confirmed Faulkner's conviction that his material lay here, in the Yoknapatawpha materials, but it was a flop with the editors at Boni and Liveright, and not published in the original version until 1973. The bulk of his fiction after *Sartoris* (the title of the revised version of *Flags in the Dust*) helped define the shape of his new cosmos, but the novels mostly sold well or badly, and received laudatory or hostile notices for other reasons. Although now he is firmly rooted in the American consciousness as the creator of a world on the scale of Thomas Hardy's, with its maps and ancestors, its history and mythology, its parallels and commonalities, for much of his career a lot of those who read him did not think of him in this way.

It is important to remember this when one tries to assess the importance of the Snopes trilogy in Faulkner's career. In one sense this family never left him alone, and he sometimes wrote to his publishers complaining that his preoccupation with their stories was preventing his getting on with other books. Yet his career is best understood not only by how he pieced together the story of his imaginary county as it came to him, but also by how he dealt with what Yeats called our daimon, the destiny that 'would ever set us to the hardest work among those not impossible'.[19] For Faulkner, it was telling stories that convey the complex nature of experience. For him, this involved representing how an impressive range of mixed-up people reflect on things, why this process is so often so impassioned and so difficult to convey adequately, why the experiences they have are as shifting and evanescent in their minds as the selves to whom they happen, and why being conscious of being conscious entails paradoxes that are endlessly interesting to play with and extraordinarily difficult to resolve. In other words, during the years that he wrote about the Snopes family and Yoknapatawpha, his mind was on many other things as well.

The last chapter is dedicated to four novels from the end of Faulkner's career, *Intruder in the Dust*, *Requiem for a Nun*, *A Fable*, and *The Reivers*. Anyone interested in Faulkner the intellectual or the 'fierce and rigid concentration' in his novels will feel very much at home here. Not only does Gavin Stevens, the resident thinker in the late fiction, play a significant role in two of these works, but the first three are full of ideas about American history, the nature of the self, the concept of justice, the sources and longevity of human civilization – the list is a long one – and even in *The Reivers*, Faulkner pauses to muse about the relations between the present and the past, making his last novel in part a study of what he refers to there as 'the inescapable destiny of America' (800).[20] In using these books to think about America and Western culture, he offers readers a proleptic view of how an increasingly secular, materialist civilization might evolve. Oscar Wilde once remarked that 'A map of the world that does not include Utopia is not worth even glancing at, for it leaves out the one country at which Humanity is always landing.'[21] Faulkner is not much given to utopian thinking, but his ideas about the world that we keep failing to create haunt these last works and give them much of their complexity and power.

2
Early Faulkner

In 1925, having finished his first novel and about to start another, Faulkner reviewed some books by Joseph Hergesheimer, a popular writer of the time. In the review, he criticizes one of Hergesheimer's novels, *Linda Condon*, for its artificialities and escapism, its lifeless characters and lack of movement. Yet the fact that the author has immersed himself in such a world is strangely moving for Faulkner, and he concludes that 'the book troubles the heart, the faintest shadow of an insistence; as though one were waked from a dream, for a space into a quiet region of light and shadow, soundless and beyond despair. La figlia della sua mente, l'amorosa l'idea [literally: the woman of his mind, the idea of love]'.[1] Faulkner leaves it at that, the Italian unexplained and untranslated, and moves on to the next novel to be considered. The phrase is a quotation from the novel he was reviewing, and Hergesheimer got it from a poem called 'Aspasia' by the nineteenth-century Italian romantic writer Giacomo Leopardi.[2] In *Linda Condon*, the poem is cited by a strange old man who tells the novel's eponymous heroine, at the time a young girl, a story about the mythical past, when hermits rose to Paradise after praying, and all was 'angels and archangels', 'black castles', 'broad meadows', and 'silk tents with ivory pegs and poles of gold'. He goes on to evoke the image of 'the loveliest of women riding a snow-white mule' along with her dark double 'on a leopard with yellow eyes', tells her that love constitutes an 'escape from the fatality of the flesh', yet insists that the body is involved in its mysteries, which only the artist can put into words, 'incredibly lovely in actuality and still never to be grasped'.[3] Then he quotes the lines from Leopardi's poem (also without attribution), and his speech trails off rather bathetically. His odd attempt at surreptitious seduction over, he rushes from the room.

In the Leopardi poem, the lines referred to are as richly significant as the lush setting *Linda Condon* provides for them. They are addressed to a lady, and they recapitulate some of the points made by Hergesheimer's character. The speaker praises the lady for her divine beauty, compares its effect on him to music, and notes that both reveal the mysteries of Elysium to the uninitiated. Imprisoned by mortality, the beholder confuses his desire with reality. What he loves is *'la figlia/Della sua mente, l'amorosa idea'*, the idea represented by the beloved, and not her physical body. The consequences – for him, for her – when he realizes his error are extremely unpleasant. Leopardi's point about the excesses of desire is the focus of his poignantly rendered hymn to human fallibility. So, in its ornate way and slightly dated way, is Hergesheimer's.

Both the literal meaning of this poem and its metaphorical implications are a useful introduction for the material to be considered in this chapter. In his early work, Faulkner explores the gap between desire and its object in the conceptual sense by having his characters speculate a lot about it. The locales in which such reflections take place are often as exotic as the ones the old man evokes in *Linda Condon*. And the irony at the heart of Faulkner's vision, the elusive essence of the thing desired, lucidly conveyed by the Italian poet a hundred years earlier, is the stumbling block for these characters as they try to bring their erotic fantasies and their aesthetic visions into alignment. Blundering through the world, mistaking their own ideas for some kind of reality, intrigued by visions that blend the menacing and the perverse with the bucolic and the voluptuous, eager to make a grand gesture in the name of love and unable to participate in the mutual exchange necessary if love is to mean anything, the men in both Leopardi and Hergesheimer resemble the yearning, baffled, striving, defeated creatures that inhabit Faulkner's world. They are fiery and languid, comic and tragic, fiercely reflective and grimly active by turns. Too ambitious to settle for what they have when they do find what they are so desperately seeking, or too frustrated by their inability to hold onto to it, they tend to become very unhappy. Tracking these subjects in Faulkner's early work will help us understand the assumptions with which he proceeded at the start of his career and their implications for the major work that was to follow. His characters' mental isolation and their rigid concentration on ways of breaking free of it are vividly reflected in poems and novels that constitute an extended search for something – an insight, an art form – that will deliver what earthly beauty cannot.

Faulkner was a lyric poet for most of his twenties. He once defined poetry as 'some moving, passionate moment of the human condition distilled to its absolute essence. ... there's no room at all for trash. It's got to be absolutely impeccable, absolutely perfect.'[4] This is a revealing definition, combining aestheticist yearning for an idealized union of form and content with an imagist's minimalism. The absence of any reference to narrative or drama and the emphasis on something distilled suggest that Faulkner has the lyric in mind. Working out this perfection in verse proved difficult, mostly because it effectively meant leaving out all the 'moving passionate moment[s]' in human experience that so intrigued him. By surveying his early work, I hope to show how influenced he was by this mixed background, how much he had to learn, and how useful it is to see the work he published during his first decade as a writer as a propaedeutic for the novels that were to follow.

The Marble Faun (written in 1919, published in 1924)[5] is a would-be erotic poem about bodiless sex, one that gives a whole new meaning to the phrase arch self-consciousness: 'Why am I sad? I? Why am I not content?' (12), and so on. Cheesy, pretentious, call it whatever you want, this question and the answers it elicits are central to an understanding of Faulkner's first literary life. What happens in *The Marble Faun* takes place in that hermetically sealed world that he often creates in his early work. There are seasonal changes, but the emphasis is on the timelessness of endless cycles. Spring figures prominently in the poems, but mostly because it too is so sad and the birth it celebrates so painful. Pan makes the occasional appearance, but this goat god is a fairly gloomy guy as well, blowing sorrowful notes and, like the faun, wrapped up in himself. He also does a lot of staring into pools and has a similarly disdainful impression of nature's eternal return. All is 'soaring silver', 'cool / Virginity' (17), and thin dreams, and Faulkner's faun is disgusted by his own body and dreams of turning his beloved's into some sort of rarefied liquid. In conveying all this, the poet shows considerable interest in sex but not much talent for the erotic. As the commentator in Nabokov's *Pale Fire* says: 'In the temperature charts of poetry high is low, and low high, so that the degree at which perfect crystallization occurs is above that of tepid facility.'[6] Articulating the links between one's own desires and the things that excite others depends on understanding this point about adjusting the temperature and having more than a 'tepid facility' for expression.

When the change to summer comes, the verse picks up a bit, as if the poet was getting verbal energy from the slender bodies the faun sees. Nevertheless, no matter how many strange adverbs ('bluely flashing', 'spreading liquidly') and rich colour schemes he deploys, Faulkner needs more material for the persistently vague sense of frustrated desire to work on. Some of the most interesting images are the most implausible – 'like a spider on a veil / Climbs the moon' (29) – and the whole exercise risks seeming a trifle mechanical. David Minter is surely right in suggesting that the poem 'brings Pastoral art and modern aestheticism into a conjunction that ... exposes the weaknesses of pastoral poetry, particularly its artificiality'.[7] That said, pastoral poets like Spenser and Sidney, without the help of modern aestheticism, seem to have got round this difficulty on their own. Incipient arousal, chronic depression, intense self-absorption, Faulkner has already found his subject but is still looking for the right medium.

The 1921 collection of poems entitled *Vision in Spring* has been described as 'the pivotal work in Faulkner's self-apprenticeship'.[8] I want to concentrate on part of one of them, 'Love Song'. It begins with what for all the world reads like Eliot's 'The Love Song of J. Alfred Prufrock' recited by someone with an imperfect memory or a quirky sense of humour: 'Shall I walk, then, through a corridor of profundities / Carefully erect (I am taller than I look) / To a certain door ... and shall I dare / To open it? I smooth my mental hair' (55), that kind of thing. Before Eliot's poem is taken up again in earnest with a repetition of all the famous phrases ('I have measured time ... I grow old ... And do I dare'), Faulkner manages to represent an intriguing picture of the mind in the process of observing its own processes. Here is part of a whole section that reveals some of the difficulties the poet is wrestling with:

> Change and change: the world revolves to worlds,
> To minute whorls
> And particles of soil on careless thumbs.
> Now I shall go alone,
> I shall echo streets of stone, while evening comes ...
>
> But enough. What is all beauty? What, that I
> Should raise my hands palm upward to the sky,
> That I should weakly tremble and fall dumb
> At some cryptic promise or pale gleam; –
> A sudden wing, a word, a cry?
>
> Evening dies, and now that night has come
> Walking still streets, monk-like, grey and dumb;
> Then softly clad in grey lies down again;
> I also rise and walk, and die in dream,
> For dream is death, and death is fathomed dream.
>
> And shall I walk these streets while passing time
> Softly ticks my face, my thinning hair?

> I should have been a priest in floorless halls
> Wearing his eyes thin on a faded manuscript.
> The world revolves. High heels and scented shawls,
> Painted masks, and kisses mouth and mouth:
> Gesture of a senile pantaloon
> To make us laugh.

$$(58–61)$$

Chesterton neatly summarizes one part of the problem with this sort of writing when he notes that 'Youth is almost everything else, but it is hardly ever original.' He goes on to characterize the emotions typical of such verse as 'furious and headlong', and points out that 'its only external outcome is a furious imitation and a headlong obedience.'[9] When Faulkner went looking for an appropriate language for the combination of timidity and self-assertion he wanted to communicate, he found it in Eliot's poem. Those afflicted with writer's block are sometimes advised simply to copy out favourite passages until they find their own voice. The result is something with all the eclecticism and impersonality of a young writer's commonplace book, the means by which he pays his ultimate homage to his spiritual guides and, in offering slight variations on what are practically quotes, takes short, aided flights from the security of simple recitation. Faulkner no doubt admires Eliot for many reasons, but one of the most important is the skill with which he recounts the pleasures of poetic despair, and that is very much the subject here. The emphasis in such verse is on the contrast between outside and inside, the cosmic and the humble consciousness. Whatever actually partakes of the physical world Faulkner can remake more or less successfully in language – for example, the first and last stanzas quoted – whereas posing makes for a language that poses.

The poetic argument of *Vision in Spring* turns on the question 'What is all beauty?', a rather large one that shows clearly how hard it is to 'think' in this kind of poetry. Similar difficulties attend the speaker's tendency to 'weakly tremble and fall dumb'. It is hard to fall upon the thorns of life a hundred years after Shelley did it, without sounding excessively self-regarding, or without confirming the reader's sense that the cross-century dialogue with precursors is getting in the way of facilitating other contact. However much the speaker wants to discuss beauty in the abstract, or communicate the frustrations of love unrequited, it is the night like a monk in grey, the priest with fading eyesight, the ascetics in a world of voluptuous ecstasies enjoyed by others ('kisses mouth and mouth') that make an impression. And, as we shall see, it is these details that survive the transfer to fiction, often intact.

Faulkner is forthright about his desire to emulate the genius of his poetic mentors, and he was a shrewd enough critic of what he produced to know when he had not succeeded. He has characters in his early fiction make fun of his own poems, for example. Yet all these years of imitation were necessary for him to work through to an acceptance of how different he was from Swinburne, Eliot, and Conrad Aiken *et al.*, how his work might complement theirs instead of just imitating it. Some have argued that that moment came relatively early. Judith Sensibar, for example, the critic who led the way in showing just how interconnected Faulkner's poetry and fiction are, sees *Vision in Spring* as much more ambitious than a mere 'obsequious' paraphrase,[10] as a parody of 'Prufrock', of Faulkner's persona Pierrot, and of himself. Ambitious the poem certainly is, at least in places, and the case for parody is a compelling one. Yet those looking for the healthy scepticism, lack of respect for authority, wry humour, and insightful critique involved in the best parody may not be completely satisfied with this reading. Faulkner is still feeling his way towards the creative imitation that involves speaking from the security of an achieved position: Pound on Browning, Beerbohm on Conrad, E.B. White on Hemingway, Swinburne on himself. The supposed intimacy of the lyric makes us feel we know the author in ways we could not if he were (say) writing a novel, and that very intimacy is often the first object of the parodist's attack. And of course parody and lyric poetry can exist alongside each other, in the same poem or even in the same line, particularly where an author like Faulkner is concerned. It is equally important to note that *Vision in Spring* is as much dialogue as monologue. Such poetry is a convenient way to talk about oneself, not to any vaguely imagined reader in his own time, let alone to some distant posterity, but to the poets who have already engaged him in a conversation, to Swinburne and Eliot themselves. They are kindred spirits: both loved mimicry and did remarkable things with pastiche, sometimes the way a master magician pulls an extra rabbit out of the hat to please the crowd between tricks (Swinburne's 'Nephelidia', Eliot's 'Burbank with a Baedeker'), but more often as an integral part of their major poems, as in 'Atalanta in Calydon' and *The Waste Land*. Of all the poets Faulkner was reading at this time, they would have understood what he was trying to do.

At the same time that he was writing so much verse, Faulkner was experimenting with a prose poetry that yielded some fascinating results. In 1922 he published 'The Hill',[11] one of the earliest records we have of his interest in depicting mental struggle in the midst of uncertainty and doubt. It is just a short sketch, featuring a man who, at the end of a day's labour, walks up a hill. We are witness to 'the terrific groping' (91) of the character's mind, which is also described as 'an internal impulse'. Although nothing much happens when he does respond to this impulse, his revelation is real enough, an understanding of 'the devastating unimportance of his destiny' (92) when confronted by the power of the changing seasons. Here, in embryo, is the process through which count-less male characters in Faulkner's fiction end up going. Like this figure, they are abstracted from the world by something that keeps them from participating fully in its illusions, they lovingly note all the serene attractiveness of nature, and they work hard at ignoring the ashes, rust, and detritus generated by an acquisitive society. Here the institutions that inevitably entangle them are seen as corrupted: there is a court-house, for example, 'discolored and stained with casual tobacco' (91). Up to this point the labourer's mind has been untroubled by moral questions, but that time is now gone. The only escape is a twilight visi-tation of fauns, nymphs, etc., to which so much of this early work is dedicated. They might come, they might not – that does not seem to be much of an issue. If they do, it would constitute merely a temporary respite from the rhythm of the seasons that he has rightly embraced, an alternative to the humdrum and soul-destroying daily grind in the town, which, without really comprehending when or why, he has rejected. Again Faulkner remains true to his aesthetic forebears. The Swinburne who spoke contemptuously of 'the market-places of the Philistines', praised the artist for his unconscious leadership, readily acknowledged the indestructible nature of evil ('evil everlasting, girt for strife / Eternal, wars with hope as death with life'[12]), and scoffed at the hopelessness of any vision of a linear march towards perfection on the part of the human species – this energetic and opinionated figure would be proud of his twentieth-century counterpart here.

An expanded version of 'The Hill', 'Nympholepsy' (written in 1925, not published until 1973),[13] adds sex and death to the fable recounted in the previous sketch. This time the worker coming home from his hard day in the fields is distracted by a nymph running through the woods. Chasing her, he falls into the water. Suddenly she is there, wrapping herself around him, her thigh like a snake, her breasts digging into his skin, trying to drag him under. He just manages to escape. This is a more earthbound affair than the one in *Vision in Spring*. The physical sensa-tions are powerfully registered, and much attention is given to detail: 'stretched branches sloped the sunset to unwordable colors; – they were like the hands of misers reluctantly dripping golden coins of sunset' (332), that kind of gorgeous thing. This sits alongside locutions like 'if only to prove himself the soundness of his integral integrity' (334), the other part of Faulkner's stylistic signature. When it comes to representing the mental processes of this character, he opts for idiosyncratic formulations like 'he felt, through vision without intellect, the waiting dark water' (334), or 'he thought only a relaxed body in a sorry bed, and waking and hunger and work' (336). The body can make more useful contact with the world by avoiding mere ratiocination, and the intellect can think the body in these early works, both ideas that Faulkner would explore throughout his career. Seeing the girl, he is excited: 'For a clear moment there was an old sharp beauty behind his eyes'. This is *l'amorosa idea* again, the thing he thinks he sees and wants to identify with. What renders her deathly is not just female malevolence but what his lust makes him feel for her: 'his once-clean instincts become swinish got him lurching into motion' (332). The clean instincts were the ones that made it possible to see the 'flame' of this wisp and distinguish it from the setting sun; the unclean ones are those that make him want to drag her back to earth and 'copulate' (the word used in this story) with her. Dallying with nymphs in their poetic environs for too long can tempt one to divide up the world in some prudish and unhelpful ways.

The year 1925 was a productive one for Faulkner: in the first half of it he wrote his first novel, *Soldiers' Pay*, along with an impressive array of stories, sketches, and poems; in the second half, he left for a five-month trip to Europe, during which he worked on an autobiographical novel, 'Elmer', which he eventually abandoned. The poems outlined above had prepared him well for his new metier. As Michael Millgate says, *Soldiers' Pay* is noteworthy for 'the recurrent images and symbols, the associations established between particular characters and particular natural objects or phenomena, the elaborately "poetic" nature of much of the language, the almost Spenserian obsession with similes.'[14] Faulkner downplays narrative and chronology for simultaneity and fragmentation, singleness of tone for a range of effects, specificity of place for the unlocalized and the diffuse. A mortally wounded soldier named Mahon, just back from the war, serves as the centre of the action, and around him turn the various characters. One has just lost her husband and feels sorry for him, another loves but cannot have her, a third is engaged to Mahon yet gives herself to another, and so on. Sex is a sort of figured bass that provides the harmonic structure of the motley group of instruments that make up the ensemble.

The language used to create the eroticism that hovers over so many scenes is keyed to the way the actors think about the world, and the aesthetic distance this enables them to have on their own experiences. The following example is taken from a scene in which one of the female characters is lying in bed, contemplating the irony of her having received news of her husband's death just after sending him a 'Dear John' letter:

> She turned feeling sheets like water, warmed by her bodily heat, upon her legs.
> Oh damn, damn. What a rotten trick you played on me. She recalled those nights during which they had tried to eradicate the tomorrows of the world. ...
> Her shoulder rounded upward, into her vision, the indication of her covered turning body swelled and died away toward the foot of the bed: she lay staring down the tunnel of her room, watching the impalpable angles of furniture, feeling through plastered smug walls a rumor of spring outside. The airshaft was filled with a prophecy of April come again into the world. Like a heedless idiot into a world that had forgotten spring. The white connecting door took the vague indication of a transom and held it in a mute and luminous plane, and obeying an impulse she rose and slipped on a dressing gown.
>
> (26–7)

Sex is always in the air in Faulkner's apprenticeship novels, particularly the idea of using it in an attempt to hold onto fleeting moments. Sentences meander as languorously as the days unfold, and even the fantasies that remain unrealized have a transformative power. For all the physicality of the curving body and liquid sheets, sex can be bodiless too, a prophecy and an escape, a breeze and a promise of change. Hence the contrast between the open and the closed, that which beckons and that which limits, the 'mute and luminous' access to the outside and the 'smug walls' and the 'tunnel' of the room. There is a sense of connoisseurship in this world, abetted by the easy and distinctive eloquence, something that suggests only those sensitive enough to respond to their environment in this way can escape the traps it sets for the unwary.

When Cecily, the girl betrothed to Mahon, dances, George Farr, the man who will elope with her in the end, watches, a little like the figure in the scene just quoted, 'wallowing in all the passionate despairs of spring and youth' (195). He too is jealous at not being able to have what he wants, and the same potent mixture prompts Faulkner to explore the vocabulary of fantasy to find words adequate for his purposes:

> The music beat on among youthful leaves, into the darkness, beneath the gold and mute cacophony of stars. The light from the veranda mounting was lost, the house loomed huge against the sky: a rock against which waves of trees broke, and breaking were forever arrested; and the stars were golden unicorns neighing unheard through blue meadows spurning them with hooves sharp and scintillant as ice. The sky, so remote, so sad, spurned by the unicorns of gold that neighing soundlessly from dusk to dawn, had seen them, had seen her – her taut body prone and naked as a narrow pool, sweetly dividing: two silver streams from a single source.
>
> (155)

Is this as 'an ornate burst of *fin de siècle* language that is clearly meant as parody'?[15] Faulkner has hit upon a clever way of characterizing George's naïveté and erudition, but deciding what is being mocked here is tricky. Like *Vision in Spring*, the passage exists in that borderland where parody, pastiche, and the desire to render something hauntingly beautiful exist together in typically Faulknerian fashion, and in many ways it recapitulates the pattern we have been tracking. Once again, buildings constrict and darken, hemming in the merely human, while mythic and natural worlds waft us away, hinting at another realm in which other-worldly desires can be realized. True, when Faulkner cues the unicorns, not just once but twice, one might well be struck by the overwrought, breathless quality of it all. This sort of thing, we say to ourselves, is precisely what young novelists go on to outgrow. Although it seems natural to see Faulkner's verbal impressionism as a manifestation of the effects of immature imitation, it is not a single thing and it does not disappear. Clearly he considers it a sort of hyperrealism at one remove. This is, after all, the reverie of a drunken youth lusting after a seemingly unattainable girl, and the stunning image that concludes it represents her type perfectly, bodiless yet sensual, someone who at this stage can be conveniently swept away by similes into the imaginative realm where only ideal unions can be consummated.

One of the ways in which these early books help teach us how to read the later ones is that they are the place where the shift from the nymph/faun dalliance to more earthbound desires takes place. Duane MacMillan notes that sex in early Faulkner is all 'innocence and innate purity' or dirty and calculating; and Daniel Singal has analysed this aspect of the novel in the greatest detail, arguing that 'there is no hint of erotic passion'[16] in the lovemaking between Mahon and his fiancée Emmy, that they are just stand-ins for their poetic counterparts. Yet even this would seem to be qualified in the context. 'I could feel his hand going right slow along my side as far as he could reach and then back again, slow, slow' (100), says Emmy, recalling part of the experience, which will sound passionate enough to some. Eroticism also inheres in what is not said, and even in this early novel the silences speak volumes. Faulkner's characters function fitfully in stock roles, only to revert to their complex humanity fairly quickly. This particular nymph wakes up 'cramped and wet and cold', and is greeted when she goes home by a father who calls her 'whore' (101) and threatens to kill her. However transcendent their lovemaking is, it certainly takes place this side of paradise, where physical attitudes and acts have actual consequences.

Soldiers' Pay is an extraordinarily talky book, yet the endless conversations seem inconsequential beside passages such as the ornate one just quoted, and the reader eventually realizes that this verbal impressionism is the most reliable guide to what is actually going on. As such passages gradually supersede the reported speech, the world of lovers' fantasies takes over from the realistic one in which soldiers are wounded and come home to die. Two other examples will suffice to illustrate the point. Towards the end of the novel Faulkner divides the text into segments designated by time's passing ('Nine-thirty', 'Ten o'clock'), segments that read like prose poems. There are more imitations of Swinburne's verbal ingenuity, particularly his skill at making abstractions concrete. For example: 'Silence carried them away, silence and dark that passing along the street like a watchman, snatched scraps of light from windows, palming them as a pickpocket palms handkerchiefs'. More jealous waiting, more lascivious looking, and then we are launched again into that in-between world that eros always evokes in Faulkner's fiction:

> [George] had lost his body. He could not feel it at all. It was as though vision were a bodiless eye suspended in dark blue space, an Eye without Thought, regarding without surprise an antic world where wanton stars galloped neighing like unicorns in blue meadows. ... After a while, the Eye, having nothing in or by which to close itself, ceased to see, and he waked.
>
> (188)

This is a strange passage. If Emerson's 'transparent eyeball'[17] is being alluded to, then it obviously recapitulates the theme of transcending the natural world and crossing boundaries generally, which helps explain those ubiquitous unicorns, denizens of an order of being that the speaker aspires to. Yet this reading works only fitfully. In 'Nature', Emerson escapes to the woods, not a dream world: his feet stay on the ground while he takes his journey. Human relations drop away along with his sense of identity, something that does not happen in the novel. For Emerson too, 'mean egotism' vanishes at this point, whereas it is obviously in the ascendency by the end of the scene in question, when George and his sometime rival for Cecily's affections, a unusual figure who is half-man, half-faun named Januarius Jones, engage in a series of scuffles caused by jealousy. Faulkner is more likely to have been inspired by a poem like Aiken's 'Senlin', with its lines about silent stars and white unicorns and its hero haunted by sea-girls and erotic last rites, and used the image here to convey all the innocence and power that inheres in it for him.

In a coda to this scene, representatives of the older generation and the younger, a minister and a soldier, survey the scene and the future it portends. Night has fallen, the houses are sleeping, and the two men walk out of the town into a world of moon, mist, and wordless music, this time supplied by the hymns from a church for the black labourers. We read: 'Within it was a soft glow of kerosene serving only to make the darkness and the heat thicker, making thicker the imminence of sex after harsh labor along the mooned land; and from it welled the crooning submerged passion of the dark race' (256). Lines like this locate the novel firmly in the 1920s South, with all its stereotyping and prejudices. This is after all the same narrative voice that in *Sartoris* compares blacks to mules in their 'impulses and mental processes' (780). This is also a semi-pastoral ending: all passion is about to be spent and re-spent, but this time by workers rather than nymphs associated with the indigenous flora. In his *Bucolics*, Virgil has soldiers who return to Arcadia to die; in Faulkner's novel, they have to compete for possession of the pastoral with those who already inhabit it. In any event, the horror of war has now become almost completely unreal, and all is lyric soaring and a sense of breathless anticipation implied by the language to which Faulkner routinely resorts in such circumstances.

The actual ending seems similarly evocative. To judge by Faulkner's revisions, he originally intended the two men to walk under the moon and pronounce their own epitaphs. He wisely omitted these, and settled for some suggestive imagery instead: the singing dies, 'fading away along the mooned land inevitable with tomorrow and sweat, with sex and death and damnation; and they turned townward under the moon, feeling dust in their shoes' (256). This may be a vision of the wasteland, as various critics have claimed, but it is a singularly ambiguous one – for the blacks who are anticipating 'the imminence of sex after harsh labor', for the old Rector and the young soldier who walk past 'moon-silvered ridges above valleys where mist hung slumberous' (255), and, ultimately, for the reader who is left to make sense of the shower of images, each more mellifluous and suggestive than the previous one. One could just as easily argue that all is potential, and that the moon oversees this scene, as it has so many of the night scenes in the novel, because its transformative power makes plain the pan-sexual character of the Southern landscape. Even the lusty, pseudo-Pan figure Jones is chanting hymns to it and intoning verses from Omar Khayyam in the scene that immediately precedes this. And the dust can just as easily be seen as fertile, a substance that links these characters to their environment. To read the ending as a version of the dusty bleakness at the heart of the modernist vision is to impute to early Faulkner an identity that sits somewhat uneasily on him at this point. It has a certain formulaic appropriateness, but a re-encounter with the actual lines suggests something more nuanced and ambiguous is going on there.

His second novel, *Mosquitoes* (1927), has been discussed as a group portrait of Faulkner's New Orleans friends and acquaintances and a writer's self-reflexive meditation. It features a number of artist figures (the main one is a sculptor), definitions of art, attempts to show how art is an improvement on life, and an assessment of the attractions and dangers of aestheticism. Its satiric jibes at the expense of a collection of dilettantes make it seem in retrospect an odd book for Faulkner to have written. Parini notes: 'It relates awkwardly to the later books' because it is 'so different in tone and style, subject and approach.'[18] Yet in this novel too there is a focus on moments of lyrical self-definition and on mental processes that link it with the work of this period. 'A portrait is not an identificative paper but the curve of an emotion',[19] says Joyce in an early essay, and that neatly characterizes Faulkner's difficulties with the novel here. All the artist figures brandish their papers ostentatiously but Faulkner is still looking for what will enable him to get that 'curve of an emotion' right.

In the novel itself, Faulkner's literary forebears are again omnipresent but more cleverly disguised. For example, he describes New Orleans as 'an aging yet still beautiful courtesan in a smokefilled room, avid yet weary too of ardent ways' (262), an allusion to a villanelle composed by Stephen Dedalus in *Portrait of the Artist as a Young Man.* Joyce's conviction that intellectual activity is free in a way that the emotions are not, that the soul emerges from our animal nature, and that the apprehension of beauty is a function of the senses and the memory – all these are ideas Faulkner explores in *Mosquitoes*. What occasions the reference to Joyce is a visit to a sculptor's studio, in which there is 'the virginal breastless torso of a girl, headless, armless, legless, in marble temporarily caught and hushed yet passionate still for escape, passionate and simple and eternal in the equivocal derisive darkness of the world' (263). This is the same combination of forces that was arrayed at the end of *Soldiers' Pay*, conveyed by the sort of vivid but vaguely puzzling epithets (what is 'equivocal darkness' and how can it be simultaneously 'derisive'?) that Faulkner uses in such striking ways throughout his career. Once again, the earthy natural rhythm is laid over against the idealized one, and antitheses like dark-light, life-art, blood-stone, decadent desire-pure passion are set up early.

When the brittle chitchat subsides we get the sculptor's anguished stream of consciousness: 'o cursed of god cursed and forgotten form shapes cunningly sweated cunning to simplicity shapes out of chaos more satisfactory than bread to the belly form by a madmans dream gat on the body of chaos le garçon vierge of the soul horned by utility o cuckold of derision' (292). There is a certain sense of strain here, but some useful information as well. The artist would seem to be a cuckold because he has been betrayed by dark desires of the physical world, and a madman because he believes that he can, god-like, impose form on chaos. Aesthetic aloofness is identified in some oblique way with sexual abstinence. Subsequent passages juxtapose an ascetic male impulse with a natural female creativity, and the male creator alternates between mocking himself for wanting a woman and acknowledging the power sexual desire has on him. Though less articulate than Stephen Dedalus, Faulkner's sculptor is obviously just as mixed up, at least as far as sex is concerned. Like the character in 'The Hill' and 'Nympholepsy', he seeks temporary solace from such meditations in a world where real work is being done – the dock, the warehouse – but his vocation cuts him off from such plebian settings too.

The last scene in *Mosquitoes* presents another version of the situation at the end of *Soldiers' Pay*. As the novel winds down there is the same combination of symbolic settings, timeless and time-bound characters, a small group of speculative individuals set against the backdrop of an omnipresent, lurking, fertile, brooding nature. The dénouement opens with a passage in dream italics, and this alternates with the drunken meditation of the characters. In the dream, all is grey despair, brought on by the sight of three hooded priests and a beggar beneath a gate. Rats sniff out the beggar's private parts, and the nightmare seems to darken. Faulkner wants to broach again the 'curse of our dual nature' question by comparing two world views, the religious with its secrets, its furtiveness, and its denial of the body, on the one hand, and the aesthetic, with its sumptuousness, its yearning, and its miseries, on the other. The problem with approaching the question in this way is the difficulty of retaining the reader's interest in impressionistic accounts of such things. What Roland Barthes says about recounting one's dreams the morning after also applies to retelling incoherent dream visions: lots of people like to do it but not many like listening to them.

When the three characters arrive at what seems like a brothel, the wild desires of drunken, impetuous youth are rampant, and speculation turns again to the aesthetic. There is an assertion on the part of one of them that the sensuous, exotic things of this world matter far more to him than the intangible hints of another, and Faulkner arranges to have Fairchild, a writer figure modelled on his friend and mentor Sherwood Anderson, pause and define 'genius':

> It is that Passion Week of the heart, that instant of timeless beatitude which some never know; which some, I suppose, gain at will; which others gain through an outside agency like alcohol, like to-night; – that passive state of the heart with which the mind, the brain, has nothing to do at all, in which the hackneyed accidents which make up this world – love and life and death and sex and sorrow – brought together by chance in perfect proportions, take on a kind of splendid and timeless beauty.
>
> (533)

It may be just the inebriated state of his characters, but this seems somewhat garbled. Is it genius that enables those gifted with it to apprehend the significance of such moments, or do such moments confer this ability? How exactly does the heart apprehend something? And how lasting is the ecstatic sense induced by its perceptions? Nevertheless, such a problematic definition, with all these questions hovering over it, ultimately serves Faulkner well at this point in this novel. He is not ready to do what Joyce does at the end of *Portrait*, namely have his hero define an aesthetic schema and move on. The lyric, the form in which according to Stephen 'the artist presents his image in immediate relation to himself',[20] Faulkner now knows will never be his form. Like Joyce, he realizes that any theory used to explain the origins and attributes of aesthetic vision, has to make room for the accidents and chance that life throws up. The means by which this material becomes 'timeless beauty' are still to be determined, but the idea of creating that is still very much of interest for Faulkner.

Fairchild goes on to give examples from history but they are also inconclusive. He mentions Yseult and Tristram, and a queen about to be decapitated, and then trails off with the image of 'a redhaired girl, an idiot, turning in a white dress beneath a wistaria-covered trellis on a late sunny afternoon in May' (533). The images are puzzlingly inconsequential, but reading across the early novels can help readers hear the curious echoes and half-echoes that in part explain them. The restless widow in *Soldiers' Pay*, it should be recalled, feels a 'prophecy of April' that resembles 'a heedless idiot [come] into a world that had forgotten Spring' (27). In that novel the idiot is the personification of a season; in *Mosquitoes* it is a person. But the pattern formed by spring and idiot, moon and passion, suggests that something beyond narrative is on Faulkner's mind and the minds of certain characters, something that brings together sex and death and writing in a new configuration. The links with Benjy the 'idiot', standing by the fence in the spring, the symbol of dispossession and yearning and thwarted expression, suggest how crucial this sort of crystallizing moment was for Faulkner, and it was an image that was to haunt him as he experimented with different narrative forms throughout his career.

Sartoris was Faulkner's third novel, published in early 1929, a radically revised version of *Flags in the Dust*, which had been refused by the senior editors at Boni and Liveright, much to his chagrin. My copy of *Sartoris* from the 1950s is subtitled 'A Novel of a Proud and Passionate Family'. On the cover a Gary Cooper look-alike in a leather jacket looks menacingly at nothing, while a semi-clad female admirer leans on him and tries to intercept his gaze. On the back flap we read about Old Colonel Bayard, 'valiant' Aunt Jenny, 'young and lovely' Narcissa, and young Bayard's 'date with a fatal destiny'. Those who sought to sell copies of Faulkner's novels realized that the romance formula was the best way to make their appeal. Sentences like 'It showed on John Sartoris' brow, the dark shadow of fatality and doom' (559) helped encourage such convictions and inspire such a jacket. One of the many things Faulkner disliked about working in Hollywood was the prevalence of this mindset there.

In this novel, he found not so much his subject as his subjects, the individuals and families in a small part of the South, their history and interrelations. More important for my purposes, it marks the end of the beginning for Faulkner's attempts to build a novel around another set of male characters and their reflections. It presents us with two brothers-in-law, around whom the two main stories and many ancillary ones are organized. Young Bayard Sartoris is the central character, but he is the sort of laconic hero from whom one does not get a lot of words.

Horace Benbow, a lawyer, is the other, and his dreamy prolixity and stimulating reflections more than make up for his counterpart's moody silence. In this novel too Faulkner's narrative voice feels freer to extemporize on various subjects relevant to the main action.

For the first time Faulkner shows an extensive interest in how a family's legends affect the way the past presents itself to the minds of the living. Old Bayard and the attendant ghosts of his ancestors stand guard in the family mansion over these stories and we learn about them from such figures. Yet these meditations, like the ones in the previous two novels, are thoroughly grounded in the real. Early in the novel old Bayard studies the semi-sacred objects – duelling pistols, a sword – that represent his family's history. They constitute fading proof that the past existed and we get to see it through his eyes. Faulkner is a master at not telling us what his characters are doing, a technique that works particularly well with his strong, silent, Sartoris types. Not great talkers anyway, they stomp down a passage, enter a room, open a chest, finger an object, and we go along, looking over their shoulders as it were, only gradually understanding this display which is not really meant for us. If a lyric poem is not heard but overheard, these sorts of encounters in Faulkner are not seen but overseen, caught in a glimpse that militates against instant comprehension. The furniture in this particular room in the Sartoris house resembles 'patient ghosts holding lightly in dry and rigid embrace yet other ghosts', which makes the room 'a fitting place for dead Sartorises to gather and speak among themselves of glamorous and old disastrous days' (613). The words 'dry' and 'rigid' are the Faulkner signature in that sentence, the ones that hint at how passion and spontaneity have leaked out of the family, leaving only decaying objects and what he likes to call the abiding dust.

These deaths are recorded in the family Bible, which seems to be turning into the elements from which it was made, its texture 'like that of slightly moist wood-ashes, as though each page were held intact by its archaic and fading print'. This last is a nice touch, at a stroke inviting us to think about how and for how much longer its language and its precepts can do precisely what the physical object has done: hold together the generations who read it even as their families succumb. The language of print is contrasted with the names handwritten on the flyleaf, the ones that mark the generations, 'growing fainter and fainter where time had lain upon them'. With a marvellous economy Faulkner conjures up the past in these 'faint, soft mottlings of time', in a blank space where there was something and now there is nothing, no memory, not even a name and a date, except the knowledge that once there was a

name written and a person doing the writing. The narrative voice provides the details that the family in question could hardly be expected to
admit: 'Sartorises had derided time, but Time was not vindictive, being
longer than Sartorises. And probably unaware of them' (615). That
'probably' is magisterial: does Faulkner not know, some part of us
wants to ask. And the answer is that he does and he does not. Yes, of
course, there is nothing personal, no grudge against this particular family that gets its names put in the Bible at regular intervals, only to have
them effaced by the force that put them there in the first place. And yet
this family does seem to be singled out, doomed to die tragically and to
take it hard. No Sartoris would ever inveigh against the heavens,
bemoaning their implacability or his fate. Yet in the dark, in the quiet
of this room, looking at this book and reading what is left inside it,
this particular Sartoris senses that there might have been some hubris
involved when his ancestors derided time, and some revenge taken,
when it took its inevitable victory.

Writing the names in the Bible is described as 'a good gesture, anyway', for reasons that are not far to seek. Bayard says this in the past
tense and then, like so many Faulkner characters, thinks about the
language that we use to convey difficult things. He muses about usage:
'Was. Fatality; the augury of a man's destiny peeping out at him from
the roadside hedge, if he but recognize it' (615). The reverie puts him
in mind of a near-death experience in the war, a point at which destiny
forked and he was not killed, but he saw, literally, the skull beneath the
skin and became aware of his mortality in a new way. Thinking like this,
on past and future, may be a kind of vanity. Pride in one's family history is identified as precisely that in this passage, with the proviso that
those who do not care about their lineage are equally vain in their anti-
snobbish gesture. The point seems to be that life is a collection of illusions anyway, the illusion that one's family puts one above it all, that
there is an escape, that a single individual has a single destiny, and so
on. Even heaven here is included as one of those illusions, not in any
antireligious sense, but rather the reverse. The only way old Bayard can
imagine it, given what he has seen of life on earth, is as a place 'filled
with every man's illusion of himself and with the conflicting illusions
of him that parade through the minds of other illusions' (616). That is
not a bad description of the solipsistic universe defined by a typical
Faulkner novel, or at least of his preferred mode of character development. It also marks the most sustained attempt by this Sartoris to muse
about the nature of experience and about the language used by those
determined to undertake such meditations.

The quintessential early Faulkner scene, the one in which characters gather to come to some sort of understanding about themselves, with nature providing the mood music, returns in a new guise. The first example is the one in which young Bayard tells his grandfather about the dogfight that killed his twin brother. The passage features a striking combination of a bluntly colloquial, fighter pilot's jargon, all sharp angles and clear details, and a melancholic, lullaby-style prose that establishes the context. This is a life and death struggle, seen through the eyes of one of its haunted participants.[21] The narrator comments:

> [Young Bayard's] voice rose again as he talked on. Locust drifted up in sweet gusts upon the air, and the crickets and frogs were clear and monotonous as pipes blown drowsily by an idiot boy. From her silver casement the moon looked down upon the valley dissolving in opaline tranquillity into the serene mysterious infinitude of the hills, and young Bayard's voice went on and on, recounting violence and speed and death.
>
> (576)

Making its third appearance in as many novels, the 'idiot' this time is a stand-in for both Pan and timelessness, mindless noise and haunting melodies. Even a single word like 'opaline' suggests the way certain precious stones give back the eerie, seemingly self-generated quality of moonlight, leaving us a vague impression of other power sources, of things beyond the merely natural. Bayard has no access to any of this visionary company, so his banishment to the finite world and death is inevitable. This novel confirmed Faulkner's extraordinary capacity for not only rendering both worlds but also for making them meaningful. He had found his medium.

The second example features Horace. At one point he lies in his bed, and we are told 'that wild, fantastic futility of his voyaged in lonely regions of its own beyond the moon, about meadows nailed with fir-mamented stars to the ultimate roof of things, where unicorns filled the neighing air with galloping, or grazed or lay supine in golden-hoofed repose' (683). Faulkner's heroes have problems with their relationships, not so much because they are passionately attracted to the wrong person, but because their fantasies are such full-time preoccupations. In the early books these dreams are filled with unreal creatures that enable Faulkner to make his point picturesquely. Horace's fleshy mistress Belle wears strong perfume and has strong desires: her love is what Donne would call 'dull, sublunary love whose soul is sense';[22]

Horace's is 'beyond the moon'. The unicorn, pressed into service again as a symbol of strength, purity, magic, chaste love, and sexual magnetism, what you will, an animal that transcends sexuality and represents fertility, is his imaginary ticket to the escape world he arranges to inhabit nightly via these journeys.

In contrast to Bayard and his furious, laconic, determined march towards death, described in clinically objective detail as the rickety plane he is flying disintegrates, Horace is languid, garrulous, and undecided as he leans away from life. The sort of self-conscious meditation that this gives rise to must have seemed self-indulgent to the editors who rejected *Flags in the Dust*, and Faulkner cut it substantially when he turned to it into *Sartoris*. The portrait of the intellectual as weary aesthete is there in both versions, but what is omitted from the second is important. In both novels Horace pens a letter, full of idle chitchat and indiscreet desire, to his sister. In *Sartoris*, he mails it, the chapter ends, and we are back to Bayard's story. In *Flags in the Dust*, he takes a walk into town to pick up something for Belle and think about things. His reflections during that walk make it clearer that Horace is a more complex version of the Marble Faun in a human body, metaphorically jotting down his impressions about his inability to have impressions. Spring beckons, but not for him. Like the character in 'The Hill', he sees the spread of civilization as a blight, 'rank fecundity above a foul and stagnant pool on which bugs dart spawning' (849–50). What he sees on his walk is reality, and he flees it, or rather tries to, for avoidance of any real contact is his *raison d'être*.

Once again, the protagonist's wandering meditation brings him into conjunction with some real people making music in the dark, this time a group of blacks gathered around a fire, chanting and singing. Once again, all the sensuous details that take over when labour is done are accentuated. These people, we are told, make love in the fields when darkness falls, and the implied contrast between them and the intense, unhappy lives of the white characters who are permanently cut off from their world is unmistakable.[23] Horace is excluded from this dark reality too. Appalled by a machine resembling 'an antediluvian nightmare' that is working beside them in these fields, and musing on his situation, he thinks: 'Man's very tragedies flout him. He has invented a masque for tragedy, given it the austerity which he believes the spectacle of himself warrants, and the thing makes faces behind his back' (853). Self-consciousness supplies the irony that mocks any pretensions he might have about assuming a tragic pose, and he is left with his own absurdity, which he sees as representative of the human condition. This somewhat facile view nonetheless corresponds neatly enough with the life that he has lived.

The novel's conclusion features Horace's sister Narcissa similarly isolated, but seen from the outside rather than from within. And she, like so many of her counterparts in the early novels, is on the inside looking out: 'the maroon curtains hung motionless; beyond the window evening was a windless lilac dream, foster dam of quietude and peace' (875). All the emphasis here is on the impalpable and ephemeral. Once again, a window opens on a limitless space where there is no weather ('windless'), at least no weather of the exciting kind that her husband Bayard, now dead, supplied. The obligatory music in such scenes is this time supplied by the piano. The echo of Keats's 'foster child of silence and slow time'[24] at the very end suggests that the evening, like the urn it resembles, is being characterized by an admiring romantic prose poet here, for what it tells and withholds, for the action and stasis it so calmly and forcefully represents.

The final take on this question of how successful the attempt to find an aesthetic design in the crazy quilt of experience can ever be involves a reference, the first of many, to 'the Player' and 'the game he plays'. Typically, Faulkner suggests that there is some other-worldly force that influences our destiny, only to repatriate it almost instantly, giving humanity the responsibility for defining the rules that determine success or failure:

> He must have a name for His pawns, though, but perhaps Sartoris is the game itself – a game outmoded and played with pawns shaped too late and to an old dead pattern, and of which the Player Himself is a little wearied. For there is death in the sound of it, and a glamorous fatality, like silver pennons downrushing at sunset, or a dying fall of horns along the road to Roncevaux.
>
> (875)

Roland, Charlemagne, legend, high tragedy, ancient history, empire building, all these are evoked by the single word at the end, a name in a paragraph about names. A story full of violence, rivalry and jealousy, a name that does not die with a body, the means by which a cult is infused with value, and the description of the process by which the collective memory of the people left behind turns history into myth – in all these ways Faulkner's third novel resembles the epic he refers to in seemingly offhanded fashion at the end of *Sartoris*. The passage recalls the one from *Mosquitoes*, the reverie in which Yseult and Tristram are evoked by Fairchild and friends as they walk through the slums of New Orleans. But now there is a family and a tradition to ground these mythic figures in real-life events. After the publication of this novel, along with Compson and McCaslin and Sutpen, Sartoris became the name of the 'game itself'. Faulkner bet a whole career that he could find an audience willing to think hard about the meaning of Southern history, and he went on to convince millions of readers, captivated by such names and their magic, that they could find their own stories in it.

As this stage of his literary life came to an end, Faulkner had learned a number of things. First, what he was interested in writing about was not attracting a large readership. The amatory problems of a certain type of young man had not struck the respondent chord he was hoping for, nor had the self-reflexive concerns about the plight of the aesthete in an unappreciative world. Unicorns, centaurs, seraphim *et al.* had served their purpose; other ways of representing dreamy and passionate reconfigurations of the real must now be found. Adopting the point of view of an observer, male, detached, erudite, and interested in reflecting on a range of subjects, must have seemed as promising a course to pursue as ever, given the different sorts of work Faulkner had produced since the early 1920s. The idea of giving this point of view and his stylistic resources to someone other than an artist figure, someone preoccupied with or suffering from something more urgent than the vague anxieties that afflict marble faun-type characters and their limited worlds, must have gradually come to seem a logical next step. Becoming that much more specific about the whole question of women and the sexual interests they have and elicit would also help to ground this point of view and this language, and attract more readers. Even if Faulkner did say to himself as he finished revising *Flags in the Dust*, 'Now I can go seriously to work on exploring my own "postage stamp of native soil"',[25] it is important to realize how much he had already done to facilitate that exploration, and what an interesting mix of innovation and continuity was implied by that conviction. Of course the transformation that turned Faulkner the apprentice into Faulkner the consummate master must remain something of a mystery. His determination to find a form capable of doing justice to the complex thoughts and feelings that he was trying to express did not change. His ability to immerse himself in and invent others' stories, including the ones that came to represent a significant part of the history of his own region, was to make all the difference.

3
Major Achievement I

Accounts of modernism often turn around a series of contradictory propositions. It has been described as a celebration of the unorthodox and as corrupt, canonized orthodoxy, an exploration of epistemological loss and the source of a new kind of knowledge, an illustration of how things fall apart and of how they fall together, the anatomizing of the destruction of the simple subject and the triumphant reassertion of that subject's position in an indifferent or hostile world, a movement that reveals the bankruptcy of metanarratives and one that legitimizes their stultifying homogeneity, the precursor of postmodernism and something that simply subsumes it, a major aesthetic breakthrough and a decadent amusement for the leisure class, a word that designates the solitary work of some very different, very gifted creative artists and one that describes a communal enterprise in which a great deal of creative effort is turned over to the reader/spectator, and so on. Still, the idea that modernism represents something new in a new way retains its force, and its preoccupation with consciousness and introspection, openness and ambiguity, limited or multiple points of view, and complex temporal sequences are all rightfully emphasized as crucial for an understanding of it.[1] These are the sorts of issues raised by Faulkner's best-known novels, the ones he published between 1929 and 1942.

The Sound and the Fury has been discussed from all these perspectives and a host of others. With the possible exceptions of *The Scarlet Letter* and *Moby Dick*, more has been written about it than about any other American novel. Even armed with this fearsome amount of commentary, we can still feel disoriented when reading it. Not just by the seemingly disconnected sections of Benjy's monologue, but by Quentin's obsessive interest in self-destruction, the attractiveness of energetic evil in Jason, the absent Caddy's ubiquitous presence, the Christian 'resolution' that resolves nothing, and so on. Even the title that announces the banishment of meaning from the world comes from a soliloquy in *Macbeth* that occurs at the precise moment when meaning is about to be restored to that world. No doubt some of this disorientation is part of the novel's point, but we can attempt to face it head on by looking more closely at the subjects that guided our deliberations in the previous chapter. In what follows, I propose to examine in turn scenes involving each of the three Compson brothers, with a view to studying both their 'fierce and rigid concentration', their efforts to understand, and the forces arrayed against them that make that task so difficult. In the process, the ways in which different, even contradictory ideas about modernism can help those interested in understanding the shape of Faulkner's career should become clearer as well.

The first section of *The Sound and the Fury*, so famous for its impenetrability, destruction of the simple subject, and avant garde techniques is as remarkable for all the things it says quite clearly about characters, the similarities it compels us to notice, and the way that these anticipate the concerns articulated in the rest of the novel. Like his brothers, Benjy has a singularly isolated take on the world that leaves him unstuck in time, vulnerable to things he imperfectly understands and pathetic in his protest against them. Like them, he has particularly acute senses, and the seemingly excessive reactions that the world elicits from him occur as if by short circuit, because what stimulates them has bypassed the intermediate links in a decoding and classifying process. Like theirs, Benjy's monologue begins in confusion and ends *in medias res*, with everything about to happen, everything that has been foreshadowed or foretold. These parallels are all the more remarkable because the differences between the three brothers are so striking.

Listening in on Benjy's monologue means doing a lot of inferring. Faulkner arranges it thus so that readers live vicariously his way of experiencing the world and slowly acclimatize themselves to the one the novel presents. After a few pages, we have learned that Quentin is a babe in arms, a female, and the same mental age as Benjy. By this point we already know that there is another Quentin, a male, and that he is in the cemetery with his father. These must be two of the people in Benjy's family who have died, one two years after the other. Benjy is thought to have premonitions of their death. We also know that Versh, Benjy's former keeper, has gone to Memphis and been replaced by T.P., that the name of one of Benjy's siblings is not spoken because she is disgraced, that that sibling is a mother, that saying her name bothers him, that Roskus is an older servant who disapproves of the way Benjy's family has handled things, that the servants think the family is doomed, that Dilsey is very practically minded, that her mistress, Benjy's mother, is not, and so on. A lot of this is conveyed in conversations that could not be more natural, more sharply recorded with a view to tone, cadence, vocabulary, and emotional inflection. This makes the first section a brilliant anatomy of a certain, very limited way of registering impressions of the world, a phantasmagoria that seems to move arbitrarily in time, a dazzling sequence of slices of conversational life, and a collection of de facto stage directions that set up the entire novel. Benjy's impressions are minutely recorded in the novel to tell us about this reality. Jason's malevolence, his attempts to dominate his niece, Mrs Compson's neglect of her offspring, Mr Compson's drinking problem, Quentin's early obsession with his sister's sexuality, and Uncle Maury's philandering and sponging off his brother-in-law – all these and literally hundreds of other things we are able to deduce from reading and rereading this chapter.

Faulkner's task in this section is to stay true to the simplicity of his character, while at the same time making his account as informative and as moving as possible. The reader must accept the literary convention that Benjy thinks in words and that the sentences in this novel constitute a transcription of those thoughts. The result is much more than a mere *tour de force*, as brilliant as this chapter is. Here is Benjy at the end of his monologue, back in time, a child again, reporting as if from the present, recording the impressions that flood his consciousness while he goes to sleep in a room with his brothers and sister. 'Caddy held me and I could hear us all, and the darkness, and something I could smell. And then I could see the windows, where the trees were buzzing. Then the dark began to go in smooth, bright shapes, like it always does, even when Caddy says that I have been asleep' (934). Simple words, short clauses, and co-ordinating conjunctions predominate, as does a minimalist vocabulary to convey Benjy's on the surface reactions to the world. But his surface is the reader's depth, and here is summarized, eloquently, even elegiacally, the life that he has had and, by implication, the one he has not been allowed to live. Like so many characters in these crucial situations, he looks out through an opening (door, window, transom, trellis) and sees framed there the world in all its mysterious power. Richard Rorty praises Freud for showing us that every human life is an 'attempt to clothe itself in its own metaphors', and judging by this criterion this is Faulkner's most Freudian book.[2] For it shows us how even someone like Benjy, with his seriously limited conceptual and expressive abilities, can make a coherent story by 'trying to say' with the figures of speech available to him.

Like so many modernist writers, Faulkner wants to explore the means by which mental life can be understood, and *The Sound and the Fury* is filled with examples of how he goes about such an exploration. Some of the techniques highlighted at the start of this chapter are obviously crucial for this purpose, and Quentin's monologue is a sort of *locus classicus* in this regard. He is the most interesting of the Compson brothers, the most thoughtful, and the most disturbed, and his characterization illustrates Faulkner's distinctive take on how the thoughts and feelings of a complex character can be represented. With someone like Quentin to study, there was no more need for characters to imagine coupling with sinister mermaids or to yearn to ride away on a unicorn. In what follows, I concentrate on three scenes, the one in which Quentin muses in general about the meaning of his life thus far, the time he remembers almost killing his sister, and the discussion about women he has with his father.

The story of his failure to perform in the role that he has scripted for himself makes Quentin's tortuous meditations some of the most interesting in Faulkner's work. Here is a typical passage:

> I seemed to be lying neither asleep nor awake looking down a long corridor of grey halflight where all stable things had become shadowy paradoxical all I had done shadows all I had felt suffered taking visible form antic and perverse mocking without relevance inherent themselves with the denial of the significance they should have affirmed thinking I was I was not who was not was not who.
>
> (1007)

For all its impressionistic character, this is a superbly realized account of mental anguish, occasioned by Quentin's reluctance to recognize that his conviction that the world should affirm its significance has no force. Like the speaker in Hardy's poem 'Hap', Quentin is willing to accept the pain of existence if he can just look back and see a pattern and purpose in the events that have produced it. But they will not sit still long enough. His thoughts here finally break down into two claims and two questions, all problematic. What does it mean to assert that I existed ('I was') when all the evidence of it is so shadowy and shifting? But the counterclaim ('I was not') is equally uncertain, since common sense suggests that the past and the kaleidoscopic collection of memories and desires it consists of enable me to affirm that I did indeed exist, and that therefore my present uncertainty on this point may be a permanent feature of the human condition, the result of trying to get an objective angle on something that will never come into focus. So much for the two statements. The two questions lead to more uncertainty, despite the painstaking attempts to hold onto some sort of assertive formulation. First there is 'who was not': that is, what unitary identity exists to make claims about existence, positive or negative, given the fragmentary nature of the self that reflection constantly throws up? The phrase 'was not who', which repeats the point, shifts the emphasis to the past, and foregrounds the play with permutations that makes this sort of questioning such a squirrel cage experiment, one that reinforces the very sense of isolation that Quentin is desperately trying to escape. Sartre remarks that the purpose of alarm clocks is to save us the anxiety associated with deciding when to get up. Quentin is troubled by the thought that there will be no self to get up when the clock goes off.

The scene between him and Caddy in the swamp, the one in which he contemplates murder and suicide, is another powerful memory that forces its way into Quentin's consciousness during the day that he prepares so carefully for his own death. The context for this meditation is important: the genteel outing that Quentin is invited to participate in by some of his Harvard classmates, the way young men talk about women on such outings, his meeting with the immigrant girl he is accused of kidnapping while he wanders the woods near Cambridge, all this is given us in fragments, as preparation for the moment in which Quentin remembers looking at his sister lying in the water near their house. It is a scene filled with great tension – will he try to kill her? – but it is also an erotic scene, with 'the water flowing about her hips', the feel of her heart pounding when Quentin puts his hand on her breast, and the smell of honeysuckle overpowering him synaesthetically. When their exchanges begin in earnest, except for the lack of punctuation and upper-case letters for the start of the sentences, the reader has relatively little difficulty in following what transpires. This is a 'he says', 'she says' discussion, mediated through Quentin's consciousness, with helpful indentations every time the speaker changes. When Faulkner wants the readers to follow closely, he uses a very straightforward dramatic sequence. When his interests change, and he wants to reflect Quentin's inner life by examining how his mind jumps from this extended memory to a series of related ones, we get the fragments and the quick cuts that many readers associate with the modernist text.

Quentin hesitates, knife poised, and the tension increases. 'Between the motion / And the act, / Falls the Shadow', as Eliot has it in 'The

Hollow Man'.[3] That shadow, composed of ambiguity and irresolution, stops Quentin's hand. Interestingly, during their exchange, his sister is not looking at him but past him: distracted by the strength of her own desire, her mind is on other things. When Quentin accidentally drops the knife, it is lost for a moment under them. The physical world reasserts itself, and the bodiless, ephemeral self, yearning for non-existence, disappears. The high drama of the sacrificial gesture is lost in the goofy fumbling: 'its funny how you can sit down and drop something and have to hunt all around for it' (994), the most innocuous line in the scene, is also one of its most poignant.[4] Caddy asks what time it is, the moment of quasi-solipsistic isolation has passed. The two are in the world where people just go on, just endure. Here a knife is just a knife, not a symbolic anything, and Quentin's unilateral suicide pact is a shabby, pseudo-romantic denial of passion, a cowardly refusal to hear what the blood in Caddy's throat is saying, a hopelessly shallow reading of human life, and a refusal to engage with it.

What happens after the knife is abandoned, left to be found in the morning, is as interesting as the narrowly avoided murder. He and Caddy are walking up the hill away from the swamp and he is looking at the horizon. Quentin thinks: 'the gray it was gray with dew slanting up into the gray sky then the trees beyond' (994). The little stutter and repetition at the start of the line are curious. Is this a jolt occasioned by Quentin's - re-entry into a world where weather and time and the gloom of another day all reassert themselves? By his difficulty in getting a firm grasp on that gray world he is so unhappy in? Is it the start of a sentence he has trouble finishing, because he does not want to be there? An assertion to confirm the reality of the memory? Whatever we decide, such an exchange becomes that much more resonant, with the reader playing a director's role deciding how a given word or set of words is to be pronounced, where the emphasis will fall, and how the tone will be modulated. How does dew slant 'up into the gray sky' anyway? Is this simply mist, but then why call it dew? An external confusion to mimic his internal one? A question of perspective, as so much in this novel finally is? The questions pile up, and this in a good sense, precisely because of all that actuality arraigned, the range of human situations creating the range of emotions.

One of the ways Faulkner makes such scenes seem so momentous is by focussing on this sort of hesitation and on moments of hesitation in general. The novel is full of strong characters who seek to impose their will on others, but they are strangely reluctant to act at crucial junctures and preoccupied by the emptiness that afflicts them every time they attempt introspection. A.D. Nuttall points out that 'in the evolution of our notion of private self, mere hesitation assumes a curious importance. In some way, hesitation is the locus of self.' He supports his contention by drawing on comparisons between the typical hero in a play by Aeschylus and his counterpart in Euripides: the latter hesitates, notes Nuttall, when confronting 'a contradictory set of imperatives', and 'in the hesitation a new entity makes its presence felt'. He concludes that 'the very hesitations of a Hamlet or a Raskolnikov ... loom larger than the decisions of a Caesar.'[5] Quentin is a modern tragic hero in this tradition, and, like his great predecessors, Faulkner uses such moments, as in the scene above, to explore his character's attempts to deal with irresolvable conflicts. Like Hamlet, Quentin has to define the responsibilities of a self, the dangers of idealism, and the pathos of mortality in a world that seems indifferent to all of them. Like Raskolnikov, his idealism sets him off in a way that makes him seem monomaniacal. The new entity that manifests itself when he pauses to reflect upon the efficacy and significance of grand gestures is what the Quentin section of *The Sound and the Fury* is trying to define.

The other interesting example of 'fierce and rigid concentration' in this section is the exchange between him and his father, and it is another detailed investigation of contradictory imperatives and their potentially paralyzing effects. Here too Faulkner is very careful to keep the reader informed about who is speaking when, because he wants, not confusion, but clarity, right down to indicating the speaker with 'and he' and 'and i'.[6] This makes *The Sound and the Fury* typographically different from a more conventional novel, but only a little. The lack of an upper-case letter for 'i' is unusual but hardly disorienting. The passage is worth looking at in detail, because it contains an attempt to conceptualize the problem at the heart of Quentin's tragedy. Like us, the two men read their lives for symbols and meaning, and the moral positions they sketch in are central to understanding how the conceptual process gets represented in this novel.

The exchange begins with a biblical allusion, a reference to Christ's casting out the demons from the madman: 'I could hear whispers secret surges smell the beating of hot blood under the wild unsecret flesh watching against red eyelids the swine untethered in pairs rushing coupled into the sea' (1012). This is a parable about power and fear, one that, like Quentin's story, begins in chaos and ends in an awful serenity. Those enamoured by the notion of a violent difference between the pure and the impure, by the possibility of concretizing and quantifying good and evil, tend to be fascinated by this story. Significantly, Quentin begins with the parable, whereas his father asserts that morality is relative, not absolute as in the Bible story. Mr Compson says that the sum of human experiences is 'carried tediously to an unvarying nil', and ends with a 'stalemate of dust and desire' (972). The phrase is intriguing, for stalemate in chess is the end because there is no end, because no winner or loser is possible. All moves are illegal, or every move results in a dreary, conclusion-less repetition. As we saw in *Sartoris*, the dust against which desire does battle has a lot of staying power and is spoken of respectfully by Faulkner whenever this battle is evoked. Nevertheless, in *The Sound and the Fury*, desire compels the other characters to engage in such a struggle, and the struggle itself is the point: it may not add up to anything more than nil, but that just shows the limitations of this particular metaphor.

Father and son move on to the subject of incest. The symbolic significance of incest in Faulkner's fiction is intriguing, but like Horace's, Quentin's illicit desires often strike us as incest lite, and their virtual absence in *Absalom, Absalom!* confirms this. They are a complex mixture of a nostalgia for lost innocence and jealousy of others' affections, and he controls them because they are weak enough to be controlled, unlike some of his Romantic avatars who really did want to make love to their sisters and often did.[7] This makes incest something of a device, as Mr Compson astutely sees and as Quentin actually admits when he says that he wants to isolate his sister 'out of the loud world' (1013). Quentin's problem is with time and mortality first and foremost. Sex, of which he has only caricatural notions it would seem, is often subject to the harshest sort of representation in Faulkner. No one is better at depicting all the vile ways it can go badly wrong, and the immediate and long-term consequences of sexual desire are often appalling in his fiction. He can be surprisingly sentimental about any number of things, but about the intimate things people do or dream about doing behind closed doors he never is.

After incest comes suicide. In a famous passage, G.K. Chesterton says: 'The man who kills a man, kills a man. The man who kills himself, kills all men; as far as he is concerned he wipes out the world.'[8] This is precisely what Quentin is contemplating: obliterating categories, moral nuances, the throes of temptation, everything that constitutes the complexity of life on the planet. What is so striking about his father's response is how insightful he is and how heartless at the same time. He tells his son that his suicidal thoughts are an evasion: 'you are not thinking of finitude you are contemplating an apotheosis in which a temporary state of mind will become symmetrical above the flesh and aware both of itself and of the flesh it will not quite discard'. He is of course right about Quentin's self-deceptions and the death-in-life plan he has hazily envisioned, wrong in assuming that this discussion will free his son of those illusions. Note too that Jason Compson, Sr mimics the reader's activities here, by analysing Quentin's character so lucidly that he anticipates and abets our struggle to understand. At the same time, he shows how ultimately unfeeling such an understanding actually is. Quentin stands revealed to himself and to us, but he dies as a result of it. So too with the next bit of analysis: 'you cannot bear to think that someday it will no longer hurt you like this now' (1013). Speaking of the death of his beloved five-year-old son, Emerson wrote: 'I grieve that grief can teach me nothing',[9] because he was appalled by the way his own experience had confirmed the cliché about the passage of time healing all. The long view, which Mr Compson identifies quite rightly with the attaining of middle age, is the one that he articulates here. One need hardly point out that this bit of worldly wisdom may be fine for someone like him but disastrously relativistic for someone as impressionable and confused as his son.[10]

What Mr Compson specializes in – and it is what make this novel so rich – are the metaphors of dissolution and decay that he uses to characterize the downward journey in human life. So lyrically and seductively does he phrase them ('every breath is a fresh cast with dice already loaded', 'love or a sorrow is a bond purchased without design and which matures willynilly and is recalled without warning'), one can forget just how powerfully they are likely to affect his interlocutor, since they appeal to his sense of despair and his aesthetic sensibility. Mr Compson too is committing suicide, and killing the world as he does it, but more slowly and more decorously, one bottle of liquor at a time. When he says that Quentin will not commit suicide, that he will come to believe that even Caddy 'was not quite worth despair perhaps' (1013), the word that gives us pause is the last one. It is one of Faulkner's favourites, and he likes the latitude it gives him to walk all the way around the explanation of something, to leave an aura of ambiguity, and to keep a sense of mystery intact. Who am I to presume total knowledge, to explain all? says this word. It is part of the self-deprecating stance that makes the narrative voice so changeable in his novels. More particularly, here it drives home the point Mr Compson is making. He is, as always, right and wrong, right for himself, wrong for his son, right for his own age, wrong for a youth trying to sort a clutch of things out and not succeeding. So sure is Mr Compson that the reductive view of the human enterprise he takes is the only one possible, so glib is his assumption that the same view in Quentin will manifest itself as simple hedonism unencumbered by ethical self-interrogation, that he in effect unwittingly announces the imminent death of his son even as he denies it as a possibility.

The final lines of this exchange are poignantly evocative. When Mr Compson says that 'temporary' is the 'saddest word of all there is nothing else in the world', he is making the nihilistic point just sketched in. But he adds: 'there is nothing else in the world its not despair until time its not even time until it was' (1014). Until what was? The passage takes us back to his first meditation on the subject. There he points out that time is something that can be measured, that is, subjected to some kind of rational control, and something that eats its children. This is what the Greeks called *chronos*, but he knows about *kairos* too, the moment that cannot be quantified. It is the thing that is here and gone in the same instant, the very essence of experience, and the very real but evanescent phenomenon that serves as the basis for our attempts to define the nature of the self. This makes 'it' in the cryptic phrase quoted something as vague and all-encompassing as 'life itself', the indivisible moments that we have to divide and thereby denature in order to talk about them. Life is temporary in this sense in that it is only understandable as something that exists in time, but the paradox Faulkner emphasizes here, the one that Quentin cannot get beyond, is that only when the life he thinks about is past can it be present, and then it obviously cannot be what it is.

Presumably Quentin keep repeating 'temporary' throughout this scene, because it is a way of accepting and banishing the hard lesson his father is teaching. In doing so, he strikes a kind of tonic chord that resounds to the end. His anxiety about his sister's sexuality is just a temporary feeling; his sparring with his father is temporary; his worrying about the ethical dilemma in which he finds himself will soon come to an end. His sense of time passing gives the edge to these meditations, and brilliantly sets up the ending of the chapter, the end of Quentin's life, as he puts everything in order in his room before going off to drown himself. The last paragraph is exactly the opposite of all the punctuationless, ethical give-and-take that plots the mind's battle with itself, the one that Faulkner loves to document. Everything in the end is the assertion of order, measurable movements, hard objects, and the first person pronoun. Some twenty clauses in the last paragraphs of the Quentin section begin with 'I'. The self about which he was so unsure gives way to the one that moves around in the physical world. The lower-case letter in Quentin's furious dialogue with his father becomes a capital as it is about to disappear.

Jason's meditations are also fierce and rigid enough for our purposes, but his thoughts are a study in contradictions of a different sort. He is a person who says he does not care about the loss of

Compson dignity even while he cares profoundly, someone utterly contemptuous of women but obsessed with their purity in a very Compson-like way. He is totally absorbed in himself yet deeply concerned about how others see him, repulsive in his cruelty both planned and gratuitous, and perversely attractive because of its eloquent and energetic articulation. In his comments on *The Sound and the Fury*, Faulkner calls Jason 'Logical rational contained and even a philosopher in the old stoic tradition' (1137). This seems odd, given the Stoics' insistence on the importance of virtue and their interest in universal love, but their rejection of the immortality of the soul, impatience with metaphysics, and condemnation of the passions can help us make a sort of sense of that remark. Otherwise, Jason is anything but stoical: his paranoid diatribes against women, big city financiers, lazy black servants, and the iniquity of a world that seems to have been created deliberately to thwart all his designs make the third section of *The Sound and the Fury* a study in the outrage that animates so many of Faulkner's characters, and a comic masterpiece. The language in which Jason's cynicism is couched sweeps us along alike that of Richard III or Iago, and the pleasure of listening to him vent his wrath like a standup comedian often short-circuits our moral indignation.

There are other, quieter moments, when Jason has finished his rant, that enable us to watch his mind at work in a mode a little different from his cynical, take-no-prisoners one. The scene I want to concentrate on here comes near the novel's conclusion. It features an important pair of journeys: while Jason goes in search of the police and the money his niece has stolen, Dilsey and her family go to church. As the examination of Faulkner's early novels showed, he often uses conclusions to focus on the sublime yet oddly reassuring indifference of nature, using the serenity of bucolic rhythms as a background for the incidental noise that human beings make. So too here. The rain has stopped, and the sun emerges 'beyond the trees and roofs and spires of town' (1098), not to shine down serenely on the main players but to illuminate the hills in the distance.

On the way back from his fruitless search, Jason sees the people going to church as a shabby group involved in a meaningless ritual, as those whose acceptance of things as they are constitutes in itself an affront to him because it is a refusal to share his outrage. Jason cannot feel the human links that they do, the ones that constitute the community as Faulkner would have us understand it. That evening he sees them again as someone drives him back to Jefferson:

They drove on, along the streets where people were turning peacefully into houses and Sunday dinners, and on out of town. He
thought that. He wasn't thinking of home, where Ben and Luster
were eating cold dinner at the kitchen table. Something – the
absence of disaster, threat, in any constant evil – permitted him to
forget Jefferson as any place which he had ever seen before, where his
life must resume itself.

(1118)

This is almost the end of his story, the last time we get inside Jason's head.
The world he watches, closed off to him, the functional families in it that
make such a contrast to his, the line he moves in that subtends the arcs
their lives inscribe – all this is straightforward enough. The stage direc-
tional 'He thought that' reminds us once more how misleading it is to
describe *The Sound and the Fury* as an opaque phantasmagoria that betrays
the lack of a desire or ability to communicate. Nothing could be clearer
than a blunt statement like this. Jason is thinking what he sees. This
desire to fix his thoughts in the here and now is a survival mechanism,
something that will help him survive the fraught journey home, but it is
also the first time one of Faulkner's isolates identifies bourgeois comfort
as the thing into which he would like to reintegrate, as improbable as
such a move might seem.

The modernists often fall back on aesthetic wholeness in the face of
various kinds of division, and it is something Faulkner celebrates in the
lines he uses to describe his book. He spoke of writing *The Sound and the
Fury* with an 'emotion definite and physical and yet nebulous to
describe ... that ecstasy, that eager and joyous faith and anticipation of
surprise which the yet unmarred sheets beneath my hand held inviolate
and unfailing.' More succinctly, he advised a friend to read it because it
was 'a real sonofabitch.'[11] Ultimately, the book is his attempt to share
that exultation. Readers should feel something akin to it when they
finish the novel, when the shape of the vision represented in it comes
home to them. It may be true that human history is the Compson family
history writ large, as full of sound and fury as life is for Macbeth. But a
novel whose subject is the complexities involved in any search for
meaning reminds us that to claim, as he does, that something signifies
nothing presupposes the existence of a realm in which it could signify
something. Ultimately the interpreter must decide. After all, who is
Macbeth to assume that he has said the last word about tomorrow, let
alone about 'the last syllable of recorded time'?[12] In his case, after all,
right after he makes his gloomy assessment of human achievement,

impossible prophecies come true, the rightful king defeats him in battle, and the social order is restored to a world that seemed to be characterized by a lust for power and the disappearance of all compassion. Once again, an aesthetically pleasing harmony defeats the forces of fragmentation, until the next ambitious Macbeth-type comes along of course. So too in Faulkner's novel. In the end Jason is defeated. Dilsey is there, holding things together, a representative of what is best in humanity,[13] and there are other decent people in the wings, like her family and the Jefferson sheriff. Julio and his sister are bringing new energies to America. The South and the North are at least interacting, even if they do not understand each other. Our experience of the novel recapitulates our complex reaction to the tragedy from which it takes its name. Both make possible other views of history and culture, of the human capacity to create, and of its need for love and justice. Faulkner wrote *The Sound and the Fury* because he was resigned to writing fiction that would please himself if he could not please others, because he was reconciled to being bypassed by history. It was to become one of the books that helped to make sure that he was not.

Faulkner's new novel pleased him enormously but did not sell well (the print run was only 1789 copies). American readers were obviously not ready to spend money on a book that made so many demands on them and, for a range of political reasons, many writers were eager to stake out progressive positions and defend them in their work. This made it a difficult time for someone like Faulkner to make his reputation. A number of other forces were at work as well. In 1930, Hoover's administration had started to make the series of interventionist mistakes that would turn the recession of 1929 into a decade-long economic crisis. The golden age of radio was underway. Mickey Mouse and Blondie and Dagwood started their lives as comic strips. Grant Wood painted American Gothic. Sinclair Lewis became the first American to win the Nobel Prize for Literature, on the strength of realistic novels like *Main Street* and *Babbitt*, and Thomas Wolfe published *Look Homeward, Angel*. The Southern Agrarians, some of whom were to become great admirers of Faulkner's work, took their stand in a manifesto against industrialism, comparing it to the economic system that was foisted on Russia by the Bolshevik revolution, and condemning its speed, its encouragement of consumerism, its perpetual dissatisfaction with the status quo, and its antipathy to art.

Faulkner had just got married, bought a rundown antebellum mansion, and was saddled with debts of all sorts. Like most authors, he was intent on writing for pleasure and publishing for money. Faced with the poor sales record of his first three novels, and the uncertain reception of

The Sound and the Fury, he tried to do what Hawthorne and Melville before him had done, namely adapt to the public taste. He went to work in earnest on the first version of *Sanctuary*, and finished it in May 1929, hoping its lurid subject matter would make it a best-seller. But his dissatisfaction with the finished product meant major revisions, and it was not published until two years later. In October 1929, a month after *The Sound and the Fury* came out, as if in reaction to all the guessing and compromising, the self-conscious attempt to reorient his career, he opted for another declaration of aesthetic independence. He began *As I Lay Dying*, a novel about a hapless family on a doomed journey to bury their dead, and finished it in less than three months. It is another novel in which Faulkner basically sets out to define what thought is for a range of characters, and explores the subjection of the rational faculties to other powers. In the process, he wrote one of the most brilliant novels of the century. By listening to four of the voices that speak in *As I Lay Dying*, we can see how Faulkner uses such explorations to capitalize on his strengths as a writer and to define new possibilities for the genre. This consummate modernist masterpiece constitutes Faulkner's second permanent addition to American fiction.

Critics have pointed out the differences between character conceived as a voice and as a participant in the fictional world we expect a novelist to create, noting that the net result in *As I Lay Dying* is a 'mosaic of monologues'[14] that is not even internally consistent, making it impossible to answer questions about who is speaking in this text. All this is true but does not constitute a major obstacle: most of the time the voices do speak 'in character', and the proof is that the exceptions stand out, forcing us to ask questions like: Why does Vardaman sound like Darl or the extradiegetic narrative voice at this point? How can someone report on things he has not seen? The issues raised by such questions are interesting but of secondary importance for me here. *As I Lay Dying* retains our interest because it challenges all sorts of preconceptions that readers bring to a novel, including this one about character and voice, describes how ordinary people involved in a series of ordinary and extraordinary crises think, and offers ways of representing these reactions that constitute a sort of verisimilitude at one remove.

The idea of representing a poor Southern family as they see themselves is a first, something new for Faulkner, for fiction written about the South, and for American fiction generally. What Sherwood Anderson in *Winesburg, Ohio* and Edgar Lee Masters in *Spoon River Anthology* did for the frustrated and unhappy inhabitants of the American small town, chronicling their thoughts so as to reveal their hidden desires and secrets generally, Faulkner does for the working poor in Mississippi. Erskine Caldwell published *God's Little Acre* three years later, his study of Georgia sharecroppers and their hard lives. Its steamy realism created something of a sensation, but it is of historical interest only now. It was much more rooted in the actual details of farm life than *As I Lay Dying*, but that is precisely the problem. As a novel it is any man's work. Because we learn only sketchily and indirectly about the Bundrens's land, their farming methods, their poverty, and their attempts to make ends meet, all that part of their existence remains somewhat notional. The novel is a marvellous portrayal of these misfits' everyday lives, full of working, drinking, travelling, standing, dreaming, and so on, but those activities involve the family in such a grotesque series of catastrophic mishaps that the humdrum aspects of their world seem faded by comparison. The effect is exacerbated by the astonishing clarity that Faulkner manages to give their inner lives. His interest in the ambiguity of introspection, with all its comic consequences and tragic implications, figures as prominently in *As I Lay Dying* as it does in *The Sound and the Fury*.

Before looking at this technique in detail, just a word about the title, because it too has a direct bearing on the representation of mental events in the text. Faulkner took it from Book XI, the Book of the Dead, in Homer's *Odyssey*. The words are spoken to Ulysses by Agamemnon, as he recounts his demise at the hands of his adulterous wife. Ulysses has just escaped captivity on Circe's island and is about to be lured by the Sirens, so his pause to chat with the denizens of Hades is a sort of respite from violent adventure. Faulkner's novel is a similar interlude, a conversation in the interstices of a series of events that mark one family's violent adventures as they take their own journey.

As the title suggests, the dead do speak in the world the Bundrens live in: people die at home and the family talks to them, grieves with them, and comes together to bury them. Faulkner can represent all this because he has lived it and is tuned in to the frequencies that people like Addie use to communicate. Her impatience with language – 'words dont ever fit even what they are trying to say at' (115) – is often cited out of context as Faulkner's own. She may think little of words and finish her sentences with superfluous prepositions, but she is very good at using them to convey what she is thinking, and the person who puts them in her mouth seems impressed by their power and quite good at demonstrating it too. The contempt here is for formulaic words, the ones that enable the speaker to take part in an empty ritual. She also compares language to 'the cries of the geese out of the wild darkness in the old terrible nights, fumbling at the deeds like orphans to whom are pointed out in a crowd two faces and told, That is your father, your mother' (117). The novel is full of powerful moments like this, in which words do what we are told they cannot, namely help someone make contact. Such similes catch exactly the eerie quality of the cartoon nightmare Faulkner created here. In a way, the Bundren children too are those words, the fumbling orphans, looking for their parents, as cut off from them as they are from each other. The only links they have are with language, and their story is in one sense then an account of their fumbling attempts to find the words that say themselves, words that say words in an infinite regress.

What Addie thinks, about language in particular and life in general, gives her an impressive array of what are in effect literary lives. She can be seen as an articulate advocate for a provocative homespun philosophy, a determined proto-feminist, and a proletarian spokesperson for one of post-structuralism's most potent insights, the gap between language and reality. And because she does with words what she says one cannot, i.e., make things real, she actively subverts the subversions she embodies. In a famous passage her husband's name becomes a dead word, Anse, 'a shape, a vessel', into which he moves 'like cold molasses flowing out of the darkness into the vessel' (116), a movement that tells us everything we need to know about how alive this dead word is. Addie can also be described as a tragic monument to lost opportunity, someone who has missed out on life, love, and happiness by being born at the wrong time in the wrong place and choosing the wrong husband. With almost equal plausibility, by downplaying the importance of her upbringing, something only hinted at in this elliptical text, and therefore not an integral part of any reading experience, one can make the case for seeing her as the perfect example of a cruel, embittered, untrustworthy malcontent with an ineradicable grudge against life, someone who dislikes her own children, as she tells us so unforgettably in sentence one of her monologue ('I would go down the hill to the spring where I could be quiet and hate them' [114]), is profoundly depressed by the change of the seasons, is resentful about having been born, and gets much of her pleasure by inflicting pain on others. The both/and rather than either/or quality of this text accounts for a great deal of its power and the multiple responses it invariably evokes.

Addie's only female offspring, Dewey Dell, is not nearly as lucid as her mother, nor do her formulations push language into new shapes, but she is as interestingly introspective. Seductive words have pushed her into a new shape, and now she is trying to arrange a miscarriage because she is pregnant out of wedlock, at a time and in a place where such things matter. She does represent another sort of challenge though, in that her name indicates how Faulkner is indifferent to realism's protocols. When Trollope gave the name Quiverful to a character with 14 children, Henry James complained: 'We can believe in the name and we can believe in the children but we cannot manage the combination.'[15] Trollope's *Barchester Towers* is a clever satire that offered itself to be judged by conventional criteria, but they were not James's; Faulkner's *As I Lay Dying* succeeded in defining the criteria by which it would be judged.

Anyway, she is no 'dewy dell', no earth mother, but a reflective, tortured soul in her own right, engaged in trying to make sense of things. With a masterful laconicity, Faulkner conveys all her longing and doubts, her refusal to take responsibility and determination to act, the querulous fatalism of someone who knows but cannot believe, who wants but is unsure. She pauses over a phrase like 'womb of time', and then uses it to explain her own life as 'the agony and the despair of spreading bones, the hard girdle in which lie the outraged entrails of events'. Thus her pregnancy becomes a metaphor for the existence pressing down on her and pushing her aside. As here, her voice can suddenly become more insightful and articulate than her actions or previous interpolations have led us to believe possible. When she describes a nightmare, we get a frenzied, iterative, searching account that conveys how she must struggle for articulateness: '*I couldn't think what I was I couldn't think of my name I couldn't even think I am a girl I couldn't even think I nor even think I want to wake up nor remember what was opposite to awake so I could do that*' (78). In the drum beat of these single syllables Faulkner offers a new take on dream consciousness; or rather dream and reality merge, and this girl realizes that, pregnant and alone, she has moved into a place where she can lose her identity, language, everything. A change in the vocabulary available to this particular voice offers Faulkner another way of adjusting its modulations. At one point Dewey Dell says 'stertorous', meaning to breathe making a snoring sound. This is not a word she is likely to know, but then we have not seen much evidence in her of the sort of sensibility that would come up with the impressions like 'Beyond the hill sheet-lightning stains upward and fades' (42) either. Such details act as markers, the sign of a transition into the lyric/descriptive mode that Faulkner uses to convey how this character's yearning realigns the verbal universe that he controls on her behalf. Whatever conclusions one wishes to draw from that display of authorial power about the arbitrariness of any given sign are there to be drawn.

Vardaman is of course in one sense one of Faulkner specialities, the inarticulate, earthbound absorber of powerful impressions, for whom the writer fashions, not a plausible vocabulary or way of thinking exactly, but a lexical and syntactic simulacrum of simplicity. We come to his sections, expecting them to be prosaic and full of action words that convey with an obsessive's specificity and a child's incomprehension of the nature of his involvement with the family's journey. And in the first part, that is certainly what we do get. His attack on Peabody's horses is a case in point. He feels the life in the horse 'running through the splotches, smelling up into my nose where the sickness is beginning to cry, vomiting the crying' (36). After two pages of this extraordinarily effective representation of uncomprehending adoration and his reaction to something as heartrending as the death of a mother, we 'know' Vardaman.

And yet, as if to punish us for complacency once we have decided that this is all he is, we come to the following in the same chapter:

> It is as though the dark were resolving him out of his integrity, into an unrelated scattering of components – snuffings and stampings; smells of cooling flesh and ammoniac hair; an illusion of a co-ordinated whole of splotched hide and strong bones with which, detached and secret and familiar, an *is* different from my *is*. I see him dissolve – legs, a rolling eye, a gaudy splotching like cold flames – and float upon the dark in fading solution; all one yet neither; all either yet none.
>
> (38)

This character knows horses, from the inside as it were, but here the vocabulary is more complex, the sentence structure more sophisticated, the emotion more diffuse, and the effect more heterogeneous than in the previous description. This is how his thought processes might sound if, *per impossibile*, he could articulate them. It is an interesting way of drawing attention to the language, and of drawing attention to the point of view by suggesting that for this character, so inarticulate, so lost, it exists just as powerfully in some notional prelinguistic state. Disarticulating the horse in this way recalls his reaction to the dead fish – 'all cut up into not–fish now' (36) – and to his famous 'My mother is a fish' assertion, except that the palpable aliveness of this animal has all the soothing force that is needed to counteract the disruptive, torturous thoughts that have put him in a frenzy. This is solipsism with a vengeance, described as it takes over its subjects and turns everything in the field of vision into an illusion. Faulkner ends up sacrificing verisimilitude in the strict sense of character portrayal in order to convey the implications of the tragic realization that he wants Vardaman to epitomize.

Like *The Sound and the Fury*, then, *As I Lay Dying* is a novel about how thought refuses to move along rational lines and how a hypnotic fascination with the physical details of solid objects often alienates the perceiver from the merely human. Faulkner is also interested in showing how a certain kind of madness is involved in the attempt to find a logic in experience. Having seen a dead rabbit and his dead mother, Vardaman is intent on denying the latter by concentrating on the former. He concludes that if his brother nails up his mother's coffin, she is dead in a different way from the rabbit, for which death simply means cooking and eating. Grammar breaks down for him ('I saw when it did not be her' [43]), but Vardaman is right in the sense that the two dead things are distinct, wrong in supposing that nature cares for our insistence on such a distinction. The seemingly impossible changes that something as innocuous as the passage of time creates leave him, understandably enough, convinced that identity is fluid. 'Then it wasn't and she was, and now it is and she wasn't' (44), he notes, still comparing the dead rabbit to the mother, whose death keeps her out of the present tense here. The combination of passion and hopeful logic leads to the grotesque: Vardaman drills holes in the nailed up coffin to give his mother air to breathe, making holes in her face in the process. The constituent parts of the body are indifferent to the sophistries we invent to protect them from time. Not the least interesting thing about such meditations is how much they recall Quentin's battle with articulating how the time passing feels and anticipate Harry Wilbourne's attempt to conceptualize similar things in *If I Forget Thee, Jerusalem*. Different characters, extended family resemblance.

As in Faulkner's early fiction, the thoughts that dominate in *As I Lay Dying* belong to the character with an artist's sensibility. Just looking at a scene through Darl's eyes gives us the chance to listen in as his mind processes and records a series of impressions, often visual. Like his creator, he has a sharp eye for the incidental detail, particularly when it is in motion. Concentrating on it as he does tends to depersonalize and make strange the human actions that are the occasions for these descriptions. Ostensibly interested in how the boards for his mother's coffin are sawn, he ends up watching the shadows of the figures doing the sawing: 'The air smells like sulphur. Upon the impalpable plane of it their shadows form as upon a wall, as though like sound they had not gone very far away in falling but had merely congealed for a moment, immediate and musing' (49). The questions raised by such a meditation involve the effects of sorting out an idiosyncratic synaesthesia, one that enables the perceiver to register smell as palpable, see it as a surface for shadows, and imbue those shadows with the power to muse about things. This blurring affects the perception of time's passing as well by arresting impressions in a virtual present. Faulkner's intensely visual style is also useful for signalling schizophrenia. The haunting quality of all these ambiguities gets transferred to Darl, making him a case study and a collection of strangenesses that render his meditation on the world he sees much more compelling.

When Darl thinks in general terms about humanity, he adopts the vocabulary and even the cadences of Jason Compson Sr: 'How do our lives ravel out into the no-wind, no-sound, the weary gestures wearily recapitulant: echoes of old compulsions with no-hand on no-strings: in sunset we fall into furious attitudes, dead gestures of dolls' (139). Thus Darl near the end of *As I Lay Dying*, just before the Bundren family makes a cast out of concrete for his brother's broken leg. The idea is typical of the novel from which it is taken, an unusual mix of lyric hopelessness and black humour, penetrating insight and patent absurdity. Darl can see what is happening in a way that Anse, another prodigal father who is trying and failing to meet his responsibilities, obviously cannot; but, like Mr Compson, his lack of compassion works to distance him as a character, while the pathetic and ineffectual fumblings of the family make them objects of sympathetic understanding as well as contempt. The idea of the family as dolls or a broken set of figures suggests that the deity, imagined as part practical joker, part malevolent trickster, may well have lost interest in his creation. To 'fall into furious attitudes' constitutes a sort of motto for a host of Faulkner characters, in two senses. They often see themselves as withdrawing from a game, as here, assuming a self-protective stance that precludes action, but shows it was once possible and might be again, if only the actual mechanism can be repaired. They seem frozen, like the characters on Keats's urn, but that too is an illusion. For they go into action in a frenzy of feeling brought on by the conflicts that pit them against each other, the mute, dogged, desperate battles for land, treasure, love, or glory that Faulkner chronicles so memorably.

Like the other characters, Darl sometimes speaks with different voices. Once in a while he is allowed to intone gnomic utterances like 'all people are cowards and naturally prefer any kind of treachery because it has a bland outside' (87), or details from Yoknapatawpha history like Flem Snopes's auctioning off the Texas ponies. Bland, confident, worldly wise, this narratorial voice is used by Faulkner to advance the plot, explaining things like Jewel's acquiring a horse, or Darl's own realization that his sister is pregnant. He also figures most importantly as the novel's poet-in-residence, of imagination all compact with the madman. His is a modernist poetry of precise statement, contained in observations like 'Life was created in the valleys. It blew up onto the hills on the old terrors, the old lusts, the old despairs. That's why you must walk up the hills so you can ride down' (153). What Darl says here can be construed as a cryptic account of human history, how we began by clustering together for warmth, for generation, and then were blown about the hills by our own destructive impulses, and how dealing with those emotions is the interminable part of the Sisyphean version of human life he outlines. The resonance of this sort of lyrical utterance is one of the most striking features of *As I Lay Dying*.

Darl's gradual detachment from a world in which words signify certain things generates the high style that constitutes his distinctive perspicuity. He notices and describes things in a way that we do not. Barthes tells an intriguing story about a conversation with the woman in a local shop on the subject of the weather. The exchange is animated until he permits himself a remark about the quality of the light, and she goes silent. He knows why: in making such an arcane discrimination he has made a point about class, about the different one to which he belongs, one that allows him the luxury of admiring something that cannot be represented.[16] So too here: cultured, sensitive, meditative, inquiring, Darl does not talk like the rest of his family, and the details he notices and the things he makes of them are one of the main ways that Faulkner signals his difference. He is cut off from them by the aesthetic stance he takes on experience.

His tendency to put a frame around whatever moves into his visual field makes him a lucid observer and a dangerous person to have around in an emergency. As Gillespie's barn burns down, he notices 'the coffin on the sawhorses like a cubistic bug' (147), and that the firefighters are 'like two figures in a Greek frieze' (149). Critics have suggested that Darl picked up an interest in modern art during his time in World War One France, and that his fascination with geometric shapes, the flattening effects of the two-dimensional, and the disorientating effects of the collage, have their roots in the painters Faulkner knew and learned from.[17] No doubt this link is significant, but Faulkner's distinctive use of their techniques is also worth noting. Painters like Picasso or Duchamps or Braque illuminate and freeze movement to create a sense of furious energy. Darl sees this arresting process as deeply flawed, calling it 'fury in itself quiet with stagnation' (110), and his disinterested contemplation becomes part of the stagnation he sees.

At crucial points in their respective stories, Quentin and Darl are seized by fits of laughter: Quentin as he contemplates the irony of his being arrested as a threat to the morals of the young, Darl as he thinks of the asylum where he is finally sent. This laughter hits hard because it marks their recognition of the revenge that reality takes on the articulate observer contemplating his patterns in isolation. The grotesque way that their journey refuses to take on the necessary *gravitas*, the refusal of Addie's coffin to play its decorous role, nature's indifference to the family's suffering, all these look comic if one assumes Darl's detached perspective. Both he and Quentin have trouble getting the words out when they see the black humour in things as they are. This hesitation constitutes another of those moments that, as in tragedy, identify the locus of the self discussed earlier in relation to Quentin. But the string of 'yes's' that follows this pause and constitutes Darl's last words could mean any number of other things as well: yes, I accept the absurdity of the world that the Bundren journey has reaffirmed; or, yes, life goes on despite everything; or, yes, the repetition of this vocable is the degree zero of human language, a long sustained hissing sound that marks mere mindless assent and a failure to communicate. We choose. Bleikasten makes a strong case for seeing the ending as a devastating indictment of civilization: 'From the depths of his own madness, Darl discovers – and makes us discover – the madness of the world.'[18] Of course if Darl's laughter and frenzied assent do that, they also speak to the sanity that enables us to make such an assessment. Faulkner prepares for this ending by making Darl someone who can speak authoritatively about his world, and by using a range of tones and vocabularies that emphasize its multifaceted nature. The risk of opting for an exclusively tragic note as a conclusion here is that one ends up solemnly endorsing a sentiment that the novel invites and undermines simultaneously. The risk of not doing it is to reduce this extraordinarily powerful story to the status of splendid farce.

The Sound and the Fury and *As I Lay Dying* helped confirm Faulkner's sense that his future as a novelist involved continuing to search for new ways to please himself, as well as writing books that would have a broader appeal. That was the obligation he imposed on himself as a writer. Accepting that the energy created by so much fierce concentration on such vividly embodied questions will always move in unexpected directions, even when we think we have mastered it, is the obligation these novels impose on us.

4

Major Achievement II

Even while Faulkner was making a date with posterity by revolutionizing American literature with novels like *The Sound and the Fury* and *As I Lay Dying*, he was working on other kinds of fiction: the rewrite of *Sanctuary*, the proofs of which he received in January 1931, and an impressive group of short stories, most notably the ones that appeared in a collection called *These 13* that same year. For all his interest in continuing to experiment with multiple points of view and fragmentation, he was clearly committed to a range of fictional approaches. In this, his reluctance to imitate himself was as important as his desire to reach a larger audience. He continued to work at conveying how the world is processed by the aesthetic sensibility, while adding other ways of seeing and experiencing. The result was two novels, *Sanctuary* and *Light in August*, that took him beyond close-knit groups or single families, focussed on sex and violence, featured a clutch of strange characters whose reflective abilities are inextricably bound up with their incapacity to understand what has happened or is happening to them, and took Faulkner's stylistic abilities and willingness to experiment with different modes of narration to new levels.

The reworked *Sanctuary* had a mixed reception from the beginning: it was dismissed as cheap attempt at sensationalism, praised as an innovative contribution to the genre of the *roman noir*, and analysed in a range of ways, as a grubby naturalistic take on human life, a dream vision, and a psychological thriller. Faulkner's account of its genesis is interesting. He says he 'speculated what a person in Mississippi would believe to be current trends, chose what I thought was the right answer and invented the most horrific tale I could imagine' (1029). Faulkner was the one who was horrified when he saw the book in galleys, and he went about revising it extensively, eliminating and shifting scenes that had made Horace Benbow the central character, simplifying the plot and improving the pace. Less overtly experimental than the two novels just considered, *Sanctuary* nonetheless involves subtle narrative and structural shifts that make it difficult for readers to orient themselves. Writing for a particular audience meant designing the book 'from the outset as a *product* to be sold.'[1] By choosing to retell the story of an imprisoned virgin and her lascivious captor, and drawing on gothic and detective fiction for models, Faulkner made *Sanctuary* derivative in ways that none of his previous novels had been, attractive to a range of readers, but very much his own as well. The outrage some of its scenes evoked (one reviewer claimed the novel was 'a case of art that has lost its values'[2]) helped create a good deal of publicity, but the publisher's financial problems prevented Faulkner from cashing in the way he should have on the sales of his book. As in *The Sound and the Fury* and *As I Lay Dying*, his interest in portraying how his characters' intense reflections enable them to make sense of their experiences remains unchanged, but considerations of plot and character make him proceed somewhat differently here. Tracking what happens in the minds of the novel's two main characters will help with the subject we have been pursuing.

Temple Drake, one of Faulkner's great creations, is interesting because of the odd ways in which she registers impressions and the way he communicates this phenomenon. That may seem an excessively clinical view, considering all the lurid activities she ends up being involved in, but I want to make a case for it, before considering in detail how the second incarnation of Horace Benbow thinks in a new situation. Even the first time we see her, 'lounging in attitudes of belligerent casualness', her eyes 'cool, predatory and discreet', her waist 'slender and urgent' (198), we are struck by how hard Faulkner has to work the language to get her into focus. The way her mind functions is just as interesting, and as problematic. For example, when Temple imagines a football game that she wants to go to, everything is denatured, 'the players, crouching, uttering short, yelping cries like marshfowl disturbed by an alligator, not certain of where the danger is, motionless, poised, encouraging one another with short meaningless cries, plaintive, wary and forlorn' (204). Faulkner liked American football, and was good at describing it, but his character here sounds like a sportscaster from another planet. By staying on the surface, concentrating on sights and sounds, he actually defocalizes the narrative, taking us out of Temple's consciousness, as significant as her visual impressions are, and giving us the sense of how the game would look to someone seeing it through a filter set to render opaque human meaning and purpose.

This technique is one of the things that gives the novel its surreal quality. The attention Faulkner pays to the minute particulars of a given scene casually turns the ostensibly realistic into something vaguely monstrous. Even an action as innocuous as eating a sandwich partakes of this unreality. With Popeye in the car, Temple sits 'motionless, gazing straight at him, her mouth open and the half chewed mass of bread and meat lying upon her tongue' (277). That 'upon' is the distinctively Faulknerian touch, and this grisly vividness in the physical detail provides the backdrop for all the mental activity that goes on in *Sanctuary*. When Hollywood went to work on turning the novel into 'The Story of Temple Drake', the dramatic potential of such scenes must have been deemed minimal, and this little cameo role for a sandwich never made the final cut. The combination of gothic ideas of evil, the inevitability of tragedy, and a naturalism out of Zola helps give the characters' meditations a context. The style that conveys the interaction of such forces was what made the novel Faulkner's own.

He uses the same technique for conveying Temple's reactions to things. The violence of *Sanctuary* is powerful stuff, but the way she registers and reports it is what readers must first react to. The car accident that leads to Temple's meeting with Popeye is another example of the curious way her mind functions in this regard. As he often does when violent things happen in his fiction, Faulkner gives the reader a sense that they are taking place in slow motion: Temple watches 'rigidly and quietly' as she sees the car about to hit the tree. Not normally at a loss for words or for sensationalist gestures, she becomes strangely passive as soon as something dramatic occurs. As the car crashes, she is described as 'carrying a numbing shock upon her shoulder and a picture of two men peering from ... the roadside' (205), another odd formulation, suggesting obliquely that, like Dewey Dell's words, her sensory impressions do not exactly belong to her, that they exist on a plane in which obvious differences between the randomly visual and the tactile count for nothing. The oddity of the locutions ('carrying a numbing shock'?) is cognate with the violence depicted. Predictably enough, in the account of the aftermath of the accident we get, not Temple's feelings or an account of her injuries, but what the onlookers are wearing, what they are carrying, and their reactions generally. Making her alien is much more useful for Faulkner's purposes than making her sympathetic.

In this novel, then, the reader's disorientation is not the result of Faulkner's blurring anything, or sketching in seemingly random details that we must then make sense of, like the ones in Benjy's monologue, but rather of his making them as sharply delineated as possible. In the same sentence we can move from registering Temple's vivid impression of what is happening to uncomprehending, outsider status. When she tries to escape, Faulkner uses the same technique: 'Still running her bones turned to water and she fell flat on her face, still running' (205). It is not clear whether this means that her legs keep moving until she hits the ground, or that she is still running in her own mind, or that she is thrashing around in a prone position. Once again, the inaccessible quality of Temple's impressions are what make her that much more compelling as a character.

The confession in which Temple describes the rape is the most important scene for anyone interested in how her mind works. It also demonstrates the shifts between action and passivity that characterize her time in Popeye's company, influences the reader's response to her appalling mendacity in the courtroom, and prepares us for the final scene in the Luxembourg Gardens as she tries to put America and her past behind her. It is described as 'one of those bright, chatty monologues which women carry on when they realize that they have the center of the stage', a strange mix of the mundane and the bizarre, observations about the noise of a shuck mattress that sit alongside something like one of Darl's deadpan flights of fancy, e.g., 'breathing goes down. You think it goes up, but it doesn't. It goes down you' (328). Describing her reaction, Temple fantasizes about becoming a boy, a corpse, a buxom middle-aged woman, and an old man, while Popeye remains a disembodied hand. Such a monologue reinforces his impotence and spectral presence while it constitutes a splendid example of her capacity for self-creation. She ends up having a penis in her fantasy; he must resort to raping her with a corncob. The result is not only one of the most famous, most morbidly fascinating, and anti-erotic sex scenes in literature, but also one that leaves notions of guilt or blame curiously underdetermined. We get this disorienting version mediated through Temple's perceptions and respond accordingly, in a range of contradictory ways, while the people assembled in the courtroom hear only the prosecutor's moral indignation, see the bloody instrument itself, and bask in their predictable indignation and outrage. Temple's interiorized monologue, by emphasizing her detachment, makes her seem less wronged and more real, while it actually effaces Popeye, making him more shadowy but also more pathetic. The fact that it is left to Horace to moralize this whole sequence also contributes to the distancing effect.

Having used such a passage to sketch in a real-life atmosphere that is simultaneously the stage set for something grand guignol, Faulkner might have kept the doors closed and proceeded by hints and circumspection. One of the things that made the book such a scandal was that he made precisely the opposite choice. The narrative immediately returns to the scene in which, as a result of the rape, Temple is bleeding in the car. Whether it is what she says to Popeye ('"It's still running ... I can feel it"' [274]), women chatting about what has happened ('"that blood'll be worth a thousand dollars to you, honey"' [279]) or the doctor going to work on his patient as Temple listens 'to the secret whisper of her blood' (282), this is rape and its aftermath, in prose written to arrest. Norris and Dreiser, for all their groundbreaking explicitness, never came close to shocking sensibilities like this. Of course not everything before *Sanctuary* in Southern literature had been decorous bodice ripping and timely swooning, but no one had had the imaginative audacity to describe the body in anything like this way before Faulkner.

Only after the physical facts have been firmly established does he turn to the consciousness of the victim, and even in this he proceeds idiosyncratically. The extended meditation on the rape precipitates the sort of passage that we have been studying in novel after novel, the place where the narrative pauses, the scene outside and inside is carefully set, and the emphasis shifts to largish questions about humanity and the cosmos. Remarkably, Faulkner manages to avoid every trace of sentimentality, as he makes Temple lucid, dreamy, confident, terrified, hallucinatory, and reckless by turns. The china ornaments in her room assume poses of 'voluptuous lassitude', a genteel parody of the people in the brothel. The timelessness attested to by their static quality represents a false repose, since the clock on which they sit measures time in a world where quasi-meaningless sex and things like rape with real-life consequences really do happen between people.

Here is Temple is looking at that clock:

> She watched the final light condense into the clock face, and the dial change from a round orifice in the darkness to a disc suspended in nothingness, the original chaos, and change in turn to a crystal ball holding in its still and cryptic depths the ordered chaos of the intricate and shadowy world upon whose scarred flanks the old wounds whirl onward at dizzy speed into darkness lurking with new disasters.[3]
>
> (283)

In the mystical tradition to which Faulkner may be making an oblique reference, the transition from 'original chaos' to 'ordered chaos' is characterized by the appearance of other spheres, namely the sun and the moon, the two lights signifying the ability to interact with and understand the other. Eros and the dark places of the universe are the first things born of chaos, hence perhaps the frequency with which the pairing of eros and chaos occurs in Faulkner, for example, in the passage from *Mosquitoes* quoted in Chapter 2 about how a sculptor works. In *Sanctuary*, Faulkner is the faithful chronicler of the modern counterparts of this ancient process, and he inserts such passages whenever he thinks they are necessary. Temple is the means by which we listen in on these reflections, but in effect this collection of symbolic spheres is precisely what she does not see. As we learn in the next paragraph, she is simply wondering what time it is.

If we turn now to the last scene in which Temple figures, the pattern of associations that Faulkner is setting up becomes that much clearer. She and her father are in Paris, doing the contemporary version of the grand tour, and passing a dreary afternoon in the Luxembourg Gardens. Low-life Memphis is a world away. The park is a humdrum, dusty place, offering a hint of the organic world but also nature acculturated. The band is playing Berlioz for the grey people assembled in the grey light. It is fun to think that the references to the 'crash of music' that sounds 'like tortured Tchaikovsky', and 'fading brasses' all point to Berlioz's 'Symphonie Fantastique'. It includes sections in which a madman imagines he is being marched off to the gallows and another in which he is being tortured by goblins, music that would serve as an appropriate backdrop for the novel's commentary on the human anti-matter that courses through it, but the band is probably playing something more anodyne for this crowd. The statues of 'tranquil queens' (398) assembled to listen make another group of still unravished brides. They provide an appropriate conclusion to a novel in which consciousness is both the means by which aesthetic form is imposed on chaos, and as something as empty and detached as the minds of the statues, waiting in the rain for the musicians to leave the air undisturbed again.

Temple is there, a bit like Jason driving back to Jefferson, looking at everything and thinking nothing, her mind a blank slate on which a set of images inscribes itself. As in the brothel scene, Faulkner emphasizes all the different circles and semi-circles that reproduce themselves, a pool, croquet balls, umbrellas, Temple's compact, a 'semicircle of trees' (398). They form a design that suggests a geometric harmony existing independently of the human mess inhabiting the same world. Emerson says that the eye is the first circle, the horizon the second,[4] but his invitation to interpret such similarities as proof of the universal soul linking observer and world is firmly rejected in Faulkner. And yet ... the banality and emptiness of Temple Drake's Paris stands in sharp contrast to the one Faulkner experienced just five years earlier, during which time he wrote this very passage, the description of the Luxembourg Gardens that was to serve as the conclusion for *Sanctuary*. He told his mother in a letter that it was so beautiful that he was 'about to bust.'[5] Ironically, these intimations of aesthetic perfection on his part were to become the coda for the most sensationally desolate book he was ever to write.

Besides the narrator, Horace Benbow is the only intelligent, compassionate commentator on what happens to Temple or to everyone else in *Sanctuary* for that matter. Twinned with Popeye by virtue of his narcissism and impotence, linked to perversions by the hints concerning his incestuous desires, ineffectual and fastidious in ways that Miss Reba, the madame of the brothel, is not, Horace is still the only character in the novel who has the ability to form a comprehensive view of what happens. He has been dismissed as a balding and effete shadow of Quentin Compson, lacking the courage of his own convictions, but this presupposes that another character, with all those forces of malevolence, ignorance, and prejudice arrayed against him, would have handled things much better. His spectatorship makes him a voyeur, but it also makes him an important witness, capable of judging harshly both what he sees and his own culpability. And phrases like 'The long sound of the rain', the 'gentle dark wind blowing in the long corridors of sleep' (332) blend his consciousness and voice with the narrator's at the end of the novel. As in the conclusion just mentioned, this voice tells us that art is only intermittently a solace from this world, that it offers no solutions for the problems it poses, and that it exists rather as a counterforce of sorts to the sordid acts and the base instincts it so faithfully chronicles.

The argument that, in a world of sleaze, Horace and Popeye are moral equivalents because both nurse illicit desires that dehumanize their potential victims is undermined by their differences. Horace is an intellectual, Popeye does not learn to talk until he is four. Horace is an expert at self-laceration, Popeye cuts up kittens. Horace is haunted by his lover's daughter and indulges his desires as fantasies; Popeye's only affective link with human beings would seem to be a casual interest in killing them if they get in his way. In other words, Horace does not belong in the moral nulliverse that Popeye inhabits. He is a misfit and a mystery, but that is a long way from being a rapist and murderer. Colin McGinn has observed that it is easier to distinguish right from wrong than it is to learn French,[6] and my own experience with both Faulkner and French has convinced me that he is right. In *Sanctuary*

Faulkner's task is not to cast doubt upon conventional notions of evil but rather to show how insidious, multifaceted, and recognizable it is. Besides, compared to the self-absorbed crew in Faulkner's early poems, Horace starts to look like one of Yoknapatawpha's more concerned citizens. The last thing he does in the novel is telephone Little Belle to say something that never does get said.[7] The emphasis in the passage is all on him and his reflections. While he is waiting for her to answer, a line from a poem, 'Less oft is peace', comes to mind. It is an allusion to Shelley's 'To Jane: The Recollection', 'Less oft is peace in Shelley's mind, / Than calm in waters, seen.'[8] As a number of critics have pointed out, the allusion creates a set of references to spiritual unrest and unrequited yearning, and a soupçon of incest.[9] When Horace quotes that line, he is being self-conscious himself, at least self-consciously literary. As in all those novels examined in Chapter 2, the human drama is commented on by the symbolic natural surroundings. In poem and novel, there is a wind blowing in through the open window and the 'light airs of the summer night' are described as 'vague, disturbing' (386), because they make Horace think of lost youth and unfulfilled desires.

The poem he chooses to quote is itself revealing. It begins with a conventional romantic setting: there is the link between an atmospheric outside and the high emotional temperature inside. The discussion of passion and the difference between it and idealized desiring that ensues also sounds familiar. The beloved in the poem is a figure on an urn ('ever fair and kind'), created this time by the imagination of the lover, inspired by but different in kind from the flesh and blood model of it. The speaker contemplates the perfection of nature reflected in the surface of a pool. But, just as a mere breeze can disturb his reverie and efface the 'dear image' of his sister, so too can troubling thoughts take him out of the seductive abstraction of nature reflected in glass-like surfaces and leave him trapped in his own consciousness. Horace is similarly afflicted. In the end, the attempted conversation with little Belle is a flop, and its painfulness (at least on his end) is recorded at some length. Romantic poets are used to singing one-sided lyrics to figures whom that poetry recreates, and their twentieth-century admirers are used to quoting them. Life is messier than literature, so they are often doomed to mumble fragments of such poems to the wind. The whole thing short-circuits any genuine exchange of emotion, and makes a self-contained, pathetic, and ultimately harmless circle.

By having Horace think through the implications of the images, Faulkner brings him and Temple together in ways that help orient us in this strange book. It is not just illicit sexuality and its potential to shock that stand out, but the emptiness of a world in which low affect is the norm. Horace's gloomy contemplation of 'the pattern of evil' is transposed into an even longer meditation on absence. Once more it is evening, the border state, and once again there is a non-human harmony at work; here insects buzzing at 'a low monotonous pitch', a sound that is compared to 'the chemical agony of a world left stark and dying above the tide-edge of the fluid in which it lived and breathed'. This is his garden scene blighted by the human machine that has marred the American pastoral, but he actually registers it and responds to it. The moon that presides over this scene resembles the one in the earlier novels we looked at, except that it gives no light, and the landscape resembles the one that surrounded his solitary counterparts in all those other texts. The clarity of vision needed to define grand things like good and evil is missing, and that is what makes Horace's conclusions so tricky to read and so difficult to credit. As he moves from a naturalistic take on the noise he is half-hearing – it is the buzzing of the insects – to a mystical one – 'it was the friction of the earth on its axis, approaching that moment when it must decide to turn on or to remain forever still' (332) – he poses the problem in stark terms. The squalid emptiness of the lives of Popeye and company belongs to the first world, the buzzing insect one. The aesthete's response he manages to articulate, anthropomorphizing the world by making it a being capable of choices that affect our lives, belongs to the second. It sounds more exalted, but it exists in uneasy parallel with the first and has no power to transcend or subsume it. One of the many things that distinguishes this novel from the early ones is Faulkner's increased interest in inviting readers to hold these two visions in mind simultaneously.

It is hard not to see Faulkner's next novel as an attempt at another compromise between his interest in pleasing the public and his determination to please himself. Like *Sanctuary*, *Light in August* is a novel in which a great deal happens. There are three interwoven stories, each one full of violent desires fulfilled and frustrated. Once again, though, the focus is as much on the characters' attempts to understand how the circumstances in which they find themselves came about, and the way men reflect on and converse about the things thrown up by everyday life is Faulkner's subject. Once again, the questions posed by the meditative scenes and the way he deals with subjects broached in them can help us chart his development during this extraordinarily creative period.

In what follows, I concentrate pretty well exclusively on the representation of Joe Christmas. This might seem a somewhat narrow and even an ill-advised approach to the novel, given Faulkner's comment that it was his 'admiration for women, for the courage and endurance of women'[10] that made him write it. The woman in question is of course Lena Grove, one of his most impressive female characters and the figure whose story helps hold *Light in August* together. Serenely indifferent to the darkness around her, intent on finding her lover and having her baby, she represents a powerful counterforce to the ones that dominate the other action. But in this novel, as in every other one examined thus far, it is mental and emotional turbulence that is at the centre of Faulkner's attention. The sentence after his remark about Lena Grove begins, 'As I told the story I had to get more and more into it.'[11] That 'more and more' is what I try to explain in my account of this stage in Faulkner's career.

Near the beginning of the novel, two men come together to discuss their situation. The setting is late summer peaceful. Hightower, the crazed and isolated minister so often pictured alone, is talking to Byron Bunch, the man who will eventually end up with Lena and her baby. To the discriminating eye, the shadows of maples 'toss faintly upon the August darkness'. The voices in the church, like the ones at the end of *Soldiers' Pay*, are making hauntingly contradictory sounds, 'at once austere and rich, abject and proud, swelling and falling in the quiet summer darkness like a harmonic tide' (65). We begin, in other words, with all the familiar indications: Faulkner is once again going to use a series of images from the world of art and from nature as the backdrop to an exchange brought about by human conflict, an exchange in which things like perspective and design will figure prominently. The prose will notify us when symbolic equations are being made, and what the male figures talk about will serve as a commentary on the action.

Hightower is one of those characters who spends a lot of time trying to understand what has happened to him. He is a broken man, a sort that Faulkner is very good at depicting. His wife has abandoned him long before the action described in *Light in August* begins, and his creator has to choose what information about this to convey to the reader. Sinclair Lewis recounts the gradual demoralisation of a wife in a strait-laced and hypocritical American backwater, and that constitutes the entire story of *Main Street*. Hightower's wife is just a bit player in *Light in August*, but arguably her role – hysteria, madness, nymphomania, violent death – is much more memorable than poor Carol Milford's. And the tone adopted is revealing. Faulkner could have told it quietly, painstakingly, obliquely. All he needs after all is a ruined man who spends his days doing nothing but reflecting on his past and thinking about the life that goes by his door. Instead, Faulkner chose the melodramatic way, gesticulating sermons, the shunning of the wife by haughty parishioners, the attempt to force Hightower to resign, his preaching to an empty church, and KKK visits and beatings. Unable to respond adequately to the passion of his parishioners, a passion to believe if nothing else, he is equally incapable of devoting himself totally to the defence of his wife. Far from judging harshly his banishment by the community, he concludes that the community is but himself writ large, that the accusations he reads in their faces are just another version of his own self-condemnation. Like Job, he has a mini-debate with God, which he too loses, and for the same reason: God's creation has proved to be more strange and terrible, more full of unanswerable questions, than he had ever supposed. All this sets the tone for what follows. This will be a novel in which Hightower figures only intermittently but is 'on stage' in our minds all the time. What he has suffered, others in this community will suffer, and they will react with histrionics and retreat into isolation as he has done. The town will be responsible for passing judgement and taking revenge. The private matters that animate them so much will remain as mysterious and ambiguous as the ones in which Hightower and his dead wife were involved.

As prominently as he figures in scenes early and late in the novel, Hightower is a minor figure beside Joe Christmas. This character's quest for understanding is different from Hightower's, since his isolation as an adult is self-imposed. The conversations he has are mostly with himself, as is often the case with Faulkner's deeply disturbed people. How to convey what is going on in the head of someone so uncommunicative is the test Faulkner set himself in the portrayal of this crucial character, and it calls on all of his resources and innovative powers as a novelist. Joe hears 'voices, murmurs, whispers: of trees, darkness, earth; people: his own voice; other voices evocative of names and times and places – which he had been conscious of all his life without knowing it, which were his life' (476). The indiscriminate phrasing and punctuation reveal just what a disparate collection of black noise this character's mind is. In trying to give readers a range of different ways to listen in on it, Faulkner involves them in the same search that his character has undertaken. To be conscious of something is not necessarily to know it, as we saw in the representation of consciousness in *As I Lay Dying*. At one point Joe muses about who else knows which voices constitute his life and resigns himself to ignorance on that count as well. He thinks it might be a God, but one that has become distracted. Our task is to try to come up with a more illuminating answer.

'Memory believes before knowing remembers' is Faulkner's splendidly succinct, homespun way of reminding us how intuitive and essential our relations with the past are, and how only a particularly angular formulation can convey all the power of that insight. This excursion into cryptic conceptualizing reminds us that origins always explain a lot in Faulkner's fiction. In *Light in August*, there is a long flashback about the dark satanic mills that have figured prominently in Joe's childhood. The orphanage that housed him was 'a big long garbled cold echoing building of dark red brick soot-bleakened ... set in a grassless cinder-strewnpacked compound' (487). I take the lexical inventiveness in such a description (there is 'childtrebling' and 'adjacenting' as well) to be a sign that the subtle effects of this atmosphere are as challenging for ordinary language to account for as the darkness visible Faulkner has just described so lovingly. The word 'garbled' suggests something unclearly articulated or badly organized, something whose meaning refuses to come clear. In a sense, the environment of this institution is everything the blackness of the dark woods and voices is not. That is, humanity, sexuality, desire more generally, and the natural rhythms of organic life are all absent from this building, an orphanage that sounds as if it has no real people to run or inhabit it.

Anyone convinced that one of the best ways of understanding what is at stake in a Faulkner novel is studying his version of Wordsworthian 'spots of time', the dark counterparts of those moments that, when reflected upon, give the poet a sense of how interdependent his being and the world are, will be struck by how neatly such a notion fits the early life of Joe Christmas as Faulkner tracks it in this novel. Joe's initiation to sex is followed by the religious one at the home of the McEacherns, the family that adopts him. Can he learn his catechism? Unfortunately no, and the scene that follows is ugly. One thinks of the flogging incident in *David Copperfield*, the one in which young David proves incapable of reciting his lesson for his new stepfather, but McEachern is an indefatigable super-Murdstone, so self-righteous, so lacking in compassion, and so determined to eradicate the work of the devil that he seems eminently capable of beating his son to death. The violence is nightmarish, otherworldly, and the flogging goes on an impossibly long time. Yet all this is somehow background effects, stage noises. The parties to it are not low affect but no affect. The baffled, thwarted father who cannot make his son repeat the formulaic words may be profoundly, irretrievably stupid and brutal, but he is not worked up, and in this epic contest Joe shows even less emotion. This formative experience really is the obverse of the ones in *The Prelude*, all those pauses in which Wordsworth is exhilarated by the sublimity of solitude. This boy develops in the darkness of such a moment, leaving us to feel that he is holding the unremitting exchange with an opaque universe to which his isolation confines him.

William James points out that, for the behaviourist, any violent physical motion is not so much the consequence of anger as the cause of it, that we often get angry because we lash out at someone, not the other way round. That psychology is inoperative in Faulkner's world. Like Eula Varner's impassioned but passionless suitors calmly squaring off in the woods to do battle, or Henry Sutpen about to murder Charles Bon, Joe and his foster father exist beyond conventional emotion, in a world informed by the heroic ideals of Boys' Own Fiction, romantic principles of characterization, all laid across a naturalistic set of circumstances. A director filming this scene would have to blend the gritty realism of hand-held with the phantasmagoric filter effects of a very bad dream. This combination means that the text moves between different modes of representing reality in ways that are profoundly disorienting, in which the emphasis is always on a lack of emotion. For example, the violent outburst in which Joe murderously attacks his stepfather is presented as the product of a strange sort of restraint. He is also dumbly uncomprehending as his 'girl' screams out her denunciation of him. Brutally beaten by her pimp, he lies perfectly calmly, eyes staring up at nothing.

After Joe has been punished, the boy's body is compared to wood or stone, 'a post or a tower upon which the sentient part of him mused like a hermit, contemplative and remote with ecstasy and selfcrucifixion' (516–7). That last word is the one that has naturally attracted a lot of attention in a book about a 33-year-old with the initials J.C. who is persecuted and killed by a community that does not understand him. Joe is an unlikely Christ figure for all sorts of obvious reasons, but he is certainly other-worldly enough to qualify.[12] And Faulkner is an angular symbolist, keen on getting readers to entertain all kinds of awkward and incongruous equations in order to undermine conventional associations. Many of his male protagonists are would-be hermits, and their detached perspective on their own feelings is as radical as any in modernist fiction. The disjunction between the self and its desires often makes carnal ecstasy impossible, and makes pain a curious sort of pleasure to be 'enjoyed'. To drive home the point, the narrator says that Joe 'felt like an eagle: hard, sufficient, potent, remorseless, strong', and then adds, in one of the rare and therefore privileged proleptic voice-overs in this novel, 'But that passed, though he did not then know that, like the eagle, his own flesh as well as all space was still a cage' (517). Faulkner likes this sort of paradoxical formulation. In his world, to count oneself a king of infinite space does not preclude the possibility of having some very bad dreams indeed.

The recurrent bad dream is of course women, and how Joe thinks about them is one of the central questions in *Light In August*. He hears early about menstruation, another unknown that intrigues him. This prepares us for the scene in which, having escaped a woman sexually interested in him, he finds himself again in the woods, 'among the hard trunks, the branchshadowed quiet, hardfeeling, hardsmelling, invisible'. The compound adjectives constitute a sign that the character seeing the world this way is being worked by strong feelings. This darkness ('not-seeing', 'hardknowing') is threatening, and the visions it encourages apparently illusory and yet mesmerizing. It is a symbol; the moon partially illuminating it is a symbol; the urns that the moon illuminates, 'ranked' and 'blanched', are a third. The urn mentioned at the outset in connection with Lena's first appearance, the haunting Grecian version associated with slow time, sacred groves, journeys that like Zeno's arrow never start and never stop, has been supplanted by a series of dark doubles. The narrator takes care to emphasize the imperfections of these urns, and notes: 'Each one was cracked and from each crack there issued something liquid, deathcolored, and foul.' Our tendency to avoid any attempt at a naturalistic explanation here is facilitated by the blatant equation between 'suavely shaped urns' and women's bod-ies. Whatever extended meditation on the representation of women in Faulkner this elicits, the two-word sentence that summarizes Joe's reaction – 'He vomited' (538) – makes laconically clear how the idea of the female affects him. Menstruation represents a force darker than any woods, and its power to frighten him is precisely what makes it so fascinating.[13]

In the same woods, among the trees, he does what Harry Wilbourne in *If I Forget Thee, Jerusalem* so fatally delays doing, loses his virginity, and thereby accelerates the process by which women become the object of his utter contempt. As always, Faulkner averts his eyes from any actual lovemaking, not necessarily out of prudery of course, but because it is so much more interesting for him to represent the way Joe approaches sex. With Joanna Burden, it is 'security and adultery if not pleasure', a somewhat unusual formulation. Forcing her into bed he feels as if 'he struggled physically with another man for an object of no actual value to either' (572), another one of those amazing sentences that was written to tease out the intricacies of a perverse union and shock the sensibilities of the reader liable to pick up Faulkner's new novel, and ended up intriguing generations of critics, particularly those who have shown how useful it can be to think of sex and gender as constructions.

Like Lena, Joe Christmas is not much of a talker, but rather a loner on the move. So before the murder, Faulkner simply has him take a walk. We get some of his thoughts about Joanna Burden, the woman he is about to kill, repeated like a sort of mantra. He stops to eat and get warm, and the day opens before him, 'like a corridor, an arras, into a still chiaroscuro without urgency' (481). This is an odd way of putting it, since an arras is a tapestry or curtain that covers an opening rather than revealing it, and it is unclear how a technique in painting that brings out subtle contrasts between light and dark with a view to delineating character represents something into which one can move. Both words are apposite though, in the sense that they evoke the notion of aesthetic representation, reality framed and reflected upon. Joe is reading a men's magazine, escapist literature, something about women and killing. And it sounds as if he does escape, 'his whole being suspended by the single trivial combination of letters in quiet and sunny space'. Here he hangs motionless and watches 'the slow flowing of time beneath him' (481). What is being evoked in this phrasing is the Grecian urn again, the one in which time produces a foster child, and life is laid out so quietly and clearly that its meaning seems almost palpable. But, again, the platonized aestheticism Keats's urn argues for so provocatively is worlds away from the sensibility under the microscope here. Brilliantly, quietly, unforgettably, Faulkner conveys another sort of aesthetic stasis that looks a lot like anomie, the dark twin of the arrested motion figured on the urn.[14] As always on one of these tours that lead to disaster, Faulkner's protagonist keeps careful track of the time. It is something regular in an uncertain world, something oddly meaningless – what difference does it make what the clock strikes? – but at the same time deeply meaningful as the fatidic hour appointed for the encounter with the woman in the isolated house approaches.

The language of the description serves as a stand-in for this inarticulate character's attempt to think through his predicament. The power of Hawthorne's symbols inheres in their rich and consistent orchestration: his dark woods are the guilty secrets and illicit desires that his characters harbour or, more to the point, expect others are harbouring. The woods are dark and deep in Frost because they stand for the psychic conflict of the observer who looks longingly into them. Faulkner's dark places signify in successive fashion. As Joe heads for his destination, the emphasis is dark on dark again, the shadows visible on him despite the fact that night has fallen. This part of town is a 'black pit', an 'abyss itself', because it is a world of easy, uncomplicated sex, 'the summer smell and the summer voices of invisible Negroes' (483), the same life of about to be fulfilled desire featured at the end of the early novels. The actual passionate world goes on out there, in the dark, not imaged on a work of plastic art to symbolize eternity, but ebbing and flowing in unseen lives. The voices Joe hears are described as 'murmuring, talking, laughing in a language not his'. Critics are right to enlist such details as proof that Joe is not black, whatever that means, but an equally important point is that the language is not his because he never murmurs, never laughs, can never feel enough for anyone to have such a reaction. Faulkner's language moves up a rhetorical notch to signal the shift, to emphasize just what this isolation signifies:

> As from the bottom of a thick black pit he saw himself enclosed by cabinshapes, vague, kerosenelit, so that the street lamps themselves seemed to be farther spaced, as if the black life, the black breathing had compounded the substance of breath so that not only voices but moving bodies and light itself must become fluid and secrete slowly from particle to particle, of and with the now ponderable night inseparable and one.
>
> (483)

Lights, voices, people, shapes, and words themselves get spliced together here to symbolize a living community. As in modern physics, what makes dark matter 'ponderable' is the kinetic energy at its core, here in phrases like 'black life' and 'black breathing'. (Faulkner has Poe's uncanny ability to make metaphoric and prescient use of the language of the scientists who come after him.) The fact that this rich darkness (and Joe's exclusion from it) is hard to convey in conventional language does not make it less real.

This is one of the rare times that Faulkner gives his character's actual thoughts: 'That's all I wanted,' Joe muses about the group he senses in the dark, 'That don't seem like a whole lot to ask' (484). This is an interesting thing for him to say, since there is so little evidence in the events narrated of his feeling it. But if this is self-delusion, there is not much evidence of that in this character either, as tough as Popeye, as brutal as Jason, as unforgiving as Henry Sutpen. Faulkner's rigorous and unrelenting account of how potentially gregarious human beings get turned into social outcasts is to follow, and it sits oddly beside the image of a would-be bourgeois, card-playing-on-the-family-porch Joe Christmas, but this curious hint of an alternative life for him survives in a separate part of the mind for all those readers who are willing to lend it credence. The victim culture that took hold of the public imagination in America with such force in the 1990s made Joe's reading of his own situation that much more plausible for those sympathetic to its principal tenets. In addition, every time one of Faulkner's utterly isolated characters imagines bourgeois comfort as an unattainable but nonetheless desirable home, we sit up and take notice, particularly because he represents that comfort in such diverse ways.

Listening fairly passively to Joanna Burden's story, one of those superb set pieces that Faulkner could toss off so effortlessly in the 1930s, a patchwork of violence and prejudice, casual murder and gratuitous cruelty, bizarre religious conversions and reconversions, deep antipathy and strange attraction between the generations, the sort of thing out of which Hollywood has made innumerable sagas, Joe says things like 'Just when do men that have different blood in them stop hating one another' (582)? Again, this is a curious thing to say for someone passionately involved in hating himself for the blood that runs in his own veins, but the keyword in it may be 'men'. Joe does not feel strongly enough about the men he fights to hate them, even the stepfather whom he probably kills, at least if we compare that feeling with the one he has for his stepmother, the white prostitute, and of course his interlocutor here whom he finally kills after insulting her in a variety of ways. He listens to her story, responds sympathetically to points made in it, and raises the question of protection of one's blood kin, the duty owed to a parent or child. Yet instead of setting up some kind of different rapport with the woman who has just told him everything, these responses redouble the hatred he feels for her, because she is a woman and because she has made some kind of appeal to him.

Faulkner presents the evolution of the relationship through the eyes of his character and with sparing but quite specific narratorial judgements. Sex with Joanna is compared to falling into a sewer that runs 'only by night' (588). This is not sin but 'filth'. The 'forbidden wordsymbols' (589) (note the reappearance of the compounds, the challenge to conventional language) get said. Beardsley and Petronius are mentioned to emphasize that this is kinky sex and no mistake. Then deliberately, revealingly, in language that could have originated in Hawthorne's reimagined seventeenth-century New England, we are told that 'Within six months she was completely corrupted' (590). Faulkner's use of this adjective suggests that to participate imaginatively in this fable, the reader must at least entertain such harsh moral notions, even though he represents their relationship so ambiguously. It is also the moral significance that the two participants attach to sex that makes it so interesting, and Faulkner's boldness in taking on a subject so far beyond the border of what was generally considered acceptable. Finally there is also the sense that, like a black hole bending rays of light, this character is such a powerful force field that he changes the nature of the narrative voice that Faulkner has created to describe him.

What Joe thinks about women is bound up with what he does with them. Here Faulkner's desire to avoid explicitness serves him well, in the sense that it allows the mystery of such reactions its full play while enabling him to visit places as dark as the ones he explored in *Sanctuary*. The downside of this narrative choice is that it requires him to avoid talking about actual pleasure, even perverse pleasure, for both characters. Little Emily runs off with Steerforth in *David Copperfield*, but because Dickens cannot even hint that she sacrifices home and poor old Ham because sexual transgression is so much fun, she ends up seeming a very one-dimensional, moral lesson of a character as a result. Joanna Burden similarly isolates herself from her past and her family, yet here too it is hard to register what she feels because Faulkner does not really say. If she exists beyond pleasure, in the throes of an insatiable desire, that is one thing, but the cold and passive end of her affair ends up looking a lot like the fiery and acrobatic beginning, just because we do not get any very precise description of either. At one point the proper daytime lady and the wild sexual adventuress are compared to 'two moongleamed shapes struggling drowning in alternate throes upon the surface of a black thick pool beneath the last moon' (591). By making Joanna an opaque dancer in a macabre ballet, Faulkner strikes the appropriate romantic note but distances us from her. How a woman like Joanna feels about sex or thinks about her life is not Faulkner's primary or even secondary interest here.

He gets around the problem of his character's limited capacity for introspection by having Hightower, his other principal victim in *Light in August*, explain why Joe acted the way he did, why his giving himself up to be killed showed he believed in fate, making him 'a volitionless servant of the fatality in which he believed that he did not believe' (605), another of those marvellous phrases that apply to so many of Faulkner's characters. Here the effects of Joe's mixed blood are chronicled in a breathtakingly literal minded way. White blood is restraint and civilized impulses, the means by which life is preserved; black blood is incipient violence and destructive self-indulgence, the thing that makes him lash out at the world. Joe's problem then, as Hightower sees it, is a weakness brought on by the mix, one that leaves Joe incapable of killing his way out of trouble and fated to surrender to his white pursuers in the end. Just why their white blood is not helping them restrain murderous impulses and embrace sweetness and light is not explained.

The account of Joe's experiences does not end there. Even when he is mortally wounded, his eyes are described as 'empty of everything save consciousness'. The fascinating thing about the novel is the skill with which Faulkner convinces readers that 'consciousness' here means and means richly, consciousness conceived as that thing that enables people to make sense of the voices that shout for attention in their head, the means by which a narrative is created from the chaos the world throws at the individual. Clearly the whole befuddled process by which Joe has tried to make sense of these voices is winding down. The eyes are 'peaceful' because they are beyond pain, 'unfathomable' because they have lost their power to signify, and 'unbearable' (742) because, despite everything, they hint at a realm of meaninglessness that Faulkner knows most will flinch away from. As a collection of hints and gestures, the passage is Faulkner's way of preparing the reader for one of those end of the day, end of the story pauses that figure so importantly in the early novels.

On the face of it, it may seem strange to compare the killing and castration of a haunted, misogynistic, murderous misfit by his obsessed pursuer, watched by an assembled crowd, one of whom is vomiting, to compare this with the serene conclusions of *Soldiers' Pay* or *Sartoris*. Yet the parallels are clear. Here is part of the famous scene in which the death is recorded.

> Then his face, body, all, seemed to collapse, to fall in upon itself, and from out the slashed garments about his hips and loins the pent black blood seemed to rush like a released breath. It seemed to rush out of his pale body like the rush of sparks from a rising rocket; upon that black blast the man seemed to rise soaring into their memories forever and ever. They are not to lose it, in whatever peaceful valleys, beside whatever placid and reassuring streams of old age, in the mirroring faces of whatever children they will contemplate old disasters and newer hopes. It will be there, musing, quiet, steadfast, not fading and not particularly threatful, but of itself alone serene, of itself alone triumphant. Again from the town, deadened a little by the walls, the

scream of the siren mounted toward its unbelievable crescendo, passing out of the realm of hearing.

(743)

The passage outlines a context in which this insane outburst of lawless violence must finally be integrated. By the time we get to the end of the first sentence, the mood is already becoming dreamy, ruminative, otherworldly, and the sentence rhythms correspondingly soothing. The narrator provides a surprising, proleptic glimpse of the future, replete with pastoral 'peaceful valleys', through which old age flows in 'streams'. There is also the subtle play with the pronoun 'it' at the heart of the passage. At the start, 'it' is clearly the blood – 'It seemed to rush out' – but that antecedent gets lost by the very next sentence. If 'they' will not 'lose it', then 'it' cannot be the blood, but it is not exactly the memory of the blood either, since the word 'memories' has already been included in the previous sentence. And if 'it' is the 'black blast', how can it be 'musing' and 'quiet'? The point is that in this most action-filled scene imaginable, the final emphasis is not on the present at all, but rather on something soaring into a memory. The crowd gathered is engaged in a communal enterprise, not gawking at a bloody spectacle but musing on the past and speculating about the future. Like the last scene in Faulkner's first novel, where the crooning rhythm of the ex-slaves serves as a lullaby for desire, the 'peaceful valleys' constitute a gesture that moves us from reality to dream, 'out of the realm of hearing' as the last line of the paragraph has it.[15]

Read out of context, such passages might well sound like purple prose or reek of rhetorical self-indulgence, but they are occasioned by concerns that have been there from the outset of Faulkner's career. His resolve to be as honest as he could be about the murderous nature of certain kinds of desire made him include such a scene and write such a novel. He knew that these events, mediated through the consciousness of a distinctive protagonist, would force him to do new things with language if he was to do justice to the complex processes involved. Finally, Faulkner's interest in simultaneously representing violence and horror, and freezing it so as to make it parenthetical, exemplifies his preoccupation with finding a medium that will do what the Grecian urn does. The material he has to work with is a little rawer, but he is as convinced as Keats is about the importance of 'breathing human passion'[16] and its timelessness, and as sure that the lyric language to which he responds so powerfully can do it justice.

The distancing effects continue to the end. As the stories winds to a conclusion, we are invited to look over Hightower's shoulder while he spreads out before him in a sort of tableau all the main players of the novel as they have been presented to us. Byron Bunch and Lena and the baby make one clear triptych. The relatively unclouded future they face represents one facet of life that Faulkner never tires of emphasizing, the fact that it just goes on. Yet Hightower is also thinking of Joe Christmas, someone whose face refuses to come into focus for him. As Hightower looks, it turns out to be a composite, a blend with the face of Joe's killer, Percy Grimm. In one sense, Grimm the white racist equals Joe, the man lost to himself: he is as violent and frustrated, and his revenge as vicious and meaningless. They seem equally passive as well, two men bound on a wheel of anti-desiring, playing out the parts assigned to them by their past and circumstances.[17] But Joe's face is described as 'confused more than any other, as though in the now peaceful throes of a more recent, a more inextricable, compositeness' (763). In the throes of compositeness: with an effort one can just imagine the active passivity involved in this energetic abstraction. Trying to put this composite together, mimicking the activity of Hightower and of course Faulkner himself, has been the reader's full-time job from the beginning.

By way of conclusion, I want to consider a couple of the best-known short stories from this period in light of the questions raised in this chapter. Faulkner published 'A Rose for Emily' in April 1930 and 'Dry September' in January 1931, and they were both included in *These 13* (1931), a remarkable collection that gives a clear sense of his range and abilities in this most difficult of fictional genres.[18] There is 'That Evening Sun', told from the point of view of nine-year-old Quentin, a poignant story of a black woman, who does odd jobs for the Compson family, in mortal danger from her estranged husband. 'Ad Astra' features a bunch of World War One veteran flyers looking for a new life now that the war is over. In 'A Justice', Quentin is 12 and learns the history of Sam Fathers, Isaac McCaslin's mentor in 'The Bear', and in the process something about the ways America's original settlers interacted with the two races that displaced them. All these stories are composed mainly of dialogue, exchanges in which, as skilfully and as obliquely as Hemingway, Faulkner probes the links between self and other, the individual and society, and the idea of citizenship and nationhood. The characters in them are mainly seen from the outside, and what we learn about their hopes, their fears, their preoccupations is mostly by indirection. The short stories I want to concentrate on here are psychological studies of a more intense kind. They too turn on how characters involved in extraordinary situations react to them. The different ways Faulkner enables us to understand the minds of his isolated, inarticulate individuals make these stories particularly appropriate for inclusion here.

The voice in 'A Rose for Emily' that does all the furious reflecting is that of the community, and it is gossipy, wayward, nosy, ignorant, and relentless. What the town thinks it sees and the means by which it conveys that becomes the subject, along with the real-life drama that transpires before its eyes. Once again, the subjection of the rational faculties to other powers comes into play in interesting ways. Chronology is scrambled, and Faulkner adroitly combines character study, sociological commentary, and a murder mystery of a distinctive kind in a few pages.

The story begins with the death of the eponymous character, the end of a life, the end of the story. The first paragraph highlights the driving forces in the tale of Miss Emily Grierson and her scandalous love affair. First there is the gossip that pushes the community to find out more about her and her private life. The importance of the first paragraph is that it hints at her secret, that she has murdered her lover, without revealing it and, in addition, introduces the reader to someone who is in on the mystery but voiceless, Miss Emily's manservant. This is not primarily a story about race, but this figure is there to represent another way of reacting to events, a stoic approach to things as they are. The other force introduced at the beginning concerns the changing culture of the South, its aesthetic excess, its effete qualities, and crucially its inability to embody a set of ideals that can withstand material progress. Miss Emily's house has fallen victim to 'coquettish decay' we are told, and the new commercial spirit is unimpressed by aging beauty of any kind. She is called a 'monument' in paragraph one and a 'tradition' (119)[19] in paragraph three, and the narrative voice fills us in on a history that locates her in that special period between the Civil War and the new century. She is the representative of what has been defeated. Subsequent references to the war accentuate the historical resonance of the story, the poignancy of what happened to this particular woman, in part because she is a citizen of a nation that has disappeared. The invocations of the South remind us of the ideals of womanhood that were such a central part of its culture, and of the consequences of those ideals for individual lives.

The language in which the slow enlightenment of the town is registered constitutes the story's most remarkable feature. The first significant encounter is the one between the town and an ageing Miss Emily, the time that the town officials go to remind her that she must pay her taxes but are rebuffed. Time has slowed in the house, and what should be light is heavy: 'a faint dust rose sluggishly about their thighs', we read, and the style begins to make its strangeness felt. Sluggish dust, thighs instead of legs – there is something viscous in the air that has permeated the humans who live in the house, and flesh is already alien and unhealthy. Miss Emily's body seems to have been 'submerged in motionless water'. Body parts are singled out in odd ways: her bone structure is described with a loaded word like 'skeleton' (121) rather than (say) 'frame'.

As the narrative moves back in time to the moment just after Homer Barron deserts her, we are told there was a bad smell around the place. On a first read through, we of course fail to make the connection, but Faulkner has so adroitly hidden everything in plain sight that the subliminal connections start to make themselves felt. Misdirection is linked to context and theme. Here the theme is dead bodies: that of her father which 'smells' or threatens to when he dies, of the snake or the rat that Miss Emily supposedly needed the poison for, of her own ('She will kill herself' [126]), and of a lover killed to prevent him from leaving. At this point this supposition is too scandalous, too melodramatic, too much like something the people in the town would think for readers to entertain it seriously.

Of course the purpose of the last section is to reveal the mystery itself. It does that, but like the ending of all great stories that go beyond the O. Henry formula of a single, dramatic revelation, often expressed in a 'now you get it' sentence, 'A Rose for Emily' does more than merely conclude with a mystery resolved. As titillating and shocking as it is to find out what was in the room upstairs, the reader is left with something that suggests that other, equally important things are happening. Like the townspeople, we want to learn about this woman's secret life, but in the end we learn as much about ourselves, our voyeurism, the way our point of view has been manipulated, and the pathos of a life denied precisely because the prying eye of the community, the community that we have made common cause with, is so prurient and obsessive.

To remind us that this is a story about Southern history, the conclusion includes two seemingly trivial references. First, there is the disappearance of Miss Emily's servant, who simply walks away when the town arrives to see what is in the house that her death has finally made accessible to the curious. An early version of this story featured a long conversation between him and his mistress about what would happen when she died. Including that would have been a mistake.[20] This man must leave so that he will not be blamed, and it is we who are obliged to infer an explanation, he who must stay silent. Then there is a reference to the confederate soldiers and their tenuous hold on the past. The point here is to emphasize the ways time bends to accommodate memory, storing up the old and rushing past the more recent. This is another of the subjects preoccupying Faulkner during these years, the complicated relationship of time and memory. The reference to the elaborate courtship rituals that belong to another era represents one last example of the changes that have destroyed the world of gallantry that Miss Emily never knew, because she was denied the opportunity to meet men by an overbearing father. His portrait gazing down on her corpse brings home the point with special force, reminding us that this is a story about death in life of a spiritual kind as well.

Only after this crucial contextualizing does Faulkner move to the description of the actual discovery of Homer Barron's body, the secret waiting in the locked room at the top of the house. It constitutes a singular test of his distinctive style. Here it is slow, careful, ornate, drawing attention to itself even while it creates in great detail the encounter towards which the whole story has been moving: 'A thin, acrid pall as of the tomb seemed to lie everywhere upon this room decked and furnished as for a bridal: upon the valance curtains of faded rose color, upon the rose-shaded lights, upon the dressing table, upon the delicate array of crystal and the man's toilet things backed with tarnished silver' (130). The sequence of prepositional phrases slows things down: for the horrific and melodramatic, something measured and controlled, for the revelation of a terrible secret, a prose that reads like a meticulous but neutral report. Again, the observer is pre-eminent, in the sense that its gaze moves around with all the deliberateness of a camera, although here we see through a different sort of observer, and the narrative voice is measured rather than flighty, comprehensive instead of narrow, restrained and keen to present the scene instead of intrusive and committed to interpreting it. This prose actually works against the gossipy, prying, vaguely voyeuristic take on things that has dominated this story from the beginning. Faulkner does not want to leave us with the demotic leveling that has been the dominant mode thus far.

The last section is obviously about sex too, sex and death, and 'the grimace of love' (130) on the face of the bodiless corpse on the bed is the phrase that brings it home. Orgasm is under-described but clearly implied by the phrase. But what does it mean to say that death has cuckolded Homer Barron? Miss Emily was faithful to him, but now she is not. Death has overcome her refusal to submit, just as it did Homer's all those years ago. The phrasing is, as so often in Faulkner, strikingly and suggestively ambiguous. The mystery is not only Miss Emily's desire to lie with a corpse all these years, but also that death regards that desire, or any human attempt to find a temporary escape from its depredations, with the same equanimity.

'Dry September' is another story about repressed desires, or as a phrase in the story has it, the 'bafflement of furious repudiation of truth' (174), another attempt to come to grips with a 'furious unreality' (175). In it, the white community bands together to take revenge on an imagined insult to one of its women, with tragic consequences for a falsely accused black man. Minnie Cooper, the woman who initiates the charge, lives out her fantasy life at the movies, the place where passion exists and is realized without consequences or compromise. The sections devoted to Minnie are all about sex, but written in a way a more decorous author than the one who wrote *Sanctuary* would describe it in 1930s America, by hint and indirection, a description of voile underthings, a phrase like 'nervous body' (174), and a focus on ancillary details from a world in which desire exists but cannot be spoken of directly. This is neatly contrasted with the male world of violence: a world of distinctive garments and nervous bodies too, but one focussing on the real, physical details. The redneck McLendon, intent on saving the white race from an imagined affront, has a sweat-soaked shirt that sticks to him. The victim chosen is Will Mayes, and the smell of his sweat distinguishes him from the others. There is also the taste of the dust, the inertia inspired by the heat, the taunts and insults in which the vigilantes decide to take action, egging each other on, all of which work together to make the male world that much more real, if that much more repugnant.

Hawkshaw, the man who attempts to stop the lynching, is clearly someone to whom we are to respond positively. After all, he does everything he can to save Will Mayes from McLendon and his half-reluctant crew of cowardly bigots. Hawkshaw's saying repeatedly 'I know Will Mayes' constitutes an attempt to take some kind of personal responsibility for the character of this ready-made victim, to individualize him and thereby interfere with the mindless, reflexive process by which a bunch of bored, weak, eager to appear courageous males can talk themselves into lynching an innocent. He alone in the story has understood what is happening; his is the voice of reason in a world of desires constantly threatening to lurch out of control. Or is it? Anne Goodwyn Jones argues that 'white people's "personal knowledge" of black people ... is at the heart of Southern paternalism'. She points out that 'what a white person actually "knows" of any black person ... is a complicated function of masks and silences that serves not "truth" but ideological peace'. The proof is that Hawkshaw also claims to 'know' Minnie Cooper ('I just know and you fellows know how a woman that never — '), a moment in which the ideological generalizations illustrate 'Southern paternalism in its gender rather than its racial mode.' Jones concludes that 'We seem to be, with Foucault, in a world where there is not truth, but only claims of truth, only discourse.' To believe Hawkshaw 'knows' is to make the story 'antiracist but still sexist: Minnie did it, not Will Mayes.'[21] What looks like amoral levelling here is done in the name of a higher morality. The premises of the argument are that one insults the female sex by endorsing the view that Minnie Cooper made up the story of the attack, and that she is guilty of murder in our eyes because her lie causes McClendon and company to react in such a grotesque and violent way. What this reading of the story reminds us is that a bald summary of the violent events or sexual encounters in all the works examined in this chapter must conjure with an absence at their very centre, the fact that they occur offstage, that we learn about them by hints and indirections, and that the way they are reported becomes an integral part of their complex reality. If ascribing greater importance to absences and ideological assumptions risks compromising readers' abilities to engage with the story's felt moments and their implications, that is a choice that readers will have to make.

So what have we learned? Five things, it seems to me, stand out. First, in this fiction Faulkner proves to be adept at finding new ways to interrupt narrative and suspend plot in order to extemporize on whatever conceptual issue – evil, sex, time – is of particular interest. Second, he continues to link stylistic innovation to attempts at conveying things about how characters reflect on their situations, in ways quite unprecedented in American literature. Third, his fascination with the complexities involved in the reflective process militates against arriving at straightforward answers to large questions. Because the characters in these novels can advance ideas in ways that tend to undermine them even as they are being espoused, or act in ways that seem to qualify them, Faulkner creates for himself an ambiguous space that helps make the reader's disorientation both essential and instructive. Fourth, he seems more interested than ever in the ways that reason is in thrall to the power of the emotions that tend to predominate in his fiction, a situation often occasioned by things that have unexpectedly momentous consequences. Finally, an excessive concern with the novels' imperfections as works of art, determined by what must inevitably be a somewhat arbitrary set of criteria, militates against being able to respond to some of the extraordinary things they do. Even a brief look at Faulkner's short fiction supplies eloquent confirmation, should it be needed, of the consistently high level of technical craftsmanship he is capable of when he wants to concentrate on that. We can count ourselves lucky that, having proved to himself that in difficult circumstances he could go from strength to strength, Faulkner eventually abandoned the idea of throwing it all up to become a barnstorming aviator, and elected to stay the course.

5
Two Views of History

In this chapter I want to look at two novels from the mid-1930s, *Pylon*, a book that has never been anyone's favourite Faulkner, and *Absalom, Absalom!*, one that did not sell well and got mostly bad reviews, but is now one of the most highly regarded novels of the century. The two books have a symbiotic relationship in his career: both come out of Faulkner's ideas about how we try to understand history and his search for a style in which to embody them, and both provide an indication of how he was going to direct his energies in the years to come.

Critics have tended to speak dismissively of *Pylon*. John Duvall calls it 'atypical, secondary, and supplemental'; Reynolds Price criticizes its imitation of other writers, singling out the allusions to Eliot and Joyce, for example, as 'unilluminating' and 'obstructive'; and Richard Pearce sees the same allusions as an example of Faulkner's 'overreaching himself'.[1] The novel is certainly a new departure for Faulkner, in its use of faceless, sometimes nameless characters, its setting in an impersonal twentieth-century metropolis based on New Orleans, and its contemporary, rather specialized subject matter, the world of airplane racing, but that still leaves the question of why he chose to write it the way he did, leaning on previous writers to such striking effect. Price says that any tenth-grader can see the flaws of the novel, but if that is true, why did such a shrewd critic of his own fiction and an inveterate reviser choose to publish this version? After looking at the galleys of *Sanctuary*, another new departure, he spent a lot of time reworking them, even though he was eager to get on with other things. He must have seen the 'flaws' of *Pylon* quite differently. A better sense of how Faulkner was thinking in 1934 about history and how we make sense of it might help answer some of the questions that the novel continues to raise.

Satisfied that the sequence of men led to nothing and that the sequence of their society could lead no further, while the mere sequence of time was artificial, and the sequence of thought was chaos, he turned at last to the sequence of force; and thus it happened that, after ten years' pursuit, he found himself lying in the Gallery of Machines at the Great Exposition of 1900, his historical neck broken by the sudden irruption of forces totally new.[2]

Thus Henry Adams in his *Autobiography*, published in 1907. His glimpse of the future in Paris in 1900 made him decide that the old nineteenth-century understanding of history was hopelessly outdated, that the conventional notions of cause and effect it used to explain history were useless, and that, in a world in which the building blocks of reality were particles that had to be described as a 'fiction of thought', some of humanity's most cherished assumptions about the nature of that reality needed radical revision. Working on *Absalom, Absalom!* (then called 'The Dark House') in the summer of 1934, immersed in his Yoknapatawpha material, bemused by the structure and meaning of the history of his created county as it unfolded, Faulkner may have had a milder version of Adams's revelation. In any event, he ended up putting aside his novel and starting on another. He had been impressed that year by the 'Gallery of Machines' he saw at the opening of a new airport in New Orleans. In his new book he tried to do what Adams had done, immerse himself in a different view of human history and think about the technology of his time as a moral power. Faulkner's musings about 'the sequence of force' as it manifested itself in the lives of the daredevil flyers of the 1930s helped produce *Pylon*.

We know that the demonic power of the new technology and the future its arrival portended were very much on Faulkner's mind at this time, and not just because he owned and flew a plane. In November of 1935, his review of a book called *Test Pilot* by Jimmy Collins appeared. He makes four points in the review that are of particular interest to those trying to understand what he wanted to do in *Pylon*. First, he says that what is needed in accounts of flying is a 'self-expression' of speed, a hint of how human beings would be transformed by velocity. Here he joins the futurists like Marinetti and Boccioni in their admiration for the fierceness and beauty of noisy racing machines. Second, he makes it clear that mere journalese for this great subject is not enough. He singles out the banality of Collins's descriptions of nature, and regrets that there is hardly a single figure or phrase in *Test Pilot* that 'suddenly arrests the mind with the fine shock of poetry.' Third, in his conclusion,

Faulkner shows how intrigued he was by the anti-human essence of the new machines and by the apocalyptic visions they encouraged. Finally, the last sentences of the review make clear that Faulkner had hoped this book about flyers heralded a new kind of literature. It would be 'innocent of either love or hate and of course of pity or terror, ... the story of the final disappearance of life from the earth'. He would watch them, Faulkner concludes, 'the little puny mortals, vanishing against a vast and timeless void filled with the sound of incredible engines, within which furious meteors moving in no medium hurtled nowhere, neither pausing nor flagging, forever destroying themselves and one another.'³ Such passages prepare us for the setting, the tone, and the emphasis on the impersonal in the new book.

When Quentin thinks about objects or himself as existing out of time, we feel that there is a certain urgency involved. If Mr Compson intimates that time devours its own children and works in mysterious ways, we register the classical allusion, sit up, and listen with interest. When a relatively undifferentiated observer launches into one of these metaphysical sojourns, Faulkner has more difficulty generating the reader's involvement. We notice this throughout *Pylon*. Because there is no crucially important character in whose thought processes we become immersed, the metaphors Faulkner loves to develop at length sometimes seem a touch homeless. The novel contains the requisite amounts of smouldering outrage and desperate yearning, but we see it only in those fated to occupy the margins of the action. There are, as usual, moments of truth powerfully rendered, as when the mechanic fatefully battles against having a drink in order to stay sober and work on the engine of Shumann's plane ('All he heard now was that thunderous silence and solitude in which a man's spirit crosses the eternal repetitive rubicon of his vice in the instant after the terror and before the triumph becomes dismay' [855]), but no sustained inquiry into how such reflections will affect the characters' behaviour.⁴ The result is a clear emphasis on the present tense and the spectatorial, something that Faulkner works at quite consciously and successfully but against his own instincts. The novel is full of characters who interact and think their own thoughts, and Faulkner is painstaking in conveying all that, but this is an anti-meditative book about an environment in which an intellectual pursuit of any kind seems bizarre and vaguely anachronistic.

Pylon often reads as if it was written by a jaded romancer who has developed an addiction to unusual epithets, someone determined to locate his characters in space and time by giving every noun an adjective and every object a signification. Shoes in a store window are 'slantshimmered by the intervening plate', and 'in unblemished and inviolate implication of horse and spur'. The aeroplanes are 'trim vicious fragile', then 'esoteric and fatal animals not trained or tamed'; the pilots who fly them lean in 'gargantuan irrelation' to their craft. The glass cases in a store are 'lighted suave and sourceless'; the merchandise is stored in an 'inviolate preservative'; and this is just the first page (779). The technique is deliberate, pervasive, and disconcerting. Once foregrounded in this way, the language of thick description takes over, and the hyperdetailed becomes the curiously unreal.[5]

The new airport is also the target of a low-level adjective bombardment: it is a 'soft pale sharp chimaerashape above which pennons floated against a further drowsy immensity which the mind knew must be water' (786). The chimaera, a mythical monster from classical times, part goat, part lion, and part snake, was always represented with wings, and often associated with the storm and thunder. This makes a good symbol for these new beasts that have the power to shock and awe. The last time those pennons were sighted, the reference was to Roncevaux and Charlemagne, and all the heroic exploits that the Sartoris males were determined to imitate. Here they evoke the idea of ostentatious courage in a new age. Like the knights of old, those who fly the new planes are becoming machine-like, harder, less fleshy, and they operate out of a building 'wherein relief or murallimning or bronze and chromium skilfully shadowlurked presented the furious, still, and legendary tale of what man has come to call his conquering of the infinite and impervious air' (800). This new use of the 'action in aesthetic stasis' metaphor that so haunts Faulkner seems worlds apart from the ones in the earlier novels. No more urn-like 'maidens loth' or passionate embraces for this group. Keats's semi-bucolic 'leaf-fring'd legend'[6] has become something ominously hieratic and otherworldly, freed from the human passions except for the pride of self-overcoming. One of the novel's central ironies is that the consequences of the attempt to soar above human involvement prove to be rather more ignominious than the mural's grandiose vision suggests. Outside the airport, crowds like the wandering hordes in *The Waste Land* are described as having 'moiled and milled and trickled'. The surreal airport, the robotic men, the impersonal crowds, this is Faulkner's city of the future, for the machines and the humans, the former in the ascendent, the latter revealed in all their interchangeable anonymity.

In such a world, the daily account supersedes the comprehensive analysis, the newspaper article trumps the novel. Hence the ubiquity of the roving reporter in *Pylon* and the emphasis on the news media. Like

Henry Adams face to face with what he calls a chaotic 'supersensual world',[7] the reporter is frightened by what he discovers that he has in common with the world of power: 'if he were moving, regardless at what terrific speed and in what loneliness, so was it, paralleling him' (970). And Faulkner is trying to find a way to talk about the effect of such a transformation, using the old language to come to terms with the new. At one point the editor removes a watch from a stack of newspapers that have come off the press a couple of hours earlier, and the narrator says: 'from that cryptic staccato crosssection of an instant crystallised and now dead two hours, though only the moment, the instant: the substance itself not only not dead, not complete, but in its very insoluble enigma of human folly and blundering possessing a futile and tragic immortality' (832). Modern life is more amorphous, immediate, meaningful than a newspaper summary, and it is interesting to see Faulkner here investing it with tragic status simply because it cannot be understood and because it just goes on. The lofty perspective outlined above in which the author imagines himself looking down on the puny hordes can make such things easy to forget.

That is not the end of this editor's watch, for he goes on to put it down 'in the exact center' of a line of headline caps: 'FARMERS BANKERS STRIKERS ACREAGE WEATHER POPULATION'. All those different social actors on the one side of centre, the terms referring to environmental and other factors that influence their lives on the other, and time in the middle – various equations involving time as the link between people and their circumstances suggest themselves. Some sort of speeded-up, simplified version of modern life, hinted at by the characterization of the newspapers as a 'staccato crosssection' and the block capitals, may well be involved as well, since these are all everyday matters, far removed from the exotic world of the flyers. However one decides to deal with the symbolism of a writer who loves enigmatic equations, the novel offers its own suggestion, by calling the watch that is lying face down 'the blank backside of the greatest and most inescapable enigma of all' (832). Like Hawthorne, Faulkner enjoys guiding readers in this way, and complicating matters by pointing out symbolic equivalents and meditating on their significance.

After the protagonist's plane crashes, the narrative temporarily turns inward and the world is recorded as it impinges on the reporter's consciousness. It is that time of day that Faulkner particularly loves, all half lights and quarter shadows, when people's loneliness is felt most acutely. There is a crowd busy 'moiling' again, going back and forth across the plaza. The empty bleachers are described as 'skeletonlattice', to drive home the point about death as underlying structure, a *memento mori*. As in the previous passage invoking heroic romance, pennons float above the scene. They fly in the wind, detached from the fray, a symbol of triumph and transience simultaneously. The 'concerted refulgence' (945) of the headlights illuminates them but not the lake where the plane lies buried. This marks the obscurity of that particular event, death's point blank refusal to render up any of its secrets.

Michael Zeitlin has explained why Faulkner filled *Pylon* with so many modernist allusions. Joyce was on the cover of *Time* in early 1934; Faulkner owned a well-thumbed copy of *Ulysses*; and he chose to echo the 'Aeolus' chapter from it in a range of scenes to help recreate a fast-paced idiom for a fast-paced culture, one in which the assault of the media in the form of importunate newspaper boys and screaming headlines defines the new cosmopolis. Zeitlin makes an excellent case for seeing all the neologisms and newspaper headlines, the nameless reporter and the strange cityscapes, as part of Faulkner's search for 'a vocabulary (and the conceptual modes inherent in it)' that can help him 'solve representational problems unique and historically contingent.'[8] As the novel comes to an end, T.S. Eliot's verse hovers almost as insistently as Joyce's prose. Building on the echoes set up by the title he gives his penultimate chapter, 'The Love Song of J. Alfred Prufrock', Faulkner creates his own version of this comfortingly pessimistic poem. The waves perform their 'travail of amazement and outrage' (945) in this chapter, washing over the corpse of the drowned flyer and his plane, celebrating the same sorts of emptiness and oblivion that the waves at the end of 'Prufrock' evoke. The 'human voices'[9] that might wake humanity from its somnolence in Eliot's poem chatter mindlessly about another 'tragedy' in *Pylon*. Like Prufrock, in his last reverie the reporter sees human space closing in on him. His attempt to escape the city is a failure: 'symbolic and encompassing, it outlay all gasolinespanned distances and all clock – or sunstipulated destinations' (970). It sounds as if the reporter too is destined to drown in the actual, his 'overwhelming question' about the meaning of what he has seen left unanswered.

In these ways, then, Faulkner plays with emotional distance and keeps us away from the innermost thoughts that have so interested him in previous novels. *Pylon*'s conclusion fits the pattern. The airman's death is reported in even fewer sentences than Bayard Sartoris's. What does go on for the last few pages is the account of the reactions to that death. The victim is in a plane, almost out of sight. His wife and child are watching, on the ground, and all the spectators report their reaction to her reaction, not what they saw of the actual crash. This is the news, 'up close and personal' as it came to be known on American television, the medium that has done so much to cater to the voyeuristic desires of its audience. *Pylon* is Faulkner's prescient take on how pervasive this response to the spectacle of violent death was to become.

In the end, the issue is once again words and how adequately they can summarize a human life, as exemplified by the way or rather ways that the death of the pilot is written up. The way or rather ways the death of the pilot is written up are interesting. There is a 'literary' obituary, full of clichés and 'whence's' and expressions like 'Roger Shumann got the Last Checkered Flag.' Enough said. Then there is the reporter's cool, factual version, with a joke at the expense of the pilots who dropped a wreath in memory of the victim 'approximately three quarters of a mile away from where Shumann's body is generally supposed to be since they were precision pilots and so did not miss the entire lake' (991). He concludes by inviting those who find the corpse, in whole or in part, to forward the remains to Ohio where his wife has gone. The third version is the reporter's cynical, dismissive commentary on this second summary and his announcement that he is off to get drunk and find a prostitute. Sonorous formulations about heroes of the air living on in the stories of their glorious deeds die the death they deserve here.

The reader ends up seeing these versions through the eyes of the copy boy, who is looking over the shoulder of an editor named Hagood, who is reading the obituary that will go out to the world the next day. The copy boy is, we are told, being introduced to 'not only news but the beginning of literature' (991) by reading the reporter's drafts and marginalia. This might mean that he is being made aware of the different ways a story can be told, so different in fact that heroes become villains, and tragedy becomes black comedy becomes farce. One is reminded of the multiple endings of Melville's *Billy Budd*, where the reader trying to make sense of the complex issues raised by the tale is confronted with two radically different readings, two obituaries of a sort, both of which retell the story, and in so doing mimic the desire of the reader to make sense of a mystery. Like Melville's story, Faulkner's novel leaves us with these different accounts, the heroic, the sarcastic, and the grimly dismissive, in order to represent as honestly as possible the relative status of the human in the new age he had chosen to explore.

This experiment evidently released the energy necessary to return to *Absalom, Absalom!* In turn, his new Yoknapatawpha novel provided an opportunity for exploring family and social history, and gave Faulkner greater scope to ground the reflections of his characters in situations as compelling as the dreams and desires that created them. *Pylon* became the novel in the Faulkner canon that did not fit, not because it was an inexplicable lapse in the middle of an extraordinarily rich creative period, but because he wrote it to question his own assumptions about characterization and the novel, and his sense of what constituted our humanity. *Absalom, Absalom!* was to give him an opportunity to put those assumptions to a different sort of test.

If *Pylon* can be described as an attempt to think about what the world might look like if our notions of history, sequence, and narrative were radically altered, and the human story had no real duration, but was simply invented and destroyed anew every twenty-four hours and reset in block capitals to be hawked on the streets by newsboys the next morning, then *Absalom, Absalom!* is perhaps best considered as a novel dedicated to an examination of the counter proposition. For in it, Faulkner seems to be particularly intrigued by the idea that we experience our lives as a narrative or as a series of stories, and that a combination of slow time coordinated imaginings and compassionate identification is crucial for any attempt to articulate that history. The notion that we systematically construe our selves as protagonists in a coherent story has become particularly popular in the last 30 years, during which all sorts of distinguished thinkers have made the case for it.

In a recent article on the subject, Galen Strawson cites Oliver Sacks, 'each of us constructs and lives a "narrative"'; Jerry Bruner, 'self is a perpetually rewritten story'; Daniel Dennett, 'we are all virtuoso novelists' writing about ourselves; and a number of other contemporary critics to suggest the dominance of the view that people 'experience their lives as a narrative'. Strawson draws a distinction between such people, whom he calls 'diachronic' in their approach to experience, and those who are 'episodic' in their understanding of how the self is related to the past.[10] There is a normative component to the narrativity argument that Strawson wants to highlight as well, the notion that one *should* be able to conceive of one's life as a story. He disagrees, and argues that those who situate narrative so centrally may be motivated by a sense of their own importance, that the stories we tell about ourselves are fated to be flawed by 'invention, falsification, confabulation, revisionism, [and] fiction', and that there are other, equally plausible and useful ways of construing human experience.[11]

The implications of the narrativity thesis are important for anyone interested in Faulkner's attitude to the life of the mind, in the modes of characterization he employs, in the complex interaction of thought and emotion in his work, and in what he takes the nature of the self to be. He is obviously an author for whom the diachronic and narrative – in his own fiction and in his attitude to his own life – are the dominant mode. He would no doubt be prepared to admit that revisionism and fiction are the inevitable results of the attempt to see one's life whole, but that would hardly vitiate for him the whole enterprise, as it clearly does for Strawson. Faulkner's characters in *Absalom, Absalom!* tend to find solace in the attempt to make their lives a narrative project. The novel is organized around the inventions and revisionism implicit in any attempt to seek coherence in a set of lives that constitute some part of the past, at the level of the person, the family, and the culture.

In the list of authors Strawson includes who have tended towards the diachronic and the narrative, we find Augustine, Wordsworth, Dostoevsky, Conrad, and Greene, and one part of the picture Strawson wants to draw starts to become clearer. It is interesting for our purposes here that these are all authors for whom certain key experiences – turning points, moments of vision, hesitations that turned into fateful decisions – organize their reflections. Think of Augustine and the account of his conversion in *The Confessions*, Wordsworth and his 'spots of time' discussed above, Dostoevsky and his mock execution before the firing squad, Conrad's Jim on the Patna or Nostromo with his bars of silver staring out at the ocean, or Greene's portrayal of Bendrix's decision to end his affair. These writers often give us characters who are in a sense authors of their own morality, a morality that is informed by a moment in which they suddenly understand that they have reached an important point in their development or that their lives have changed dramatically. In Chapter 3, these moments of hesitation were discussed as definitional for a kind of self-creation and, in the texts cited, this is obviously at play as well. In addition, these moments are informed by the protagonists' visceral emotional response to their circumstances, one that goes far beyond mere ratiocination. They are involved in trying to turn the episodic into the diachronic, inventing and revising the events and motivations of their own lives and those of others, and recognizing the fateful moments in them. *Absalom, Absalom!* constitutes one of Faulkner's most important contributions to this discussion of how the self might be conceived.

The title is of course from the Bible, and the number of points of comparison between the story it comes from and Faulkner's novel is impressive. The story he chose to allude to in the title of his novel has a double focus: it is about a father and his offspring, a leader and his nation. The words are spoken by David, someone whose human failings make his history as told in II Samuel and I Kings particularly interesting. He is also one of the Old Testament's most impressive figures, a king of Israel favoured by the Lord, someone whose story involves the fate of a whole people. Illicit sex, violent death, and bitter repentance are all featured in this story of alienation and betrayal, and help give the title its multiple associations. David cries out his son's name when he hears of his death, wishing he had died for him. Absalom has been in exile, and the news of his death is delivered in a confused way, in part because one of David's trusted counsellors is responsible for killing the king's son and wants to keep it secret. Things are complicated by the fact that Absalom was killed while leading a rebellion against his own father. He is also a sacrificial victim found hanging from a cross-like structure, pierced through the side with sharp weapons, which introduces a whole range of questions about his typological status.[12] David's grief is seized upon by some of his followers as a lack of commitment to them: i.e., public and private obligations work in contradictory ways to complicate matters further. Faulkner could hardly have chosen a stranger title or a more apposite one for this novel about a father and his murdered son, in a family in which questions of primogeniture are important but unclear, in a land as fraught with conflict as ancient Israel, peopled by families as riven as King David's, as subject to violent changes of fortune, secret plots, and horrific suffering, and as interested in impassioned debate about the meaning of their existence and its legacy. The conflation of personal issues with regional and national ones in both the Bible and *Absalom, Absalom!* constitutes another significant parallel.

The novel appeared at a crucial time in Faulkner's career. Many consider it his most remarkable achievement and the best of the Yoknapatawpha novels. It also marks a new stage in Faulkner's representations of mental processes. The exchanges that fill the book are spoken or imagined as having been spoken, and these reveries, far more than the actions referred to in a book that takes us through a whole century of extraordinary feats of creation and destruction, are in the end the main thing. Of course *Absalom, Absalom!* tells about the rise and fall of Thomas Sutpen, his rejection at the door of a rich landowner, his determination to succeed, his marriage in Haiti, the killing of his first son at the hands of his second, the proposed marriage to his sister-in-law, the impregnating of Wash Jones's granddaughter, which makes it a novel about rebellion, incest, miscegenation, and murderous revenge. Yet Faulkner's interest in the narrativity thesis, the way we conceive of ourselves as part of a story and the way we imagine others' thoughts and feelings as part of that story, makes this remarkable range of activity subordinate in the end.

As evidence for this hypothesis, we learn on page one that this novel, like *Sartoris*, is peopled by ghosts. In the earlier book it is Old Bayard's father and his colleagues, quietly haunting the house to whose inhabitants they have bequeathed both their penchant for violence and their haughty courage. Here it is everyone. The 'real' ghost is Sutpen, now dead but conjured up by an emotion, Miss Coldfield's 'impotent yet indomitable frustration'. This locution with its arresting oxymoron suggests that she is a sort of ghost as well, or at least an other-worldly combination of opposites, there but not there, a woman the size of a child, dressed like a widow though she has never been married, venerable but deprived of a real life. Then there is Quentin, the third ghost, another combination of opposites, someone who is 'talking to himself in the long silence of notpeople, in notlanguage' (6). This is a dialect of ghosts' *lingua franca*, and in this book it is widely spoken, because it alone can represent lives lived most intensely in the minds of the speakers who people this text.

Rosa's Coldfield's reflections are a potpourri of different sorts of texts. They are obviously not verisimilar in the sense that letters or a set of journal entries might be, but rather a means of representing how she might have thought of herself or chosen to represent her life had she been given the opportunity. In a sense that makes Rosa's monologue an example of the falsification or fictionalizing that the diachronic mode encourages, but it also underlines what a range of forces are at work in the construction of a life. Faulkner represents Rosa as knowing nothing and anticipating everything, as innocent, yet highly experienced in the vicarious sense. Using a language that is as explicit in its way as Temple Drake's, yet disconcertingly detached from any lived reality, she speaks of herself at 14 as dreaming of an 'unravished nuptial', 'nightly violation', 'a virgin's itching discontent', 'friction's ravishing of the male-furrowed meat', and being 'weaponed and panoplied as a man instead of hollow woman' (120). This is another bout of florid plain speaking, a matrix of rhetorical flourishes designed to make an emotional point. As we saw in 'A Rose for Emily' and 'Dry September', virginity and solitude are potential sources of violation for women denied the possibility of breaking through into the world of the living, as this language shows. Her story repeatedly reminds us that she has no story, no coherent narrative. Like one of Strawson's episodics, her self exists in the 'now' and proves to be as elusive and difficult to grasp as the language she falls back on in trying to explain herself. But she finds this as frustrating as his episodic self-experiencer finds it fulfilling. Lacking a past, unable to contemplate a future, living in a world with a limited cast of characters and a plot imposed on her by others, she becomes a discouraged, would-be storyteller, someone who is looking for a form in the void.

Rosa identifies parental love as a violation of privacy, partly because this is her particular situation, partly because in some sense this is how Faulkner's characters in general tend to register it: think of Jason Compson on the subject of his mother, or Dewey Dell's relation with her father. For Faulkner to imagine a world in which parents' love is enabling, he would have to people it with beings who are selfless and have the potential to feel fulfilled, and this is for the romancers writing their best-sellers, not him. Rosa puts it this way: 'I who had learned nothing of love, not even parents' love – that fond dear constant violation of privacy, that stultification of the burgeoning and incorrigible I which is the meed and due of all mammalian meat, became not mistress, not beloved, but more than even love; I became all polymath's love's androgynous advocate' (121). That is quite a mouthful. Presumably she calls love a 'polymath' because, like anyone who is impressively multitalented, it can casually assert its supremacy in a range of situations, embody contradictory feelings, burden and support, bliss and torture, and leave us spellbound and uncomprehending as it performs its most impressive activities. Her previous discussion of virginity helps clarify why Miss Rosa speaks of androgyny here. Deprived of love, fated to endure but not having had the chance to prove that she is as tough as a man, as tough as Sutpen himself in her blind pursuit of her own ends, she brings together both sexes and yet insists that she belongs to none. As an advocate, she is powerfully persuasive, by virtue both of what she says and how she acts. Faulkner uses such passages to create a sort of rapt record of pathological obsession: words defined stipulatively, the obvious denied – she repeatedly insists that she felt no love, for example, or jealousy – but convincingly replaced by a deeper, more visceral emotion, one that enables her to make a story out of absence and loss.

In every Faulkner novel, in the scenes filled with violent emotion there are characters who stay absolutely cool, not just fearless but apparently oblivious to any sense of personal danger whatever. At such moments, they become heroic characters in their own stories. For these reasons, they often seem somewhat passive. The vocabulary and syntax in such scenes create effects that help give a sense of the drama involved, but these people are unmoved by it. We have seen repeated instances of this in previous novels: Joe Christmas is obviously one of those ultra-detached types, Percy Grimm, with his blood-curdling imprecations, is one of the other sort. Roger Shumann is another example of the first type, his wife Laverne, the second. The Indians in 'Red Leaves', methodically, remorselessly, good humouredly escorting Issetibbeha's servant to his death with gentle, encouraging words are another instance of Faulknerian A-Type; the servant's passionate attempt to hold on to life makes him a moving example of someone aware of and visibly terrified by what is actually happening. The male Sartorises are part of the first group; most of those married into the family are not, and so on. Linked to this is an overwhelming sense, overwhelming for all these characters and intermittently for the reader, that there is a destiny at work in these lives that cannot be avoided, one that in part explains their superhuman self-control.

In *Absalom, Absalom!*, Rosa is the woman who assumes the role of unmoved mover. The example that illustrates this mode of proceeding is the representation of the killing of Charles Bon. The man threatened with death also presents an utterly calm face to the world. To make sure though that this does not drain the situation of feeling altogether, Faulkner includes what Rosa calls 'the tedious repercussive anti-climax of [death], the rubbishy aftermath to clear away from off the very threshold of despair' (124), and this consists of the long section on building the coffin in which to bury Bon. Just as the grotesque physical details of the Bundrens's journey ground their narrative in the quotidian, so too does the matter-of-fact discussion of how best to get Charles Bon into the ground. The irony is striking: alive, he is a voice imagined, an improbable actor in a melodramatic scene. Dead, he must be dealt with, and at length. '[T]hree women put something into the earth, and covered it, and he had never been' (127), Miss Coldfield tells us, and that represents her summary of what took place. In its devastatingly laconic way, this sentence encapsulates the whole book. The notion of enduring in the face of horror is rendered that much more powerful by virtue of the blunt way in which such a sentence records it. Everyone who remembers a first encounter with this novel as being fraught, the making of repeated attempts to deal with what seems a wilfully circumlocutory prose, should pay particular attention to the tone and structure of a sentence like this.

Rosa's soliloquy is part nostalgic reverie, part sudden awareness of the present moment, which is not a bad description of the way a great many of Faulkner's characters offer their reflections in these novels:

Once there was – Do you mark how the wistaria, sun-impacted on this wall here, distills and penetrates this room as though (light-unimpeded) by secret and attritive progress from mote to mote of obscurity's myriad components? That is the substance of remembering – sense, sight, smell: the muscles with which we see and hear and feel – not mind, not thought.

(118)

In such a passage, Rosa becomes not only a psychological case study, but a student of that study, someone with a theory about how memory functions and emotions work on the mind. Hence the curiously abstracted quality of her meditation on her own life, so intimate yet so detached. Here she articulates another version of Proust's idea of sensory stimuli holding up the edifice of memory, facilitating total recall, keeping the dead alive, but without the attendant pleasure. Although science has shown that the memories triggered by the senses are no more accurate than those caused by words or pictures, Faulkner is entirely consistent here in having his character assert the uncanny power of the senses, the way they trigger strong emotions, and the way they assert their pre-eminence over mere ratiocination. Beyond the actual experience, what Rosa is describing here is a bodily knowledge that connects us with the human past and the mythic one: that is, what she was at 14, and her bonds with 'all the unsistered Eves since the Snake' (119). She may not have experienced much in the last 43 years, brooding over Sutpen's insult, but to judge by such passages, she has done a lot of reflecting on the process of reflection.

Because they are responsible for inventing the details that can never be known, Quentin and Shreve's reconstructions of the past are central for an understanding of how the novel invites us to think about the explanatory power of narrative.[13] The process by which they conjure up the past is described as 'overpassing', which is defined as a sort of no-fault spectral creation:

that happy marriage of speaking and hearing wherein each before the demand, the requirement, forgave condoned and forgot the faulting of the other – faultings both in the creating of this shade whom they discussed (rather, existed in) and in the hearing and sifting and

discarding the false and conserving what seemed true, or fit the pre-
conceived – in order to overpass to love, where there might be paradox and inconsistency but nothing fault nor false.[14]

(261)

The passage suggests how tentative and intuitive this business of getting
at the truth of the past is, and how it in effect depends on errors and
reimaginings if the requisite co-operation is to take place. What Strawson
warns against when he talks of seeing life as a narrative, Quentin and
Shreve embrace eagerly. The criteria used to assess propositions are
nowhere specified; the desire to make the attempt and forgive those who
fall short is all.

The passage quoted also invokes the ethical component of story-
telling, an obligation to a deeper truth that Faulkner always insists on
when he talks about matters of the human heart. Quentin and Shreve
are inventing, but the 'happy marriage' referred to grounds those
inventions in the larger reality of shared desire that the novel explores.
This is a desire for heroes, perhaps, but more importantly a desire for
meaning and the sort of narrative coherence that Strawson considers a
collective delusion. J. Hillis Miller argues that 'Love here is the name
for a relation to history and to other people that may transform ideology and provide the glimpse of an escape from it', and goes on to suggest that knowledge of the past changes our relation to it by providing
'a new space within which decision and action are possible.'[15] This
space in *Absalom, Absalom!* is occupied by Shreve and Quentin while
they are talking. Their triumph over the past is as ephemeral as their
voices in the cold air of Quentin's room, the serenity they create as
transitory as the emotions they study in the ghosts they summon. Yet
the ephemerality of love or the contingent quality of the actions that
ensue from it does not make them less real or less worthy, only more
difficult to quantify as Quentin and Shreve struggle to find words to do
them justice.

Gradually their room at Harvard, characterized as a 'dreamy and heat-
less alcove of what we call the best of thought', is transformed by 'violent
and unratiocinative djinns and demons' (214). 'Unratiocinative' is of
course the Faulkner signature here, and the operative word for describing
much of the reflection in the novel. This is the power that makes
Quentin face up to his demons, try to deal with emotions such as hatred
and jealousy, convince himself that he does not hate the South, and
take the measure of a set of lives that frustrate him because they seem
fragmented or unfinished. In Faulkner's terms, a life like Sutpen's can be

heroic even though his great design is left incomplete, for it simply reminds us that every life is ultimately left incomplete: Mr Compson drinks himself into oblivion; Henry Sutpen, like his grandfather, walls himself up and waits for the end; an array of characters – Rosa, Wash Jones – sustain themselves with a thirst for revenge. Finally, the only thing such a chronicle of wasted energy and unrealized potential can tell us is that life is fickle and its djinns unpredictable. By the same token, that in no way makes these stories not worth trying to understand, rather the reverse. To participate in the retelling of the Sutpen story is to have made a history, and that too constitutes the sort of enduring that Faulkner would have us admire.

For all the imaginative freedom that Quentin enjoys in his attempt at 'overpassing' with Shreve, he remains confined by his own constructions. In the end, the Sutpen house is about to be destroyed by a rousing inferno, as every gothic dwelling must be once it has outlived its usefulness, yet its power to imprison Quentin is undiminished, because he has internalized it. There in the house he finally meets Henry Sutpen, in an encounter that resembles the one between Poe's narrator and Roderick Usher, the former full of torturous imaginings, the latter of dark secrets. They talk, but the exchange is circular and the responses automatic and inconclusive. The figure of the person who loomed so large in his imagination is reduced to a pathetic old man waiting for death. For Quentin, the exchange brings home the dingy inevitability of mortality, that thing that robs life of meaning for him as surely as it guarantees it for those dedicated to living in the moment. Like Henry and Rosa, Quentin is immersed in long time, not time past so much as the monotonous links between the present and the past. He has been temporarily transported in time, back again to the era of the story he and Shreve have created together, and then rushed forward to the present and on into the unforgiving future, as his incantatory mumbling of 'Nevermore of peace' (307) makes clear. The weird echo of Poe's 'The Raven' strikes the right macabre note, and the echo of the anxiety articulated in Shelley's 'To Jane' poem, the one about guilty family secrets, reminds us of the demon that will not let Quentin go.

The final focus is on his thoughts, not Miss Coldfield's, because this novel is about his reconstruction of her past and the way he deals with the recognition that no grand conclusions can be drawn from a retelling of that experience. The fire comes on, the house is destroyed. And here Faulkner works his particular magic, going beyond the merely formulaic devices that he has temporarily appropriated. For nothing is cleansed in this fire for Quentin. One dark house burns, the one in Cambridge, Massachusetts comes back into focus. He has not escaped because there is no escape. Sutpen's daughter Clytie dies in the fire thinking she is protecting a Sutpen. Miss Rosa dies in the ambulance, having failed to protect a Sutpen. What Quentin is witness to is the pointlessness of self-abnegation, something that is revealed to be as useless and even as potentially dangerous as all that Sutpen self-assertion and the tyranny of the past. Especially acutely Quentin seems to feel the pointlessness of female self-abnegation, he who has so many problems with female self-assertion in his previous incarnation in *The Sound and the Fury*.

All that remains are obituaries and proleptic visions, both on the thin side. Shreve pronounces Miss Rosa's obituary, and a very cursory thing it is: 'And she went to bed because it was all finished now, there was nothing left now, nothing out there now but that idiot boy to lurk around those ashes and those four gutted chimneys'. This is a pared down language for a subject that is rapidly becoming a non-subject. Words are repeated, phrases used as a refrain, and the whole thing serves as a vague verbal equivalent of the desolation being described. The four chimneys are of course the ironic markers of Sutpen's failure in his bid for exalted social status. Quentin is equally estranged from the scene, but for different reasons. When he tries to imagine it, he cannot tell which window he is looking at, the outside Cambridge one or the inside one that opens on the South. The whole idea of the South is losing its transformative power for him. Finally what he is trying to conjure up is a representation, a story, not the house but his father's letter describing the catastrophic events that took place there: 'It was becoming quite distinct; he would be able to decipher the words soon, in a moment; even almost now, now, now' (309). We note the careful repetition of the very word that Shreve has just used three times himself, with this crucial difference. When Shreve says 'it was all finished now', he means then, or rather then and now: then there was nothing and now the same emptiness reigns. Quentin reads the 'now' evoked by his father's letter as signifying the moment that an effort of fierce concentration will enable him to grasp, the one in which time present, the thisness of experience, will divulge its secrets.

Despite having come this far, Shreve cannot accompany Quentin to the end of his fiercest reflections. After all, the South is even less real for him than Harvard, and he will soon abandon the Northeast and go back home to Canada. There is a charming attempt on Faulkner's part to link the young men by reminding readers that their countries are joined by the 'Continental Trough' (213). But as Faulkner knows all too well, Alberta is a long way from New England, and those who come from a country founded on compromise will always have trouble understanding one born of a covenant.[16] What is so striking generally about Shreve's last exchange with Quentin is how unproductive it is. These two young men, who have collaborated on a story and worked it out in incredible detail to their own satisfaction, can now barely hear each other. The African blood that Shreve imagines will be triumphant is going to be fairly diluted in a couple of thousand years. Jim Bond may serve as the symbol of a process that will mix the races in a way that leaves all the fanatical discriminations made by Henry and Charles looking like the foolish and cruel things they are. But as one more 'idiot boy' (309) who appears at the conclusion of one more Faulkner novel, unaccompanied by a hint of seasonal renewal or vague promise of transcendence, he is an ambiguous figure at best. In one sense he seems less a person than a bit of background noise, feral howling. The African kings Shreve refers to would seem to have disappeared as definitively as the dream of the man who used and abused them. Their royal blood has gone the way of his self-defined nobility.

Which leaves Quentin's state of mind, his final attitude. Of course in having him deny it so vehemently, Faulkner invites us to think that Quentin does 'hate the South' (311). Like so much in this novel, his final claim is true and not true. The story he helped create is one of desolation and death, but that is now mankind's story as he sees it, so there is no particular reason to hate the South because it offers him a particularly compelling version of a universal vision. He does hate it in the deeper sense, the one that compels him to hate all life because he is convinced that it has so little to offer. Quentin rightly fears that he is about to become one of the ghosts that inhabit the house and his past, the house from his past. What was foretold on the first page comes true on the last: the dead have been brought back to life. Miss Rosa's 'outraged recapitulation' that the narrator speaks of has successfully evoked Sutpen, the object of its contempt. And that ghost is not a ghost, because the consequences of its existence for those who continue to inhabit the real world are still so profound. Yet, paradoxically, it is just a ghost, an imaginative projection of the fears of those left behind, 'quiet, inattentive and harmless'. Yet precisely because it has been evoked 'out of the biding and dreamy and victorious dust' (5), because it is that dust, in this way too it gets to celebrate its certain victory.

Faulkner went on to write other novels about people possessed by ghosts from the past, but the machines of the future continued to haunt him too. The former provided him with more scope for his various talents, the latter the material for his apocalyptic fears. In the end, he remains convinced of the efficacy of diachronic truth-telling, despite its obvious shortcomings. The idea of a dramatic break with history, a new machine age or a new materialist understanding of human desire, proved to be illusory, though it was to recur in other guises in Faulkner's fiction to the end of his life. As Alan Megill points out, 'The notion of a crisis in history presupposes what it sets out to destroy – the idea of history as a continuous process',[17] a useful reminder for those of us tempted to pronounce on things like the ill-starred destiny of America or the imminent downfall of Western culture. Our judgements, like the reporter's nihilism or Quentin's assessment of the South, may be the result of perfectly understandable anxieties, but that is not sufficient justification for our desire to universalize them. Faulkner's dialogic imagination, so prominently on display in these texts that argue with themselves and each other, was crucial for helping him to resist giving in to such a temptation in his fiction.

6
More Experiments with the Novel

Faulkner's situation at the end of the 1930s and the beginning of the 1940s has been variously described. Probably the most impressive thing about it is that he simply kept at it, convinced of the worth of what he was writing in the face of readers' indifference. He was unhappy in Hollywood but worked long hours there to gain the money to pay off his debts and buy himself a 320-acre farm. He struggled to reach out to a larger readership and stay true to his own aesthetic standards, and was as encouraged by the sales of *If I Forget Thee, Jerusalem* as he had been disappointed by those of *The Sound and the Fury*. He was unhappier than ever in his marriage, and found partial solace with Meta Carpenter, the most important of a series of young women with whom he had extended relationships. His problems with alcohol became acute, and binge drinking almost killed him in late 1940, when he became unconscious and had to be rushed to a hospital. It is simply astonishing that during such a time, with so many difficulties and so many demands on him, he managed to produce so much good work.

The three books I want to consider in this chapter, published between 1938 and 1942, are experiments with the novel form, ways of weaving together different stories, including many of the ones he succeeded in placing in popular magazines. Striking variations in tone and style raise questions about authorial control, but that of course could be said – often has been said – about practically all the novels written previously. Here too Faulkner works hard at redefining for his readers the standards by which his fiction is to be judged. Nevertheless, the novels from this period are uneven in somewhat different ways than the fiction that precedes them. Obviously one of the things he is working at is to refine the language in which his characters think about history and about the problems major and minor that it routinely throws up. Questions about narrativity also manifest themselves as an interest in stylized memories, the language of romantic recollection. What Bayard Sartoris thinks, the story that the man tells himself about himself as a boy, and the style that comes into play to communicate the emotion generated by memories of the war constitute Faulkner's subject in the stories that make up *The Unvanquished*. *If I Forget Thee, Jerusalem* (first published as *The Wild Palms*) tells two stories in which plot and its development figure prominently, but the novel's other subject is how two very different men try to think through their situations, to compose a story about them in order better to understand what has happened to them. *Go Down, Moses*, the third novel I want to look at in this chapter, is another collection of stories that demonstrates an important thematic unity with a strikingly disparate collection of tones and styles, and contains some of Faulkner's most profound reflections on how America conceives of itself and its history.

The coming of age of Bayard Sartoris is represented by a series of crucial moments, the sort in which he realizes that his life has assumed a new shape. 'Ambuscade', the first story in *The Unvanquished*, is a brilliant example of this, because it so neatly and definitively depicts the evanescent nature of childhood, ultimately revealing it to be a state that becomes that much more fleeting, no matter how much the diachronic imagination goes to work on it, precisely because it took place in a world that has also disappeared. Bayard and his friend Ringo are playing at war while the real war is about to descend on them and it almost gets them killed. Yet the end of the story reminds us that they are still children: in the hectic encounter with the Yankees they have used bad language and are to have their mouths washed out with soap. The scene takes them back in time, even as it moves them forward, giving a curiously contradictory quality to the limbo in which they find themselves at the end. They blow soap bubbles 'just by breathing' (342), making a game of it, and the bubbles, the taste of the soap, and the light of the day all fade and disappear. The scene concludes with a reference to the mountains in Tennessee where Colonel Sartoris was fighting against the North, the ones Bayard's friend Ringo has confused with the clouds that sometimes envelop them. The conflation is a simple example of childhood ignorance, but it identifies what is on view at the horizon with other things lighter than air: the hopes that took Bayard's father there to fight have disappeared just as definitively as the clouds. In the end, there are no more conversations and Bayard is left with his own reflections. He has seen the ephemeral in action and the ephemerality of action. The vividness of battle, the intensity of living in a mode of heightened consciousness, the power of a passionate cause, the cause of the South – these are all going. The South will be defeated, and its illusions will drift away like the light, the clouds, and the soap bubbles in the sun.

In 'Raid', the third story, Faulkner describes his subject as 'a boy's affinity for smoke and fury and thunder and speed' (382), which is accurate enough, but this story too is about Bayard's reflections on history and his attempt to apprehend its symbolic significance. The phrase is used in an account of his response to the railroad, and the war's attractions, its studies in the exercise of power, mystery, novelty, danger, and excitement, are usefully summarized by that dynamic list. The master trope in this story is again the possibility of arresting time as it moves people back and forth. The race between a Confederate and a Yankee engine along a railway line is described as 'an interval, a space, in which the toad-squatting guns, the panting men and the trembling horses paused, amphitheatric about the embattled land, ... and permitted the sorry business which had dragged on for three years now to be congealed into an irrevocable instant and put to an irrevocable gambit' (384). Defining the moment in which even something as complex as a war can stop for long enough to reveal a meaning was to be Faulkner's subject again in *A Fable*, and the attempt to see it as a drama with a narrative line replays the aesthetic sensibility's desire to put a frame around experience that has interested him from the beginning.

There is lots of derring-do in *The Unvanquished*, but 'Raid' pits the North against the South in a symbolic encounter in which not a lot happens. This too is a story about a superseded past, about not just something that happened once but also something that could never happen again. Everything inheres in the style of the show made, the aesthetic gesture effected by wheels, rods, stack, and fittings, the bravura of blowing the steam whistle whatever the cost in speed or distance covered. The superiority of Southern gallantry, its appeal to the eye, is what will enable it to triumph over Yankee ingenuity. In the end, the Southern train outraces the Northern one, and after the chase, the materialistic Yankees tear up the railway tracks, immune to the significance of the drama in which they have unwittingly participated. We are told that the rails have gone back to nature, 'knotted and twisted about the trunks of trees and already annealing into the living bark' (384). Bayard lingers over this detail because that twisting is significant. Literally, it means no more trains on that track, no more chances to fight the North. This makes him and Ringo, like Quentin and Shreve, inferior to all those who actually participated in the war. Metaphorically, it means no more straight path to glory. Bayard must find his own way to be a hero, to make the curved line straight.

All the references to the links between love and death, honourable death on the field of battle, remind us of the romantic ethos that informs some of the extended meditations about the war in Faulkner's work. In this novel, it is as if Stephen Crane and Hemingway and Remarque had never written, and war is once again romantic valour, clever ploys, noble sacrifices, and endlessly repeatable stories on their way to becoming myths. And one war is all wars. Although the machinery and tactics of warfare change over the years, this battle between the engines resembles 'a meeting between two iron knights of the old time' (385). As the train waits in the Atlanta roundhouse, Southerners come 'to caress the wheels and pistons and iron flanks, to whisper to it in the darkness like lover to mistress' (384). The fact that one of the most memorable scenes in *The Unvanquished* is so centrally related to the romance tradition tells us a lot about what Faulkner thought appropriate for *The Saturday Evening Post* where most of these stories were first published, and about the varied goals he had in creating this short story cycle.

The last story I want to consider, the one universally regarded as the best in *The Unvanquished*, is 'An Odor of Verbena'. Once again, the subject is fierce reflection, this time as exemplified by the language of youthful recollection, and Faulkner's task in adding this story to the series to complete his novel was to offer his readers romance without lapsing into romantic cliché. The first encounter between Bayard and his stepmother Drusilla is all resistance on his part and 'Kiss me, Bayard' on hers. Things get more interesting, but the same combination of a consciously stylized presentation of self distinguishes subsequent scenes. Here is Drusilla speaking to Bayard about the guns she is giving him to avenge the death of his father:

> you will remember me who put into your hands what they say is an attribute only of God's, who took what belongs to heaven and gave it to you. Do you feel them? the long true barrels true as justice, the triggers (you have fired them) quick as retribution, the two of them slender and invincible and fatal as the physical shape of love?
>
> (481)

No wonder critics go looking for sexual symbolism in Faulkner when semi-proper Southern women are willing to point it out so directly. Millgate describes this speech as 'grotesquely and almost ludicrously overwrought in its rhetoric and in its imagery', and suggests that

Faulkner must parody the Sartoris code 'in order to revalue' it.[1] This is also part of the pattern of extravagant gestures that exists from the beginning, when Drusilla is first introduced to the reader as 'the Greek amphora priestess of a succinct and formal violence, or described as having a 'fierce exultant humility'.[2] In Chapter 2, we saw how parody needs as its object something marked out as distinctive from the beginning, and that a certain amount of arbitrariness is inevitable when assessing its goal and effectiveness. The rhetoric of noble revenge, in the Southern context, is such a discourse, but it is hard to decide exactly what Faulkner is doing with it here, or rather it is difficult to conclude that he is doing any single thing. Presumably the sentimentality of some of the other stories in *The Unvanquished* could be characterized in similar fashion, as a subtle parody of the sentiments dear to readers of popular weeklies, for example. Parody is after all the trope of choice for the experimental novelist keen to survey different modes of expression and disorient readers, since it constitutes a serious obstacle for those accustomed to invoking absolute criteria for judgements of aesthetic value. More generally, Faulkner's most characteristic gestures as a writer often seem programmed to evoke the contradictory responses that such a passage inevitably creates.

The language of romantic recollection colours the narrative at its climactic moments. For Bayard, a sense of imminent danger is both a physical sensation and a rough assemblage of concepts that impinge themselves on his mind, but even putting it that way makes it sound too cerebral. It manifests itself physically by a quick intake of breath, a 'panting' that suggested Bayard's being generally overwrought by the death of the father, keen for revenge, and – given the explicitness of the sexual symbolism in the pistol scene – aroused by the prospect of it. Although none of these is irrelevant, Faulkner typically, deftly, redirects the reader's attention by defining 'it' himself: 'this was it – the regret and grief, the despair out of which the tragic mute insensitive bones stand up that can bear anything, anything' (483). The three epithets for 'bones' are carefully chosen: they are tragic because the father's death indicates how all who witness it must accept such an end as a part of the high moral code his life exemplifies. No amount of insistence on the power of reason or compassion in the world can distract us here. The bones are mute because, unlike Drusilla and Bayard, they do not have to resist the temptation to pose, or try to capture their feelings in memorable words. In short, there is no danger that the thing they stand for will be obscured by the attempt to transform it into meaningful language. And, finally, they are insensitive because they are made of sterner stuff than all that soft tissue with its nerves and vulnerability.

Faulkner loves silence for many reasons, and this is one of the most important. The human voice fated to go on talking after the last ding-dong of doom is estimable, because it represents the continuity of the species, but also dispiriting, because it diminishes the tragic grandeur of wordless stoicism that he so admires.

Note that in this passage we are directed not to one 'it' but at least two. Grief, the most disabling of emotions, is the first one, and the fact that people continue to function in spite of it is Faulkner's way of drawing attention to a truth that makes Bayard's bereavement more difficult, even while it makes it less. Remember Emerson on grief and the loss of his son. Something he thought was part of him is not, and what seemed a moment of truth, a chance to see more deeply into 'real nature', has come and gone and left no trace. Imminent death is the second 'it'. Our own death awaits, 'An Odor of Verbena' implies, not as some grand gesture or meaningful conclusion, but as the grimly anticipated moment in which whatever illusions we had about life will be permanently banished. Ruskin says famously that 'the only question (determined mostly by fraud in peace and force in war) is, Who is to die, and how?'[3] That question dominates in the three novels under consideration here.

The story ends with – what else? – two men talking quietly, one of them thinking about what has just transpired, convinced that the ghosts left behind are powerful, and that he has gone through a moment in which he hesitated, decided, and changed his life forever. The usual paradoxes abound as well: by not revenging his father's death, Bayard has avenged it; by not expressing his love for Drusilla, he has kept it inviolate. Once again, the ambiguous meaning of a series of violent events is emphasized, right up to the last gesture mentioned in the novel, Drusilla's leaving a sprig of verbena on Bayard's pillow. Faulkner was asked what it signified by a student at the University of Virginia, and answered that it was the sign of her recognition of Bayard's courage.[4] If we think of it in terms of the dream of a nation that Drusilla was defending for her dead husband, then the odour of verbena is part of an elaborately worked out series that includes the taste of the soap, the intensity of violent desire, and the bitterness of defeat. Each of these is powerful despite its evanescence, immaterial and yet real, obviously part of a symbolic set of images and yet very much one with a tangible South that Bayard is called upon to defend. In this way, words and symbols convey meaning and bind together the stories just as surely as themes like the plight of the blacks or the Southern code of honour. One reason Faulkner added this story to the sequence was to recreate such crucial moments in Bayard's meditation on the past.

If I Forget Thee, Jerusalem resembles *The Unvanquished* in that it organizes itself around a series of fierce reflections as well. The protagonists' thoughts on time, death, survival, and thinking itself help frame one story that makes up the novel; the narrator's ruminations on equally large questions shape the other. The allusion in the title is to Psalm 137, in which the Israelites lament their exile. Like the characters in Faulkner's novel, their plight depends upon the tenacity of memory. The phrase quoted is a dependent clause, added to a plea for punishment, should the past be forgotten. The intention of the whole verse is to articulate an impossibility and make a pledge: it is unimaginable that we exiles will forget where we came from. The verse also implies that the exiles will never give up on the attempt to get back home, which casts an interesting light on the resignation of the two protagonists at the end of their respective stories. The sentiments expressed in the psalm are bracketed by typical Old Testament sadism and vaguely masochistic melancholy, which makes them particularly appropriate for this novel. The captives make the promise because they are mocked by their captors, the Babylonians, and invited to sing a song of their homeland. In their turn the Israelites vividly recall outrages performed against their city by the infidels and pledge a hideous revenge on their enemies, replete with evocations of scenes in which the babies of their tormentors will be smashed against a rock. This too suggests links with Faulkner's novel, for in it life takes its revenge on everyone, Charlotte and Harry for their determined pursuit of pleasure, and the convict for not seeking to escape. Charlotte dies and the other two are given prison sentences by a society that (it is implied) is mindlessly vindictive because it is unable to see the deeper patterns of personal history. If one reads their stories as examples of the dangers implicit in the passive acceptance of one's situation, because a resignation to one's supposed destiny can mean self-obliteration in the present, other links with the verse from the psalm suggest themselves.

By choosing to situate his characters outside of Yoknapatawpha County, Faulkner merely transposes to a new locale the concerns that characterize his fiction in this period. The meditations on narrativizing the past in *Absalom, Absalom!* and *The Unvanquished* are replayed in a new key here. The novel can be read as a gritty, naturalistic tale about adultery, abortion and death, but that story is repeatedly set aside in meditative moments like the ones in previous novels, moments in which Faulkner engages in the sort of extended, richly rhetorical commentary on issues raised by the plot. Such self-reflexiveness applies to the nature of the story itself: when something that happens only in books – Harry's finding a wallet full of money at precisely the moment when that money will radically alter the future and make going off with Charlotte possible – actually does happen to Harry, Faulkner cleverly distracts readers while he is borrowing from that fiction to make his 'real life drama' possible: 'It should be the books,' says Harry, 'the people in the books inventing and reading about us'. Not only that: he goes on to add that what makes characters in a novel different from their real-life counterparts is that the former are *'males and females but without the pricks or cunts'* (529). It is not the least of the ironies of this strange book that it concludes with Harry wishing for a world in which he could retreat into the monastic enclave hinted at in the airbrushed literature he dismisses so contemptuously here.

This talk about books and life is part of the larger meditation at the centre of this novel on the difficulties inherent in the search for a language that can express adequately desires that are often obscure to us. Charlotte's Sutpen-like grand design, the perfect love affair, and the impossibility of its realization are Faulkner's subject here, but most of that project is conveyed through Harry's reflections. His failure to achieve what he wants is at least as interesting as hers, and better documented. I want to concentrate on two more 'males in dialogue' moments in which the narrative pauses so that such questions can be pursued at length, namely the two conversations that Harry has, the first with his friend McCord and the second with the Doctor when Charlotte is dying.

Harry's account of his relationship with Charlotte is a study in how complex men's attitudes to women are in Faulkner's novels. They have spent a lot of time together in a Walden-type setting, and it is perfect but somehow sterile. The pursuit of the ideal seems to have corrupted the ideal. Having delighted in the signs of the changing seasons, Harry foreswears all Thoreau-type praise for sensation, and thinks of Indian summer as a seduction by Nature, now dismissed as 'an old whore' (573) for fooling him into wanting her, for making him think the beautiful days would last. The sensations evoked by Charlotte fade with the disappearance of late summer. Thomas McHaney makes a compelling case for linking this unmasking of the illusory quality of human existence to Schopenhauer and the veil of Maya,[5] but it may also be an Americanized version of Sartrean existentialism, a yearning for authenticity that is stifled by routine. Harry cannot stand the boredom of his return to nature, and he is equally impatient with regimen and creature comforts. The misogynistic subtext here is complemented by a disdain for physical pleasure itself. The idea of trying to organize his life around Charlotte's sexual attractiveness goes bad, although he does not say why exactly. Perhaps his lack of sexual experience leaves him unprepared for the fading of passion that such relationships normally feature. Or maybe it is just the inability to parlay the intensity of such an experience into something that does last, into a story that is more than just a collection of moments, that so disappoints him. The discussion precipitated by this question constitutes the defining moment in so many Faulkner novels, two men, sitting alone, talking, although here the ostensible dialogue becomes an occasionally interrupted monologue fairly quickly. Harry explains to McCord that he does not want to become a mere bourgeois husband, 'the doomed worm blind to all passion and dead to all hope and not even knowing it, oblivious and unaware in the face of all darkness, all unknown, the underlying All-Derisive biding to blast him' (585). In the same way that the Old English epic poet saw the world in terms of a stark contrast of forces and used the binding qualities of alliteration to assist his hypnotized listeners' inspired imaginings, in this passage Harry inscribes himself in the glorious excesses of a Faulknerian rhetorical tradition. According to this view, such expressions are not so much stylistic self-indulgence as examples of a rhythm and a vocabulary commensurate with the world-shattering process in which Harry is unwittingly caught up. It is also a magnificent, romantic rodomontade that announces a serious, conceptual treatment of the subject, as does the reappearance of the probably non-existent but definitely malevolent god that haunted Hardy's imagination in the nineteenth century and Beckett's in the twentieth. Harry is gloomy about the quintessentially benighted status of a species that does not know its own meaninglessness.

According to Harry, virginity is a kind of physiological timelessness, an absence that makes itself felt by preventing those afflicted with it from entering time. He imagines it in the form of a rather terrifying set of images, 'dark precipice' (588) and so on, and then conflates the moment of orgasm with a human life span. For Harry, both symbolize intensity and, interestingly enough, solitude. This prompts him to propound a theory of time, no mean feat, and he gets lost fairly quickly: 'I was not. Then I am, and time being retroactive, is was and will be' (588). So far, so unenlightening, but when he compares being out of time to virginity, the point starts to become clearer. The first male orgasm is described as:

> One final fluxive Yes out of the terror in which you surrender volition, hope, all – the darkness, the falling, the thunder of solitude, the shock, the death, the movement when, stopped physically by

the ponderable clay, you yet feel all your life rush out of you into the pervading immemorial blind receptive matrix, the hot fluid blind foundation – grave-womb or womb-grave, it's all one.

(589)[6]

Or, there goes another novel, as Woody Allen quotes Balzac as saying after a night of strenuous passion. Such linguistic extravaganzas link Harry with Rosa Coldfield, two fierce, inexperienced idealists, given to provocative metaphors, intriguingly hyperbolic, pathologically dualistic, and self-consciously apocalyptic. And his project is very much hers, reacting to the violence of virginity lost, whether imagined or real. We are supposed to feel his bafflement, but there is also something self-regarding about Harry's using such words to characterize the time spent with Charlotte and to justify his disaffection when, despite all the close-ups and the work with details, the novel contains so little in the way of interactions that could confirm his reading of what has happened to the two of them.

In such passages, he sounds more like a critic in love with a theory and a vocabulary than someone trying to deal with an emotional upheaval. The subsequent references to 'the mausoleum of love, ... the stinking catafalque of the dead corpse borne between the olfactoryless walking shapes of the immortal unsentient demanding ancient meat' (590) help extend the lexical register but still leave us a little puzzled. Obviously one of the reasons Harry reacts so harshly to the waning of physical passion that everyday life imposes on couples like theirs is that no protracted, organized relationship is possible on the terms that he has set for it. In that sense, this novel features another, very interesting version of the lack of success which so many Faulkner characters studied thus far have had when trying to make sexual desire a meaningful part of an extended human exchange. The whole idea of thinking about sex in this way, as a male impulse that has a deadening effect when it inevitably weakens, is of course a major part of the problem.

As the story moves towards what is perhaps the most painful conclusion Faulkner ever wrote, Charlotte's death after her lover botches the abortion she begs him to perform, the author must proceed with great care. The risk of overwrought language for his overwrought people at this stage is a serious one. What helps him is the incomprehension that characterizes all the principals at this point. Harry does not understand what is happening. The doctor does not either, but he does not know that he does not, hence all the exclamation marks, the italics (*'This is too much! There are rules! Limits!'* [684]), the references to fornication and the like.

This is the language of conventional condemnation, perfectly serviceable as far as it goes, which, in a Faulkner novel, is not very far at all. Even Satan is invoked at one point, as if he could help explain human ills. The doctor is only 46, but he is dismissed as a 'profound and now deathless desiccated spirit which had contrived to retire into pure morality' (685). The adjectives are the giveaway here, particularly 'desiccated' and 'pure'. They are the signs that this man has ceased to matter, in the ethical sense, because human circumstances are always humid and impure in Faulkner's world. The doctor disapproves of wild passion, because it has passed him by and, although he does not even know it, because he has been so weak as to conclude that not having experienced such a passion makes him the fortunate one. Harry's choice at the end of grief over nothing is being prepared for.

When the narrative moves back inside his consciousness, we learn that the terror he is enduring is self-created, imaged as a 'black wind' that prevents his body from functioning properly. Tears, heartbeats, all this basic machinery seems not to be working, and yet it is: '*it's not that I really cant breathe*', he concludes, '*because apparently the heart can stand anything anything anything*' (685). Quentin (and Hamlet before him) resorts to similar sorts of triple repetition when he is in a state of emotional turmoil. Faulkner needs words for Harry's experience that will convince us that Harry is not simply trying to turn experience into mere words. The wind is a symbol of death, but death that laughs rather than moans, chuckles and whispers rather than shrieking like a fury, denying high tragedy, emphasizing the mundane, forcing Harry to conjure with all the details, the lamp, the door, the walls, and the silence. Around him the doctor gives furious orders and arranges for Harry's arrest; inside, Harry is passing judgement on his whole life: '*I guessed wrong. It's incredible, not that I should have had to guess but that I should have guessed so wrong*' (686). This is not so much a reference to the bungled operation or to the summoning of the doctor, but rather to the guess that he made about love, about his underestimating the importance of desire even when one has a high ideal and the willingness to pursue it. Harry looks foolish and irresponsible if one thinks this a selfish attempt at exoneration. What kind of naïveté could have allowed him such a view? It is a devastating and unanswerable summation considering all the absurdly impractical things he has done in the name of love. Yet it can also be read as a poignant and selfless claim that seems almost heroic in the face of the bad luck and hardship that have dogged him at every step of a noble attempt to make a separate peace. Faulkner's refusal to pass judgement deflects the reader's desire to pass judgement.[7]

The lovers' last moments together are represented in a language Faulkner has used before. Death is a cuckold and Harry is the lover whose place is being usurped by this dark double, something he cannot see but that is present nonetheless. This idea puts the focus on the man again, on the notion of sex in general and sexual betrayal in particular, 'the pregnancy of his horning' (687), as the narrator puts it at one point. Charlotte is lying naked in the room, her body laid out for all to see, but again Harry's thoughts about suffering are what Faulkner concentrates on. The description is graphic and surreal, like the harsh accounts of flesh and blood in *Sanctuary*. One last time, the topic of how experience becomes words in the stories we create to make sense of it is touched upon, in the form of the seemingly irrelevant thoughts that go through Harry's mind, a scene from a Western novel in which men try to keep a woman alive by walking her up and down in a bar. The subtext to everything, the thing that goes on regardless, is Harry's heart and his breathing: 'the strong ceaseless shallow dredging at air, breath on the point of escaping his lungs altogether' (693). This is a force that exists beyond the realm of the human, cognate with the wind in the trees, 'the threshing of the invisible palms, the wild dry sound of them' (695). This passage is of course the one that gives a title to this section of the novel. It is the thing that goes on, in the background, that which cannot be controlled or explained. Why the wind blows, why Harry continues to breathe and Charlotte does not, cannot be analysed. These are non-symbols in what is described in *Absalom, Absalom!* as notlanguage, one that signifies the absence rather than the presence of mystery. 'The Wild Palms' tells the story of the search for the words that can convey that absence.

The most remarkable thing about the story told in 'Old Man' is that it exists at all alongside the one just discussed. The idea of twinning these tales and using them in elaborate counterpoint is pure Faulkner. He wanted to try something new, to experiment without particularly knowing how readers would react, because he knew intuitively that the first story needed to be interwoven with this one, a very different account of a man, a pregnant woman, and the natural forces that serve as the backdrop for the drama in which they are swept up. In the passages where the great issues of this novel are presented or debated, the uneducated, taciturn, reclusive convict is linked to the garrulous young intern with a metaphysical bent, even though it is usually the narrative voice that is doing the actual reflecting. Like Harry, the tall convict thinks of turning his back on 'all pregnant and female life forever' to return to the 'monastic life' of the prison. Like Harry and Charlotte, he and his companion are both playthings of a force far greater than they can understand, 'a separate demanding threatening inert yet living mass of which both he and she were equally victims' (599). Like them, he inhabits a world in which the 'frail mechanicals of man's clumsy contriving' (603) stand in for a civilization that has now been revealed for the fragile, ramshackle concoction that it is.

Finding a language for the reactions of this simple character provides Faulkner with an interesting test. Here is the narrator, for example, describing the convict's reactions to seeing a skin hung on the wall of a hut to dry:

> from what animal, by association, ratiocination or even memory of any picture out of his dead youth, he did not know but knowing that it was the reason, the explanation, for the little lost spider-legged house ... set in that teeming and myriad desolation, enclosed and lost within the furious embrace of flowing mare earth and stallion sun, divining through pure rapport of kind for kind, hill-billy and bayou-rat, the two one and identical because of the same grudged dispensation and niggard fate of hard and unceasing travail not to gain future security, a balance in bank or even in a buried soda can for slothful and easy old age, but just permission to endure and endure to buy air to feel and sun to drink for each's little while.
>
> (668)

In such passages (and there are not that many dedicated to the convict because he is too busy surviving to do much reflecting), Faulkner articulates yet again his minimalist definition of humanity, that thing which makes us so pitiable and admirable at the same time. He does it in prose that says with all its incantatory power that this life is a contradictory combination of subsistence and bounty, the richest possible kind of degree zero. Asked to paraphrase the passage just cited, one would presumably say something like: 'The convict sees that the owner of the hut in the bayou is a kindred spirit, someone who decorates his home with a trophy from his daily struggle with nature and lives to experience sensations.' When we think of what is lost in such a paraphrase, we come to the heart of what is important in this section of the novel. Obviously, the lean summary leaves out the poetry, with all its teasingly suggestive figures of speech, and those figures are a stand-in for the quasi-ineffable richness of both men's lives. There is a natural logic that binds the two men that exists beyond the powers of their articulation. Such people give a new meaning to the word humble, for they do not even assume breathing is a natural right, and ask permission to live in the air and feel the sun, permission that is about to be denied, or redenied in the case of the convict. What differentiates them from Faulkner's grasping, acquisitive, materialistic heroes also makes them pitiful and vulnerable. They are no match for the wily, but more importantly they barely stand a chance against the ordinary. Nature is a strong but worthy adversary. The advantages offered to them by the human world – money, sex, companionship – do not seem worth the effort, so they are bound to live out their lives in this sort of solitude.

This type of meditation is mixed incongruously but relentlessly with a lot of single syllable thoughts set in italics – *'If that's it then I can do it too'* (668), *'a hog is still a hog'* (670) – to emphasize the difference between the convict's workman-like mental attitude to the problems the world presents him with and the metaphysical concerns related to them that Faulkner wants to explore. Suddenly attacked by an alligator the convict thinks, unremarkably enough, 'It looks big', but this is conveyed to us only after the narrator has offered a somewhat more evocative version of the attack: 'the flat thick spit of mud which as he looked at divided and became a thick mud-colored log which in turn seemed, still immobile, to leap suddenly against his retinae in three – no, four – dimensions: volume, solidity, shape, and another: not fear but pure and intense speculation' (669). That sentence revs up like the alligator preparing to leap, and it also contains a rather helpless definition of space, in which the three dimensions all sound vaguely the same. In an odd way, that fourth dimension, the 'intense speculation', enables us to see past this confusion to the subject of consciousness itself, the thing actually under investigation in the circumstances, the thing that makes the attack of interest in the first place. The intensity with which this character experiences his thought is what Faulkner ultimately captures in his idiosyncratic prose.

The larger pattern we have been tracking reasserts itself again: in moments of intense emotion, Faulkner makes his character a determined, fearless, almost feelingless actant, and he holds onto the idea of emotion by the lyrical sweep and inventiveness of the words that recreate the events in questions. The convict retains his simple integrity – it is not he who is thinking these high falutin' thoughts – yet his everyman qualities are precisely what make him a candidate for this lyricism. Part of this is a deep admiration on Faulkner's part for ordinary people doing ordinary work. He shares this with novelists as diverse as Tolstoy, Jack London, Upton Sinclair, and Steinbeck. But, unlike them, he usually avoids a detailed account of the minutiae of a given occupation. Of the stoic, determined man with his repetitive gestures that others see as ignominious imitations of the dumb animal, Faulkner makes a potentially tragic hero by chronicling the determination in a language that helps such a figure transcend the mundane even while he remains immersed in it.

There is a silence at the heart of such isolation that constitutes the convict's signature. He is as suspicious of language as Addie Bundren, because he keeps finding that words get him nowhere, at least insofar as explaining himself to the state machine, determined to see him an escapee, is concerned. The attempt to give himself up so that someone can help with the imminent birth of the baby is thus fraught with peril. Shouting that he wants to surrender, he is described as 'speaking to no one now anymore than the scream of the dying rabbit is addressed to any mortal ear but rather an indictment of all breath and its folly and suffering, its infinite capacity for folly and pain, which seems to be its only mortality' (613). The 'seems to be' is nicely ambiguous. Breath is not so much mortal as a force that takes possession, but for what purpose, besides prolonging the 'folly and pain' that it imposes on the breather, is not clear. Faulkner reads the natural world here with the transcendentalists' convictions and fervour, but without drawing their benign conclusions. Certainly other novels offer more positive views of the human predicament, but *If I Forget Thee, Jerusalem* takes its place alongside *The Sound and the Fury* and *As I Lay Dying* and *Sanctuary* and *Absalom, Absalom!* as records of folly and pain in which a lot of the suffering seems unmitigated.

And yet ... it is precisely at this point that the woman whom the convict has been protecting gives birth to her baby. The juxtaposition could not be more dramatic. Even though the description of that extraordinary event in the circumstances is a grim recording of more folly and pain, there it is, human life reasserting itself, impressing the reader more than it does the man who feels so obliged to assist his pregnant charge. At this point the convict becomes a member of that special group in Faulkner: males who have survived a dangerous situation with great courage, an absolute minimum of comment, no complaint whatever, and then recount it quietly, succinctly, memorably to the male company they normally keep. As the huge wave approaches, we are told that the convict 'glared over his shoulder at it for a full minute out of that attenuation far beyond the point of outragement where even suffering, the capability of being further affronted, had ceased, from which he now contemplated with savage and invulnerable curiosity the further extent to which his now anesthetized nerves could bear' (614). Again, the vocabulary shifts, and neologisms like 'outragement' fill in for their more humdrum counterparts. The convict becomes his creator here, curious to know how much more this particular human being, who happens to be himself, can take. Cut off from feeling in the conventional sense, not saying a word, paddling at the same rhythm, absolutely unmoved, he is at the same time 'savage' to know more, angry with impatience at this dull but relentless adversary that is slow to show its hand.

For the full orchestration of these complex effects, Faulkner frequently uses a technique called delayed decoding, a favourite of Conrad's.[8] This involves the description of a sequence of events as they appear to the uncomprehending eye of someone caught up in the throes of them. For example, the wave that sweeps the boat along at one point brings it parallel with a swimming deer. 'He did not know what it was' we are told, because seeing and understanding require valuable energy perhaps, energy the convict cannot afford at this particular moment. It rises out of the water and 'was actually running along upon the surface, rising still, soaring clear of the water altogether, vanishing upward in a dying crescendo of splashings' (614). This is Faulkner's way of staying true to the focalized quality of the narrative while conveying all the drama of this near escape, the fortuitous arrival of dry land at the crucial moment that seems in its way as much of a miracle as a deer running on the water and away into the sky. All that remains is pushing the woman to safety so that her baby can be born. Though he ends up face down in the mud and then underwater, the convict succeeds. Yet the baby, like the woman, is ultimately a side issue in this narrative, an accidental encumbrance. The end of the chapter is revealing in this sense: the man is back in the water as if attempting to drown himself and thus escape his doom. The newborn's cry is heard, but only as a recollection, from under the water, something seemingly other-worldly and miraculous as the appearance of an animal that can walk on it, the sure sign that life goes on, but that the convict is going to remain cut off from it.

Like his counterparts in *Soldiers' Pay* and *Mosquitoes*, the convict responds to something primordial and timeless in the darkness that surrounds him, and he finds an equivocal solace in the company of other men. Near the end, we are told that he stares 'at the wall before him until after a while the crude boards themselves must have dissolved away and let his blank unseeing gaze go on and on unhampered, through the rich oblivious darkness, beyond it even perhaps' (673). Pound wrote 'Damn "perhapses"' on the manuscript of *The Waste Land* in an attempt to make Eliot be less equivocal and more assertive. But Faulkner needs this one here as a sign of just how tentative he has to be in representing such a withdrawn consciousness. He is not sure the convict thought this; this is not a character about whom the author knows everything. There is something so private about such a deprived life that out of respect the author will not trespass more than he deems proper.

As this story moves to its conclusion, Faulkner's problem involves the difficulty of making plausible the convict's voluntary return to captivity. Gazing at the lake, he thinks *'This is a greater immensity of water, of waste and desolation, than I have ever seen before'* (680). He sees the 'forlorn passivity' of the crowds of people waiting, people 'whose race he did not recognize'. This is a vision of the modernist wasteland, the people Faulkner calls the 'violently homeless', and the convict is one of them, 'more so than any, who would have permitted no man to call him one of them' (681). This characterization speaks volumes, for it succinctly summarizes why the convict makes the decision he does. His home is with the anonymous crowd back in prison, but only because like them he has no home. He is ironically compared to Bienville, the founder of New Orleans, Napoleon, the man who made the Louisiana purchase possible, and Andrew Jackson, the leader who defeated the British at New Orleans in the War of 1812, a victory that gave a tremendous boost to the morale of the young republic. They are all people who played crucial roles at moments in the life of the city, and their names are remembered because they fought heroically or changed the course of events in which they were involved. They have found their home in its history. The convict is about to do the opposite, to efface all traces of himself in this place, by crossing the city, taking his boat up the river, finding a law officer and turning himself in. He cannot permit himself the Israelites' desperate hope and rhetorical gesture, and he finds himself in the end as isolated as they are. The unratiocinative djinns have taken him to the place where Harry Wilbourne arrived after all that reflection.

The last novel I want to look at in this section is *Go Down, Moses* (1942). *The Hamlet* was published in 1940, but it makes more sense to consider it in the next chapter along with the other novels in what came to be called the Snopes trilogy. For my purposes, *Go Down, Moses* belongs with *The Unvanquished* and *If I Forget Thee, Jerusalem*, because it is part of the search for a form that would permit Faulkner to interweave different narratives in a way that makes the whole more than the sum of its parts. It also constitutes another attempt to articulate in the language of romantic recollection how people go about the difficult business of composing a narrative that enables them to make sense of the past. As in *The Unvanquished*, the stories vary greatly in style and tone, ranging from the broad frontier humour of 'Was' and the poignancy and earnest silliness of 'The Fire and the Hearth', to the splendid economy and power of masterpieces like 'Pantaloon in Black' and 'Go Down, Moses'. As in *If I Forget Thee, Jerusalem*, the stories talk to each other by virtue of their thematic links. Here the relations between the races takes centre stage, and Faulkner uses the structures and devices we have been looking at – privileged moments, conversations designed to test ideas, and the self-conscious musings involved in such a process – to explore this theme. The idea that people with different coloured skin might actually treat each other with tenderness and compassion or feel love for each other binds this novel together. Only a writer with Faulkner's courage would have attempted it at such a time in American history. Here, I propose to examine the general question of how characters think about the past by concentrating on 'The Bear', the longest story in the volume and one that practically everyone agrees belongs on the list of Faulkner's outstanding achievements. The risk of focussing on only one story in *Go Down, Moses* is that the novelistic strengths of the whole are obscured, but that subject has been comprehensively dealt with elsewhere.[9]

'The Bear' is also a story that is central to an understanding of the shape of Faulkner's career. In it, his characters try to sum up one of the things that has preoccupied him at least since the writing of *Sartoris*, namely how a moment of time can be perceived, understood and expressed, and what all the furious reflection about the South and its identity amounts to. This, in turn, sets the stage for extended meditations on the possibility of making one's personal past or a nation's history into a coherent narrative in novels like *Requiem for a Nun* and *A Fable*. One more time, two men talk about the past and how it is represented, this time in the ledgers that record the dealings of their families. Just how important this sort of exchange is to Faulkner can hardly be overestimated. Millgate puts it well when he describes the Faulknerian dialogue generally as a 'marvellously flexible device, allowing him to dramatize even the processes of ratiocination, to manipulate time sequences, withhold information until the moment when its revelation will have the greatest impact, and, in sum, to extort narrative excitement from the most recalcitrant material.' The encounter between Cass Edmonds and his cousin Isaac McCaslin is an episode in a book organized episodically, and it represents Faulkner's attempt 'to hold in suspension a single moment of experience, action, or decision and to explore the full complexity of that moment by considering, in particular, its total context of past, present, and future, and its emergence as the often paradoxical product of many contrasted forces and pressures.'[10]

Just as Quentin and Shreve make readers forget Harvard again and again as they recreate the past, so do Cass and Ike allow the contemporary South to fade by taking us on a tour in space and time, back to the Holy Land and the Garden of Eden, and then forward through various kinds of mythic history to the present day. They are in the commissary in which records of all the transactions have been kept while America became a nation, and the South became a different sort of nation within it. This building is in effect part of their conversation. Like the courthouse in *Requiem for a Nun* and the citadel in *A Fable*, it speaks a language, changes over time, makes statements, and even asserts its own symbolic character, as when it is described as 'squatting like a portent above the fields whose laborers it still held in thrall '65 or no' (188). In this building things were sold, things that were real and pungent, things with evocative names that are no longer much used, 'plow-collars and hames and trace-chains' (189). Faulkner includes them here with a view to anchoring the conversation about the past in the world of the physically useful, the material that enabled a simple economy with an agrarian base to function. The nouns recorded in such ledgers are the humble counterparts for Melville's great lists, the ones that complement the metaphysical excursions in *Moby Dick*, and the tremendous catalogues in Whitman that ground *Song of Myself* in nineteenth-century America, even as both writers soar back in historical and geological time to give a cosmic context to the events they recount.

God in Faulkner's novel is variously called an 'Architect' and an 'Umpire', but just how present he has been, how watchfully he has presided over American history is something of an open question. In 'The Gift Outright', Robert Frost refers to Americans as 'Possessing what we still were unpossessed by, / Possessed by what we now no more possessed',[11] and this is very much Faulkner's subject too. But whereas Frost sees the pioneers as ambiguous in their commitment because they were torn between two continents, Faulkner sees forces at work beyond the merely human. His God is described as something of an arbiter still but, like the beings who owe their allegiance to him, he too is 'dispossessed'. This seems puzzling, since it is unclear how an omnipotent maker can be dispossessed of what he has made. Cass explains it this way: 'Dispossessed. Not impotent: He didn't condone; not blind, because He watched it. ... Dispossessed of Eden. Dispossessed of Canaan, and those who dispossessed Him dispossessed Him dispossessed' (191). The explanation gradually becomes an incantation in which the word takes on a life of its own. Despite the capitalized pronoun, the meaning slides between God and man here, which is a clever way of reproducing what is happening in the mythical history that is summarized so cryptically. God is dispossessed with his creation because, like a passive onlooker watching an accident and its aftermath, he cannot intervene or cannot be bothered to, or because what was supposed to be the crowning glory of his creation is a bit of a bust. Man suffers the consequences either way: thrown out of Eden, then out of the promised land, then out of the American version of that land, he is thrice denied his birthright, and turned into a nomad, an exile. The land of Canaan is doubly significant because, like all of Noah's grandsons, it is a person and a place, as closely tied to the land as Cass and Isaac are. Like them, Canaan is cursed by his ancestor and condemned to a kind of slavery by the history he inherited.

The view of history in this context is very much human-centred. This is essentially Bishop Ussher's 4000-odd-year saga being retold, while the long geographical time so lovingly chronicled in the novel is temporarily forgotten. The Christian history in 'The Bear' is a odd blend of fundamentalist faith in the Old Testament as a literal account of creation, and a humanist reading that emphasizes metaphor and factors in all the subjectivity of the scribes who contributed to the creation of the Bible. Cass's contention that 'There is only one truth and it covers all things that touch the heart' is ambiguous between a rigorously literal Christian point of view and the sort of congenial monism that can happily exist independently of any religious doctrine. In the end, it is on the humanity of the scribes that the accent must fall. It makes them 'comprehend truth only through the complexity of passion and lust and hate and fear which drives the heart' (192), and these it must be remembered are holy men. Cass's claim is another version of two ideas Faulkner has been pursuing from the outset of his career, namely how powerfully the passions refract the truth, making it difficult to see and doubly difficult to sum up, and how the truth about time's turning people and books into dust is as poignant and as compelling as the one that suggests that they should treat each other properly.

God does reveal himself again in this history, and although Faulkner's two commentators on America's origins do not use the words 'manifest destiny', they often seem to believe in some version of it. It is called 'a new world where a nation of people could be founded in humility and pity and sufferance and pride of one to another' (191). We are even told that God ordered and watched this whole process, to the point of organizing the enmity and slaughter of the native peoples so that the European colonizers would end up fighting each other to produce someone like Grandfather McCaslin. Whatever we make of this grotesque teleology, for Faulkner this man is the linking figure, someone wild and independent enough to be one with the pioneers in his love of hunting and whiskey and male company, someone free of the cash nexus that threatens to entrap his descendants, and yet someone who recognizes that the sins of the fathers are visited on their descendants.

The dusty records about which the two men talk are sacred books for those with an anthropological interest in the origins of American culture. In them is recorded 'the injustice and a little at least of its amelioration and restitution faded back forever into the anonymous communal original dust' (193). They constitute one of the means by which human history can be judged, since they are a faithful record of who and what was bought by and sold to the people who live on in the imagination of the present as a result. Of course it was precisely this buying and selling that turned these people into objects in the first place. Having gone through the description of transactions involving money and goods, slaves and their owners, Ike and Cass come to a pair of cryptic references to suicide. The question is: who are these people and why have their deaths been recorded so laconically? We learn that there is a kind of class system even among slaves, that the girl who killed herself was part of a family that, by virtue of their long history with the McCaslin family, belonged to a superior class. She is born of incest and miscegenation, the dispossessed dispossessed theme again in all its stark power. This child, one of the most important in all of Faulkner, is called 'solitary, inflexible, griefless, ceremonial, in formal and succinct repudiation of grief and despair who had already had to repudiate belief and hope' (200). That is quite a list of epithets. Any child born of such a union, the result of a supposed violation of taboos, has 'repudiate[d] belief and hope', yet 'grief and despair' are also rejected because life in all its mysterious fecundity keeps asserting itself, even in this doomed union. The child that is to cause a great deal of grief, as a symbol of the curse on America, is griefless, and never more so than now, when all that is left of her is a name in a book. She has become one with the hames and the ploughshares, reduced by time to her constituent elements, yet her existence is more real than theirs because it has come to symbolize the construction of a culture (hence the references in the list to 'ceremonial' and 'formal'). Thinking about her centrality could enable that culture to change, if it has the ability to read its own past aright. As Gavin Stevens claims at the end of *Intruder in the Dust*, the memory of suffering and injustice lasts far longer than the people to whom it occurs.

As rarefied and abstract as this makes it sound, particularly in a novel dedicated to practical matters like the 'right' of the master to sleep with his slave's wife ('The Fire and the Hearth'), or how to arrange the funeral of an executed murderer and allow his family to maintain its dignity ('Go Down, Moses'), Section Four of 'The Bear' is central to an understanding of *Go Down, Moses* because it inscribes it in a study of cultural psychology, one that suggests how to think about something as nebulous as time passing, and what that passing has to convey about the nature of truth. Here is where 'Ode on a Grecian Urn' comes in again, not just alluded to but actually read out loud, improbably enough at first glance. Ike cannot immediately see the relevance of Keats's poem, and his response no doubt mimics many readers' instinctive reaction to this very literary allusion, but it does belong here. It concludes with a recommendation that is at once a summary of venerable wisdom ('Beauty is truth') like the ones Cass has been intoning, a teasing inversion of same that is demonstrably untrue ('truth beauty'), as the history of the ledgers makes clear, and an injunction concerning how entirely this should satisfy us mere mortals who lack the urn's long view ('that is all/Ye know on earth'), its ability to hum quietly through the 'slow time' of human history. Like the ledgers, the poem is also to be found in a book that speaks to subsequent generations. Like them, it tells stories about past generations, tells them anonymously, and then generalizes from them, in a way that Faulkner is obviously attempting here. The urn has the power to 'tease us out of thought', says Keats, a point borne out by all the commentary that his poem full of teasing thoughts has generated, just like this period in American history and its multifaceted and problematic legacy.[12] It provokes by virtue of a series of paradoxes: it is virginal and amatory/orgiastic; though silent it tells a story. In a similar way, 'The Bear' invites its readers to think seriously about the paradoxes of the stories it tells. It contains the whole history of America, yet nothing happens in it except talking and hunting and talking about hunting. The old remain young in this way by staying in contact with the dreams and desires of youth. It documents the existence of a curse and indicates how it might be exorcized. It is not the least of Faulkner's extraordinary achievements in this scene that he makes the thinking literary critics do about tropes like paradox seem relevant to questions of real importance.

Near the end of their discussion, Cass falls back on the primacy of subjective feeling in any attempt to define truth. Rousseau famously offered as his proof of the existence of God the feeling evoked in him by looking at a sunrise. In someone else, watching the sunrise might evoke a quite different feeling, but the argument has the advantage of being irrefutable on its own terms.[13] So too with felt truths for Cass: they are things that exist beyond argument, things so personal that they cannot be translated into verifiable propositions, a state of affairs that frustrates logicians and appeals to writers like Faulkner. In *Absalom, Absalom!* he linked such things to notlanguage and made clear that its province was the unratiocinative essence of things as they are. We get the same sense here. What is interesting about the many pages dedicated to these ledgers and the stories they tell is that, in a very real sense, the more we hear about them the less we know. The facts about the McCaslin family history have been dragged out of the dark and exposed in the dusty light, but the disparate reactions to them, the battle of the narratives into which they can be fitted, the labyrinthine sentences dedicated to their elucidation, all these make us unsure at the end just what has been learned about the past and its hold on this family. '[T]here is only one truth and it covers all things that touch the heart' (192), 'what the heart holds to becomes truth' (220) – like the cryptic utterances in Keats's ode, such resonant propositions end up meaning everything and nothing. If we must have a final meaning, Faulkner seems to be saying, it will not be found in a gnomic utterance, even though some part of him responds very powerfully to them.

Faulkner updates the urn in the discussion between Cass and Ike by comparing one of their gestures to a stereopticon. This instrument (sometimes called a stereoscope) was extremely popular in America in the second half of the nineteenth century. Every middle-class home had one, and the images – of monuments, landscapes, great events of the day – that could be looked at through it were as avidly collected as CDs are today.[14] As Faulkner's explanation makes clear, the stereopticon is invoked as a metaphor for something that unifies and harmonizes disparate objects in a visual field: here Cass's vision of the past, the things he has seen chronicled in the ledgers and represented on the commissary's shelves, and the symbols he has decided to repudiate as an expiation for the sins of his ancestors. Like the urn, the stereopticon enables the viewer to bring together twin perspectives as if they were one, thus taking two-dimensional images into three-dimensional space. It also gives the viewer privileged access to the past and the supposedly timeless. Of course the urn has everything that the stereoscope does, albeit in less high-tech form: the great events of history, the emotions that characterized them, and the curiosity of something timeless that is nonetheless rooted in time. And both in turn resemble the commissary objects and the ledgers in that they turn over their mysteries to 'readers' who are keen to posit continuities and to resolve ambiguities. Both allow the viewer to experience life vicariously without encouraging mere passivity. Both impose an order on the vagaries of an existence by isolating its symbolic moments. Both are hard objects that outlast the cultures that produced them. Both speak silently about time past and time passing.[15]

McCaslin's argument is summarized by his gesture, a moving hand that points out a bunch of objects and some pieces of paper, but it is a dismissive one. With that sweep of his hand, Ike announces he repudiates it all, the responsibility and the shame. We find ourselves once again forced to deal with notlanguage, the one Faulkner systematically resorts to when his characters are unable to see clearly or judge adequately. Their caution should make us equally reluctant to pass judgement here. Cass's answer is another silent but eloquent gesture, one that says that Ike is no more free of his family's past than he is of human history, 'the frail and iron thread strong as truth and impervious as evil and longer than life itself' (221). The thread he speaks of is described with contradictory epithets because it represents the flesh itself, mortal but imperious, decaying but unignorable, a mere trifle but the means by which 'lusts and passions' influence human relations at the most basic level, bind us to our ancestors, and, as the stories in this novel show, end up helping to determine the course of history in a whole country. Ike says he is free 'of that too', presumably because from his material perspective, a simple act of will or a refusal to credit such a notion are gestures sufficient to allow the present to escape the past. The obstacles discovered by other characters in Faulkner who have tried to free themselves from history augur ill for Ike's success.

The ideas surveyed and the challenges posed by the discussions Faulkner dramatized in such original fashion during these years make the books under consideration here permanent contributions to American literature. As far as large questions concerning human destiny are concerned, documents, urns, and stereopticons for that matter are all helpful for those in search of answers, but they are no more capable of resolving these questions than the reflections or interactions of the characters who use them as props. In fact, their primary function is to help reconcile readers to ambiguity and irresolution. It is true that Faulkner was under extraordinary pressure at the time that he put these books together, and the compromises involved in writing to make a living manifest themselves in various ways in the finished products. It is also true that he was working out his own thoughts by arguing with himself about race and gender and the meaning of history, as he proceeded. Lest we be tempted to be too critical of what he achieved, we should give a thought to all the fiction from this era by writers such as James T. Farrell,

Josephine Herbst, Myra Page, and a host of others, the sort of progressive, socially conscious novels that Faulkner was criticized by activist commentators for not producing in the 1930s. Rediscovering *Studs Lonigan* or *Pity is Not Enough* or *Moscow Yankee*, to list the best-known titles of the writers just mentioned, can be quite enjoyable, but it also tells us all that we need to know about such books. Here ambiguity is banished and the questions surrounding self and history posed much more starkly and answered more confidently. And that is of course the problem. If Faulkner's work must sometimes be characterized as uneven, theirs is not even uneven. A good deal of it is now enjoying a modest revival as the canon continues to be redefined and a new generation of students rummages in the stacks, and quite rightly too. Whether they will reread such works as avidly remains to be seen. The worthy citizens who produced these novels documented their era; Faulkner helped to create that era by producing its best literature.

7
The Snopes Trilogy

The Snopes trilogy occupies an important place in Faulkner's career. It represents his most determined attempt to be a chronicler, to pick up stories where they leave off, tie up loose ends, and narrate the lives of a family and its connections with other lives in his invented county. Filling in the Yoknapatawpha cycle proved easy in the sense that Faulkner had many stories to tell about local characters. He continues to use the meditative moments in those stories to structure novels in which action predominates, but the balance admittedly shifts. Before taking up in chronological order *The Hamlet* (1940), *The Town* (1957), and *The Mansion* (1959), I want to consider 'Barn Burning' (1939), a story he thought of using as the opening chapter for *The Hamlet* and one that is generally considered one of his best. Faulkner's interest there in studying the male mind reacting to circumstances in a series of intensely emotional moments will serve as a helpful introduction to the subsequent discussion of the trilogy itself.

Many books have been written about the way Yoknapatawpha took shape and the unity it gave Faulkner's vision, and they constitute some of the most indispensable guides to his fiction. His imaginary county has been usefully compared to the world Balzac created in *La Comédie humaine* and to Hardy's Wessex. The parallels are indeed so numerous, so widely acknowledged, and so useful that I shall confine myself here to point out a couple of significant differences between Faulkner's mode of proceeding and theirs. If we compare the description of the protagonist's entry into a shop near the start of *Lost Illusions* and Flem's arrival at Jody Varner's in *The Hamlet*, for example, we see the principal one. Someone could start a print business in post-revolutionary France with the Balzac novel as a blueprint, whereas reading about what is in the Varner store or on the main street of Jefferson, we are forced to move more slowly, work much harder to understand, and tentatively adapt ourselves to a way of seeing a world even while we learn about that world. Balzac is a leisurely writer, Faulkner an intense one. Balzac is in the information dispensing business in this early scene; Faulkner is establishing a style. The conditions of the conflict to come are slowly laid out in the former; the conflict begins with the first encounter, with the first words spoken, in the latter. With Hardy it is the same, a wealth of parallels and some crucial differences that stand out in sharp relief. The market scene in which Henchard sells his wife and the setting for the long anecdote in *The Hamlet* in which Flem Snopes sells his horses are both typical of their authors, used to begin the respective novels, integral to the plot, bound up with the main theme of the work in question, and characterized by detailed description. Yet it is much harder to recall the physical details of the scene in Faulkner because he does not bother to draw them to our attention. If we try mentally to juxtapose Casterbridge and Jefferson, not on the basis of a map Faulkner drew in the mid-1940s but according to how their buildings and streets and activities present themselves, the difference is striking. Hardy's prose is constantly telling us to notice things, about people, their movements, their expressions, and their surroundings. Faulkner's is busy doing something else. Again, in *The Mayor of Casterbridge* the drama is about to unfold; in Faulkner it has already begun.

So too with the trilogy, as different as each of the novels is. Faulkner's characters are too busy talking and thinking, too abstracted from daily activities to do the things that make the features of a town more visible. They do not go window-shopping or to the doctor, wander aimlessly from store to store, read the news from the paper or comment on some insignificant thing that is happening in the next street. One sometimes gets the impression that nothing is insignificant, despite the superbly realized casualness. Once the setting has been described, we get long paragraph after long paragraph in which a distinctive narrative voice predominates. Because the characters Faulkner recycles often concentrate on the past or live in the strange spaces created by their own heads, it can sometimes seem as if we know more about the South in the nineteenth century than about the details of its transformation in the twentieth. He provides some very interesting historical overviews, particularly in his late fiction, but these tend towards the subjective and impressionistic, and they are often informed by a wistful sense of how badly wrong things have gone. The result is that, if one is looking for world creators because one wants to understand a human community at a particular point in time, all kinds of American writers, Upton Sinclair, Sinclair Lewis ('Upton Lewis'[1] as Nabokov liked to say, rather unfairly), Erskine Caldwell, Willa Cather, *et al.*, are, like Balzac and Hardy, more useful for anthropologically minded critics than Faulkner is.

'Barn Burning', the short story that almost became part of the Snopes trilogy, begins with a ten-year-old boy, Sartoris ('Sarty') Snopes, reacting to an overload of sensations and trying to make sense of them. Our plunge into the scene *in medias res* gives us a sense of how his bafflement afflicts him. He is at some sort of legal hearing, clearly, but who is on trial for what? The case is dismissed and when he leaves the scene there is a scuffle because someone says the words 'barn burner'. The boy's reactions are described as follows:

> Again he could not see, whirling; there was a face in a red haze, moonlike, bigger than the full moon, the owner of it half again his size, he leaping in the red haze toward the face, feeling no shock when his head struck the earth, scrabbling up and leaping again, feeling no blow this time either and tasting no blood.

(6)

Faulkner likes stringing together gerunds in this way to convey action and, as so often, the human agent in the middle of it all seems invulnerable, almost oblivious to the furious activity he has initiated. While the extraordinary things are happening, there is something that keeps the self apart, self-sufficient, alone, trying to understand.

The limited point of view is potentially an obstacle of course, but Faulkner resolves it in a typically forthright way. When he feels the need, he simply takes us into the future, when the boy would have seen things rather differently: 'Older, the boy might have remarked ... older still, he might have divined ...', and so on. Here it is also worth pointing out that, for all the ways in which Faulkner is best understood as a high modernist, i.e. someone for whom truth is relative, meaning obscured, and coherence fragmented, these editorial interpolations are a means by which he can explain the truth about certain crucial propositions. Why, the boy wonders, does his father, Abner Snopes, build 'niggardly' fires, why not prodigal ones, to match with the 'let's burn up everything' together mentality that goes with the Civil War he lived through? First, the narrator carefully explains, it is a habit; second, it is a throwback to all those secretive nights when one did not want the enemy to see one's fire; and, finally, fire equals integrity for someone like Abner Snopes, and therefore his respect for it makes him choose small ones that burn most intensely and economically. 'But he [Sarty] did not think this now ...' (7–8) Faulkner concludes, and that is that for the fire episode.

When he wants the reader to understand, even though the boy may not, Faulkner will use an oblique detail that works that much more effectively because it is so casually introduced. ' "Not that ... the wagon gear" ' (17), says Mr Snopes to his son at one point in the story, when indicating what harness should be used for the mule they are about to hitch to the wagon. If we are paying attention, we get the most powerful but understated image possible of a man who works all week as a 'beast', using the mules not to pull the wagon but to drag him around the field in human harness. Here he checks his son's instinctive move to pick up that gear to convey that it is time to go to town in a carriage like a human being.

The story proceeds quickly and inexorably towards its dénouement, precipitated by the father's smouldering resentment against the aristocratic landowner's power to exploit him. He is one of those characters whom Homer would characterize as doom hungry, and he ends up being shot for his refusal to submit to the laws that he sees as oppressive. The story's conclusion can also be seen as a moment of vision for the son, a feature of 'coming-of-age' fiction like London's *Martin Eden* or Lawrence's *Sons and Lovers*. According to this view, Faulkner describes the point at which a boy cuts loose from family ties and becomes a man. He has registered the inadequacies of the father figure he once worshipped unthinkingly, and the inconsequential nature of the family – his mother, his sisters – who merely cower in submission to the father's dictates. This reading presupposes, if not some genuine understanding of what has happened, at least some hint of more mature self-assertion that has taken place or is about to.

But the language used to describe nature in the last paragraphs is inconclusively rhapsodic, like the endings in *Soldiers' Pay*, *Mosquitoes*, *Sartoris*, *Sanctuary*, etc. It could be a threnody to a lost past or a hymn to an array of growth possibilities: a great deal depends on just where one chooses to put the accent. Once again Faulkner uses a mix of styles to communicate the nature of the consciousness that is processing all of this. Simple language for basic feelings and needs – 'It would be dawn and then sun-up after a while and he would be hungry' – is complemented by the words used for the more evocative world that beckons: the whippoorwills are 'constant and inflectioned and ceaseless'. (We saw the same combination at work with the same kind of limited sensibility in 'The Old Convict'.) Besides, an escape into nature is never a definitive answer in Faulkner's fiction. The birdsong is identified with 'the rapid and urgent beating of the urgent and quiring heart of the late spring night' (26),[2] but even that powerful call must be heard and interpreted. Trying to satisfy the deep desire symbolized by the fire and its destructive potential was precisely what got Sarty's father into so much trouble. Faulkner may well be signalling that something similar awaits this young man, someone who feels strong enough not to look back on his past, his family, and his wandering life, but someone who must, like every character in Faulkner, look back whether he wants to or no.

The stories that make up *The Hamlet*, the first novel in the series, were the product of almost 15 years' work that proceeded by fits and starts. Though less taut and less unified than a story like 'Barn Burning', they resemble it in other ways. Some of Faulkner's most remarkable strengths as a writer are his ear for colloquial expression, his sardonic humour, and his ability to create a good narrative. He tended to evaluate work sent to him by aspiring writers by assessing the quality of the story, and *The Hamlet* contains some particularly memorable ones. Few are as skilled as he at weaving a collection of episodes into a narrative whole, and this novel represents another triumph of this kind. It is also a novel composed of moments in which reflection serves as a stand-in for action. In what follows I consider three scenes in which Faulkner uses a style different from the colloquial one appropriate to the tall tale and the anecdote, taking as his subject a series of desires that exist just at the edge of understanding, or ideas that help explain the passions motivating so many of the characters in the trilogy as a whole. First there is Flem Snopes's visit to Hell, then the section featuring Ike Snopes and the cow, and finally the scene in which Armstid falls for Flem's trick and ends up digging fruitlessly for gold.

The participants in the preamble to the first scene under consideration are Eula Varner and Flem Snopes. *The Hamlet* is in one sense their story: the first two sections are named after them, and they are married by the end of the second one. However, such a description is quite misleading. Another novelist would have given us the background, the process, the intrigue, the shock, the denouement, everything involved in a short 'froglike creature's' (868) winning the family's assent to his marrying their beautiful young daughter. That is exactly how Richardson's *Clarissa* begins, for example. Faulkner instead tells a long tale about Abner Snopes and his trickery, an equally long one about a schoolmaster who lusts after Eula the way 'a man with a gangrened hand or foot thirsts after the axe-stroke that will leave him comparatively whole again' (839), and an account of the gradual insinuation of Flem and his family into the affairs of Frenchman's Bend. The actors on this stage are larger than life: the men are manic obsessives, and Eula is Woman, a field 'rich and fecund and foul and eternal', the 'mortal natural enemy of the masculine race' (869). In other words, for all its folksy, homespun humour, this is not just another realistic novel, but part fable, part romance, part tall tale, part documentary account. What the two principals are in themselves is important, their relationship is not. When the earth mother is beautiful and foul, lust a disease, and the man who triumphs a neuter, the novelist is going to be covering his canvas with fairly broad strokes.

The section ends with Flem Snopes's triumph and a visit to the devil in Hell. It is not clear from the text whose meditation this is, and the passage is unusual in a number of ways. It is completely unprepared for, different typeface, scene, characters, tone, vocabulary, genre, and yet it is juxtaposed to a lyrical meditation on change by Ratliff, Faulkner's homespun philosopher, as if it might help explain what he was thinking. Then there is the sheer audacity of it. It is hard to think of another American novelist of his era who would dare such a thing. Hawthorne puts the Prince of Darkness into 'Young Goodman Brown'. He is debonair, sardonic, intrigued by, and very involved in the human passions explored in the story, and it is set in a time when the devil did get around quite a bit, particularly in the Northeast. Fitzgerald has a devil-like figure in *This Side of Paradise*, because he wants a spooky presence as a stand-in for the power of sexual desire too. But such authors are careful not to violate the conventions of the mode in which they are working. This last consideration is possibly the one Faulkner has least respect for. As we have seen, he abides by literary conventions as he sees fit, and redefines them as required.[3] Just why he put Thomas Wolfe (first) above himself (second) in his ranking of American writers willing to take a risk has never been clear to me.

Snopes has stolen everyone's dreams, all the hopes of the young and lusty, the old and impotent ('now-glandless earth-creeping' [868]), and substituted for them the bleak truth about the power of money. That makes him diabolic in Faulkner's eyes, reason enough to send him to eternal torment for not having a soul. Hence his visit, but things appear to have evolved in Hell just as on earth. The new Prince is a lesser being, despite the ingeniousness of the torments he has invented. Gone too is his icy calm. He is now a windbag and becomes more unfrightening by the minute as he puffs out his empty threats. Snopes, the man who wants nothing, is by far the more dangerous one, although he too is singularly devoid of tragic grandeur. He is best thought of as a sort of anti-Sutpen, in that his desires are the lowest common denominator of human ambition, just relentless acquisition for its own sake in endlessly deceitful ways. He does not seek to right some wrong, because he does not recognize the existence of an affront. He makes no case, does no fierce reflecting of the kind we have been studying, because for him the question of existence is uninteresting, the purpose of it self-evident. His lack of desire must always succeed in exasperating those who seek control over him. Not to have a soul, Faulkner seems to be saying, means refusing to accept the relevance of any moral argument whatever, even the hellish version. In short, Flem Snopes is, to adapt T.S. Eliot's formulation, not 'man enough for damnation',[4] which is why his hosts in hell have no idea what to do with him. The lesser being he stands for is what makes the modern world, for Faulkner and Eliot, as dangerous as the old melodramatic one that Satan represents. The one thing he has is staying power, and Flem takes his pleasure, not in exotic illicit activities like indulging in sinful lust, but in the malady of the money-making quotidian and the bankruptcy of human nature.

The fact that the second scene under consideration is so different is itself worthy of comment. In the next section, Faulkner begins by writing a prose poem about how the coming of spring for Ike Snopes, a character who is linked to the calendar rather than the clock, defined by the order of the seasons: 'by April it was the actual thin depthless suspension of false dawn itself, in which he could already see and know himself to be an entity solid and cohered in visibility instead of the uncohered all-sentience of fluid and nerve-springing terror alone and terribly free in the primal sightless inimicality' (882–3). From the 'throes of compositeness' in *Light in August* to 'cohered in visibility' here, Faulkner is particularly adept at finding the language for such selves, those figures whose inchoate status makes them so vulnerable and unpredictable. The strangeness of the whole passage is also bound up with the casual way Faulkner provides a simpleton with the sensibility of an aesthete, keen to track the day's difficult progress from 'the moment after the false dawn' and 'the gradation from gray through primrose to morning's ultimate gold'. Having done such a masterful job of conveying how the world looks to someone like Benjy, his incomprehension, his strong desires, his poor, bare, forked humanity, Faulkner finds himself in a similar situation in *The Hamlet*, and chooses to resolve it quite differently.

So we read that Ike Snopes's rapport is 'with all anonymous faceless female flesh capable of love walking the female earth' (898); that a rain drop is a 'brief lance already filled with the glittering promise of its imminent cessation like the brief bright saltless tears of a young girl over a lost flower'; and that light is not 'decanted onto earth from the sky, but instead is from the earth itself suspired' (902). Here they are again, the exotic creatures from the rapturous early visions of the young and lusty: 'Helen and the bishops, the kings and the graceless seraphim.' They are asleep beneath the ground, but the tone here is exultant rather than melancholy. Sleep is the 'mammalian attar'; the moon is 'nympholept' (903); the arrival of dawn is marked by 500 words in hyper-descriptive mode that splendidly capture the noisy rush of the new day. When Horace Benbow in *Sanctuary* looks through Shelley's eyes at the world reflected in a set of pools, he sees something pure, abstract, desirable, yet unattainable. Ike has attained it, in the form of his bovine mate, her image mirrored in the collected rainwater. At the end of the earlier novels, when the diurnal cycle has turned, sex is the natural reward for those attuned to the languor of day's end. Here the same conditions obtain, but the group assembled in the shadows has disappeared, replaced by a man and his cow. The love scene between them plays out in an environment of murmuring pines, with the trees serving as harps or lutes. Faulkner even tries out a series of phrases for the setting: 'the azure bowl of evening, the windless well of night; the portcullis of sunset' (897). Look at how many different ways this can be written, he seems to be saying, as he extemporizes, throwing the emphasis on the inventiveness of the possible formulations.

This is what nature would look like if the permanent state of arousal imaged on the urn was available to us, and if we were nothing but sentient creatures like Ike Snopes. In a world where Flem Snopes can marry a beautiful young woman, where money is a kind of poetry and power an aphrodisiac, the love between a man and a cow can hardly be dismissed as absurd or immoral. Once more the combination of desiring idiot, conspiring spring, and lascivious nature is used to benchmark the unhappiness and frustration of the principal characters. Like T.H. Huxley with his protoplasm, Faulkner is bold enough to give a name to the force that manifests itself here: 'the strong inexhaustible life ichor itself, inherently, of itself, renewing' (903). The ensuing paean to inchoate desire provides the definition that itemizes the characteristics of this substance, whose name evokes the potent liquid found in the veins of the gods. The joke, such as it is, is on us, members of a species normally confined to conjuring up exotic dream equivalents of this kind of fulfillment.

The last scene provides a fitting conclusion for this singular series of reflections on man's angular relations to nature. In it, someone is feverishly hunting for a treasure that is not there, but realism is not uppermost in Faulkner's mind here either, and he gives the scene a mythic aura from the outset. The assembled spectators are 'traversing another land, moving in another time, another afternoon without time or name' (1072). Armstid is a whirlwind of frantic activity, but his 'fury' is there and not there, lasting and gone, 'spent and unflagging' (1073), a contradiction in terms. The spectators' interest in him is like something out of Gregor's predicament in Kafka's *Metamorphosis*, a gentle, insistent, reserved interest in something profoundly alien to them, something that at the same time stands for them, although it is beyond their powers to see the similarities. He is crazy, they are sane. He is busy, they are idle. He is preoccupied with finding the thing that will justify his present labour; they are watching to feel reassured about the mundane nature of their own lives and – who knows? – wondering if *per impossibile* Armstid might actually find the treasure which could not possibly exist. Here for Faulkner then is the human condition writ large: a man carried away by emotion, maniacally engaged in a search for the thing he is absolutely confident that he will find, and a group of people living, half disdainfully, half vicariously, by watching him prove to them what they know in their hearts is doomed to failure, even as he reenacts the dream that haunts them. The last word on the scene is Flem Snopes's, as he watches wordlessly and then clucks at his horse to take him home. It turns out that we have been looking over his shoulder while Armstid madly digs. Although we have no idea what Snopes's silent meditation consists of, we can assume it is pitiless. Like Satan in *Paradise Lost*, he does not have to make a special journey to get to Hell, since he carries his own version of it around with him.

Faulkner wrote a parody of one of the hyper-descriptive scenes from *The Hamlet*, something that would strike most people as an act of supererogation. Certainly those who have made their puzzled way through all the 'coronal of nympholept noon' descriptions in the Ike/cow scene would have difficulty imagining how such a scene could be parodied, since in itself it raises all the questions that parody does. In 1937, Faulkner read aloud 'Afternoon of a Cow' to a group that included his French translator, Maurice Coindreau, explaining that it had been written by one Ernest V. Trueblood. In it, Faulkner rewrites the scene in which Ike rescues the cow from a fire. He introduces himself and Trueblood as witnesses to the real-life version of this event. Trying to save Beulah, Faulkner ends up falling into a ravine with it. During the attempt to get it out, he receives 'the full discharge of the poor creature's afternoon of anguish and despair'. The parody turns out to be an uninspired performance. Words and phrases like 'conflagration' and 'incandescent sensation about the soles of the feet' do not get anywhere close to imitating Faulkner's lexical range. And where are all his stylistic tics, his habit of saying six times what something is 'not' before he tells us what it is, the neologisms, the pleonasms, the sentences that threaten to lose themselves in their own tangles? When Laurel and Hardy were first dubbed into French, someone inexplicably had them speak French with a British accent. Faulkner's decision to give Mr Trueblood, the man who has been writing his novels for years apparently, the same accent is equally hard to understand. The piece is also very long for a parody, which often depends on verbal economy for its comic effect. It is long because it is full of sentences like this: 'I have been told by soldiers ... how, upon entering battle, there often sets up within them, prematurely as it were, a certain impulse or desire which brings on a result quite logical and quite natural, the fulfillment of which is incontestible and of course irrevocable ...'[5] blah, blah, blah. If Faulkner were just a wordy windbag, if his harshest critics were right, this would be funny, I guess. But actually he never writes like this.

If all that is true, then how is it that someone with such a good ear can miss some of his own tones so badly? Perhaps his lack of interest in literary criticism *per se*, something that is always a part of the best parody, made him uninterested in taking his own genius apart. Michael Grimwood makes the intriguing suggestion that, in translating the vulgar into the genteel, Faulkner not only parodies his own excessiveness but also reveals the doubled authorial figure he has always been: a profane farmer and a literary translator. When their partnership finally became unbalanced and untenable, argues Grimwood, the parody was the result, Faulkner's half confession of the truth that he was a deeply divided man, a faux farmer and a faux author to boot.[6] That helps explain a very puzzling text, but it also threatens to obscure just how much creative use Faulkner makes of his deep divisions, and it downplays the extent of the continuity that exists between what he wrote before 1937 and what he wrote after. Whatever we decide about Faulkner's motives, we are still left with the fact that, in so far as parody is concerned, a number of people in this special sense knew and imitated Faulkner far better than he did himself.[7]

His interests in writing a relatively straightforward realistic novel in which the characters' daily interactions are extensively chronicled make *The Town* another new departure of sorts. The events described in it follow directly from those that take place in *The Hamlet*, and a complex series of echoes and recollections bind this text to the other two in the trilogy. In structural terms, Faulkner does a variation on something he had tried before. He explained that he deliberately created three viewpoints for the action that takes place in the novel: Charles Mallison he designated as a 'mirror' responsible for the episodes that make up more than half the book, episodes that feature the ironic, farcical, and grotesque material that Faulkner is so good at narrating. Ratliff represents another point of view, according to his creator, because he 'practiced virtue from simple instinct ... for a practical reason, because it was better.'[8] He embodies wisdom of a commonsensical sort that Faulkner evidently sees as crucial for citizens in a functioning democracy. Even the justification he offers for Ratliff's choosing virtue is pure Benjamin Franklin. Gavin Stevens's is the third voice. Broadly speaking, the battle between him and his principles, on the one hand, and the Snopes and their rapacious expediency, on the other, binds the episodes together. Stevens is the most interesting narrator for my purposes because he is the most articulate, and involves himself with a range of human reactions to complex situations. He loves abstractions, he repeatedly mistakes people, their motives and their worth, and his efforts to help often do more harm than good. But his consciousness is the battlefield on which Faulkner pits life against ideas, and in *The Town* he offers the most probing account in the novel of why people do what they do.

Our chief affliction according to Stevens is that we invent difficulties for ourselves as a distraction from the boredom of existence: 'even in the folly of youth we know that nothing lasts; but because even in that folly we are afraid that maybe Nothing will last, that maybe Nothing will last forever, and everything is better than Nothing, even lice' (119). Passion does that to reflective people in Faulkner, gives them insights into things that work at negating insight. Here Stevens vacillates between claiming a knowledge of the void and a fear of it, but ultimately the two amount to the same thing for him because his anxieties are so compelling. The capital 'N' Nothing echoes the language of the existentialists, particularly those French thinkers who convinced a whole generation that the search for an internal self that existed independently of our relations with others was fruitless. They also spent a great deal of time exploring the implications of such a discovery for the decisions we make, the stance we take on questions like free will, the limits of rationality when faced with the absurd, and the new moral universe created by a willingness to look into the heart of such darkness. Stevens's comment here is ambiguous between a claim about humanity's not being constituted in a way that would enable it to contemplate genuine nothingness, a metaphysical assertion, and a refusal to accept a gloomy view of what seems on the face of it to be a startlingly empty universe.

For the existentialists, this nothingness had worked its insidious way inward as well. Faulkner's characters can be made to sound superficially like Sartre's Roquentin and company, that group doomed to introspect the void when they went looking for an inner self. When Stevens becomes more insistent, he can fall into this mode: 'O gods! Nothing cannot remain anywhere since nothing is vacuum and vacuum is paradox and unbearable and we will have none of it even if we would' (120). In effect, what Stevens is inveighing against here is the world that Faulkner has so carefully delineated. Complain all you want, Faulkner seems to be saying in such passages, the nothing from which we come and to which we return, like the death stalking the Sartorises, is unimpressed by whatever criticisms we might want to make about it. As someone who seems not to have had many mystical bones in his body, Faulkner for the most part avoided worrying about the problem of saying the unsayable. Samuel Johnson's quip about Boehme, that if he saw unutterable things he should not have tried to utter them,[9] would probably have provoked a wry smile. But the hard-to-say things about this world, even about something as nebulous as 'Nothing', do come in for their share of discussion, particularly in the notlanguage whose various manifestations we have been tracking.

Apparently this Nothing is better thought of dialectically. As Stevens puts it, he needs such an abstract notion 'to measure my stature against whenever I need reassure myself that I also am Motion'. Motion is apparently more than simple activity, which could obviously be as empty or mindless as stasis. Faulkner has Stevens explain it this way: feelings last, or at least when the body responsible for them ages, it lays up memories of old capacities, even the capacity to feel anguish at emptiness. So when Housman writes that 'nothing cannot remain', he is wrong according to Stevens because only something can remain, or, as he puts it, 'it is Remaining which will always remain' (120).[10] Unlike some windy Left Bank exchange about being and nothingness, Stevens's reflections here serve as a prelude to a very specific example that Faulkner wants to introduce: Linda Snopes and Stevens's feelings about her. Their interactions occupy a great deal of the novel because they give Faulkner a chance to characterize a range of speakers and to orchestrate more meditations on life in post-war Jefferson. One more time 'The Love Song of J. Alfred Prufrock' figures prominently in a Faulkner text. As a poem about ageing, self-consciousness, the inhibitions of the unattractive, empty rooms full of people, and failure to touch, it haunted Faulkner throughout his career. In his mind it is obviously one of the most compelling portraits we have of the self-regarding, cerebral lover, lost in the garrulity of his endless interior monologue. The 'That is not what I meant at all' world for Stevens is the one in which he tries to express his feelings for Linda. This stuttering love interest drives the plot, and Faulkner uses it at this stage of his career to try to articulate the underlying laws of behaviour that he intuited 20 years earlier.

Inevitably this occasions one of those reverie-filled moments we have been singling out for special emphasis. In the midst of a discussion concerning the morals of the community and the effect of adultery on its way of perceiving, Faulkner shifts perspective and takes us to a place from which the narrator is 'looking back and down'. From this perspective, Jefferson is distant and ill-defined enough to resemble the town Stevens knew as a child. As the actual town recedes, one of those longer, more detached views that Faulkner is so good at orchestrating asserts itself. Stars burn 'coldly', barely visible, and the earth grows 'luminous' as if the light is pooling 'among the low places of the ground'. Cue the fireflies, or lightning-bugs as they are called in *The Sound and the Fury*, and 'you stand suzerain and solitary above the whole sum of your life beneath that incessant ephemeral spangling' (277). This makes the observer the feudal overlord to whom fealty is due, the position in which Faulkner can arrange for Stevens to survey the past yet again, artistically laid out before him as a virtual possession.

The description of the scene brings together a number of the subjects central, not only to *The Town* or the trilogy, but to Faulkner's fiction as a whole:

First is Jefferson, the center, radiating weakly its puny glow into space; beyond it, enclosing it, spreads the County, tied by the diverging roads to that center as is the rim to the hub by its spokes, yourself detached as God himself for this moment above the cradle of your nativity and of the men and women who made you, the record and annal of your native land proffered for your perusal in ring by concentric ring like the ripples on living water above the dreamless slumber of your past; you to preside unanguished and immune above this miniature of man's passions and hopes and disasters – ambition and fear and lust and courage and abnegation and pity and honor and sin and pride – all bound, precarious and ramshackle held together, by the web, the iron-thin warp and woof of his rapacity but withal yet dedicated to his dreams.

(277)

Such prose no doubt elicits a range of reactions, but it is hard to imagine someone reading it carefully and concluding that this is clearly a novelist who has written himself out. For an insightful, unsentimental, suggestive account of what it feels like to look 'back and down', one could hardly do better. As far as its function in *The Town* is concerned, Faulkner touches on a number of points that constitute an answer to the existentialist predicament sketched in earlier. First there is the empirical evidence of having existed, of growing up in Jefferson, a time and a place described as 'the center'. The light it makes is a sign of human habitation, not 'frantic and pulsing' like those fireflies, not aloof like the stars, but just there, more dark than light, the symbol of what in another evocative phrase Faulkner calls 'the dreamless slumber of your past'. It always strikes him as odd that something so intensely lived at the level of the minute particular as childhood could ever be utterly forgotten, and that is why he keeps coming back to it. Then there is the idea of the self as the centre of a series of concentric circles, both the links between the child and the larger community, and the sphere of influence defined by the artist at the centre of the world as he imagines it. Third, there is the way such scenes force the observer to think about 'the whole sum of your life'. This is a problem, because it involves a calculation that must be performed with an imperfect memory, an awareness of things missing and lost that can never be added up, things that are not the less important for being so hard to recall.

Stevens becomes, for the time that he looks back, one of Faulkner's eager nostalgists who experiences a sense of vertigo poised between the present and the past. The reality to which he constantly refers, the thing that refutes Nothingness, is defined by all the elements he joins together in one of those marvellous Faulknerian lists – 'ambition and fear and lust', etc. In the decade during which *The Town* was written, Faulkner liked giving interviews filled with those words, usually linked with that other great leveller, the co-ordinating conjunction. He has Gavin Stevens reel them off here because they help explain the complex process of self-creation that a character like him is constantly engaged in. The mix of emotions and moral categories is deliberate, if for no other reason than that the one can never exist in Faulkner's world without the other. This then is an answer of sorts to the doubts that assail Stevens, particularly when he contemplates all these hard things gone soft, bodies turned to dust, people changed into phantoms, as he will surely be in his turn. He can contemplate Nothing with more equanimity, vaguely comforted by the thought that he is not the less alive for being aware of life's ephemerality, rather the reverse.

This meditation, one of the most beautiful and nuanced in all of Faulkner, constitutes living history for someone like him. In such passages, he seeks to represent some sort of generic yearning, because he believes that any individualized version of it is linked to the same old emotions that have driven humanity from the beginning. The stars are visible when we look up, but although reason tells us their light is a message from a non-existent past, for us they no more reflect cosmic time than the fireflies do some insect version of it. The bemused quality of the passage suggests that human time is all that anyone can ever really try to understand. It also makes clear that readers who go looking in a novel such as *The Town* for incisive comments on the difference between our forefathers robbing the Indians of their land on the one hand, and their robbing the slaves of their dignity and selfhood on the other, are going to come away disappointed. The novel counts all those things into this history but they are subsumed in something larger.

In the end there is the inevitable move downward to darkness, the one that almost always occurs in some form at the conclusion of a Faulkner novel, most memorably perhaps in the Snopes trilogy. Stevens apostrophizes himself as an 'old man' and announces that 'the tragedy of life is, it must be premature, inconclusive and inconcludable, in order to be life; it must be before itself, in advance of itself, to have been at all' (279). Turgenev apparently irritated his acquaintances by referring to himself as an old man from about 35 on, but Stevens is doing more here than indulging in self-pity or fishing for compliments. The context makes clear that this is a paean to young love, seen as tragic because the young cannot see it as that, appreciate it for all it offers, or see how recollections of its perfection will envenom the simulacra that the future is sure to present. Wilde's Sir Henry Wotton is hovering somewhere close, with his stirring reminder that 'There is absolutely nothing in the world but youth.'[11] I take Faulkner to be saying here as well that, although every human being yearns for a sense of completion, the possibility of actually feeling that sense is the very thing precluded by the nature of the yearning for it. The feeling in question will serve as a metaphor for everything in life that we want intensely and can never have, including a sense of fulfilment at the end of it all. What Gavin Stevens is expressing, then, is a semi-tragic world view, as seen from ripe old middle age.[12]

The inconclusive quality of the novel's ending speaks to this notion of life's tendency not to work out in ways that seem like an acceptable conclusion. Eula commits suicide, but that leaves her as a subject of commentary for the talkers left behind. Far from summarizing the point of her life, it serves to underline the simple fact that life does not have a point. Stevens then muses, as a number of his predecessors have done, on verb tense, what 'is' and 'was' mean, only with a different kind of backward view. He decides that Eula's disappearing in this way is better caught in the words 'no more is' than 'never been', as if 'what is going to happen to one tomorrow already gleams faintly visible now if the watcher were only wise enough to discern it or maybe just brave enough' (293). This is Mr Compson without the debilitating cynicism. The somewhat oblique reference to a kind of destiny is symbolized by the lighting effects. The light thrown by the stars and fireflies, the ones that light up the dark and the past when Stevens looks back on Jefferson, now shines on the future, and Eula is on the way to becoming another imperfect memory.

The conclusion to these reflections features Stevens speaking of her in code, of the principle of male devotion to a lost female ideal, something that lies dormant for long periods, and animates the flesh of the man when the image reasserts itself. This is *l'amorosa idea* again, refined into something more selfless and life enhancing. In the process, it gives Stevens proof of having really existed, and of an image of a love that outlasts time, even if it has to be a somewhat impersonal one. He calls this the 'ectoplasm of devotion too thin to be crowned by scorn, warned by hatred, annealed by grief' (294). (It is easy to forget when one is generalizing about late Faulkner how many sentences like this a novel such as *The Town* contains.) The reference to ectoplasm recalls the phantoms of previous settlers mentioned who remain so potent despite being part of the abiding dust. Like them, this devotion survives, even when pitted against those strong emotions that might be supposed to wreak havoc with it, because it has more staying power than they do. The formula of a lonely male or two, co-operative nature, gorgeous prose, and the long view forces us to see Horace here as one more in a long line of would-be lovers, wondering about his place in the larger scheme of things because he has not been able to find it in the smaller one, singing an equivocal hymn to the beauty of solitude.

In the discussion of *The Mansion*, the last novel in the trilogy, I want to concentrate again on moments like these in which characters pause and think about themselves and the past. Although Faulkner uses Mink Snopes's single-minded desire for revenge on Flem Snopes to move the plot along, his reflections do not really become interesting until the very end of the novel. His simplicity makes him representative in another sense, and it gives Faulkner a chance to represent the insularity of Southern society. White males in *The Mansion* are divided in various ways, but the fierce independence and bitter resentment of any kind of government interference is the thing that binds rich and poor together. Faulkner's portrayal of the deeply conservative views of these people is important for anyone interested in how they think.

In this novel he sums them up in a memorable sentence. This group sees anyone attempting to interfere with them as 'communists', a label that includes 'Harry Hopkins, Hugh Johnson and everybody else associated with N.R.A., Eugene Debs, the I.W.W., the C.I.O.' (523). This list is worth pausing over, for its eclecticism says a lot about how undiscriminating such people are, how frightened of outside influence, how committed to holding onto their indigenous brand of capitalism, and how deep the anti-Yankee prejudice runs in a town like Jefferson. Hopkins was Roosevelt's right hand man during the Great Depression, and a spokesperson for the American government during the war. His politics were democratic, his sentiments with the poor. Hugh Johnson, by way of contrast, had a spectacular break with Roosevelt precisely because he, via Bernard Baruch, represented the interests of big business. The NRA (National Recovery Agency) for which he worked set up a vast series of regulations and codes of conduct for American business during the New Deal. Both of these people were political insiders, whereas the next one on the list, Eugene Debs, was a socialist who believed in the cause of the American worker and collected millions of votes as his party's candidate in successive elections between 1904 and 1920. The unions that round out the list certainly had links with communism in America, but they were very different things. The IWW (International Workers of the World, or Wobblies) had a significant impact on American culture as well as American industry, embracing as it did bohemians and the homeless, and advocating alternative lifestyles that went with their political liberalism. It organized thousands of strikes, antagonized the Federal and State governments, and was viciously repressed after a huge initial success. It also advocated sabotage in its battle with the capitalist system, a position that appalled Debs, for example. The CIO (Congress of Industrial Organizations) was, like the IWW, crucial in the development of the union movement in America, if quite a bit less radical. In articulating its blanket distrust of these organizations, the South was simply repeating what it had done in the years leading up to the Civil War, when it dismissed as abolitionists figures such as William Lloyd Garrison, John Quincy Adams, and Abraham Lincoln, who held widely divergent views of slavery.

The list also helps to set up the story of Linda Snopes's involvement with the Communists, in Spain during the Civil War and then back in America. This interest in contemporary history is a relatively new feature in Faulkner's fiction, and it enables him to supply his characters with a number of opinions on current issues. It is also true that, because political passions can never animate his more interesting characters for long, this leads to some flaccid writing in what is, by Faulkner's standards, a very long novel (almost 400 pages). The narrative does not really make a meditative pause until Faulkner takes up Linda Snopes's story in earnest, and then only after a lot of retelling of events from the previous two novels in the trilogy. Faulkner has to lay the groundwork for the battle between the males for one female that drives so many of his plots – *Soldiers' Pay, The Sound and the Fury, Sanctuary,* and *If I Forget Thee, Jerusalem* – but because Horace is such a reluctant participant in it, that battle is also less interesting than it could be.

The male/male conversation which Faulkner likes to use to work out ideas also makes for difficulties at certain points, as when Ratliff has to debate German idealism with Gavin Stevens, someone with a PhD from the University of Heidelberg. Still, even these passages are of interest for the abstract issues that Faulkner wants to wrestle with in *The Mansion.* For example, when Ratliff makes a point about darkness, namely that it is the source of German music, German ideas, in fact of anything capable of touching the human heart, his thinking runs as follows: 'In the dark there is no shadow. Shine a light into it and you get a sharp shadow, a reminder of who we are, the shape of our collective "deformity"' (450). The source of this light turns out to be female. This at least is what Ratliff, whose erudition apparently extends to the classics, claims when he laconically observes: 'Helen walked in light.' This prompts a short lesson on the enduring quality of female beauty, in which we learn that Helen retains her mythical status because she never speaks apparently, whereas Semiramis and Judith and Lilith *et al.* 'are fading steadily into the obscurity of their own vocality within which their passions and tragedies took place' (451). That is, there is something progressively less real about the tragedy of the passions that leaves it diminished by artistic repetition. (As a comic counterpart to such a discussion, the names of these mythical female figures come up in the part of the novel dedicated to Mink's journey. When he visits a brothel he looks for women 'functional' like 'Helen and Eve, and Lilith' and 'colored white like them' [591].)

The focus on Linda's story gives *The Mansion* a chance to escape male dominance.[13] Yet because in the novel women like Linda are repeatedly identified with the seductive qualities of these mythic avatars, they are exalted to diminished status. Faulkner ultimately cannot do for a character like Linda what he does so compellingly for Quentin Compson or Harry Wilbourne: make a detailed study of desire from the inside. In this novel, he is interested in exploring how male desire contributes to the creation of the object of its own obsession, *l'amorosa idea* one more time. Stevens's feelings about Linda again drive most of the action when Mink's revenge plot is not the centre of attention, but they are as uninterestingly complicated as he is weak and indecisive. In their last embrace, Stevens's hand is on her buttocks, 'as you cup the innocent hipless bottom of a child.' As critics have pointed out, it is Linda who is the experienced one by now and Stevens the child.[14] Without despair and grief as part of the package, sex writes a trifle white in Faulkner. He tries though, assuring us that Stevens thinks about Linda's desirability 'with terror' (710), but no one really believes it.

The end of the trilogy brings out all kinds of parting gestures: characters like Jason Compson, Joanna Burden, Bayard Sartoris make cameo appearances; endings are supplied for stories we know – Benjy burns down the Compson house, Jason is fooled by Flem Snopes into selling the family property – as Faulkner bids goodbye to all that. Prospero says that in retirement every third thought will be his death, and Derrida opted for every second thought in a valedictory interview. Faulkner was obviously in the same mental space when he finished this trilogy, and he took special care to communicate these reflections at the end of *The Mansion*.

Once again a small group of men is left to contemplate the world of envious desire and violent reactions that has held centre stage to this point. Ratliff and Stevens leave Mink with some money and promises for more, and we read of 'the night the moonless dark, the worn-out eroded fields supine beneath the faint breath of fall, waiting for winter' (719). The delusory but attractive prospect of endless summer has been eclipsed here, and with it the human drama fades and the camera pulls back. The stars in their patterns make their quiet comment on the seemingly patternless folly of the events recounted to this point. So far, so typical of Faulkner, early or late. But then a new note is struck. These rhetorical gestures are just the beginning of the long, sonorous peroration that ends *The Mansion*. Mink lies down, like Bartleby, to sleep with kings and councillors. The passage is worth quoting at length:

> it seemed to him he could feel the Mink Snopes that had had to spend so much of life just having unnecessary bother and trouble, beginning to creep, seep, flow easy as sleeping; he could almost watch it, following all the little grass blades and tiny roots, the little holes the worms made, down and down into the ground already full of the folks that had the trouble but were free now ... all mixed and jumbled up comfortable and easy so wouldn't nobody even know even care who was which anymore, himself among them, equal to any, good as any, brave as any, being inextricable from, anonymous with all of them: the beautiful, the splendid, the proud and the brave, right on up to the very top itself among the shining phantoms and dreams which are the milestones of the long human recording – Helen and the bishops, the kings and the unhomed angels, the scornful and graceless seraphim.
>
> (720–1)

This is a hymn to the great levelling, but it retains the vestiges of a hierarchical view of the system. Helen is there to represent the seductive deceptiveness of female beauty, the havoc it wreaks on men not strong enough to resist it, and the fact that even it must capitulate to time in the end. So too the mighty of the earth, and the seraphim are back, as fallen angels this time. In early Faulkner they were the dazzlingly attractive and seductive counterparts of an erotic vision that needed an otherworldly lexicon to communicate its intensities. Now they are 'scornful' and 'graceless' and 'unhomed', like the convict at the end of *If I Forget Thee, Jerusalem*. Even they have seen enough and are as tired of the human spectacle as he and Mink are. The poem hovering in the background of this scene is probably 'Thanatopsis'. Since everyone else has gone to 'the silent halls of death' without any fuss, says the speaker in Bryant's famous 1820 *memento mori*, you should approach your grave 'Like one who wraps the drapery of his couch / About him, and lies down to pleasant dreams'?[15] The decor is less genteel in Faulkner, but the message is the same. Note too how the rhythm of the sentence mimics the life rhythms it describes, all those short phrases groping inexorably for the lowest level as they mimic the trickling down to disintegration as 'the democracy of the dead' asserts itself.[16] The dispossessed are finally in possession.

Time and again Faulkner asks us to face up to the hard truth that we live only to decay. The case is made with great rhetorical persuasiveness, as here, yet he faithfully records our hope that such a conviction might be nuanced a little. Faulkner sees this hope as bound up with the different kinds of time represented by art, including of course the natural cycles. Like the action imaged on the urn so often referred to, Nature moves but is herself 'unmoved', as a medieval poet might put it. Faulkner does not write medieval allegory (although he did have a go at something like it in a 1926 book called *Mayday*), but he is fascinated by fable. And the lesson of this fable is that those who are immersed in the world of change, or 'Motion' as he calls it in the trilogy, cannot get any kind of atemporal perspective that would enable them to think of themselves in relation to stillness. Caught up in permanent flux, they cannot grasp – cannot be expected to grasp – the interdependence of time and eternity. If in the quasi-mystical moments associated with solitude or when creating something that has pretensions to timelessness, we get intimations of this interdependence, the power of the words used to convince us that it does not exist will paradoxically give us some reason to believe that it might.

8
Late Faulkner

The last two decades of Faulkner's life were a remarkable mix. The 1940s marked the pinnacle of his screenwriting career ('To Have and Have Not', 'The Big Sleep'). Malcolm Cowley's *The Portable Faulkner* was published, but more importantly *Sanctuary* and *Pylon* enjoyed great success as paperbacks, luridly packaged to maximize sales. Hollywood made a successful movie out of *Intruder in the Dust*; Faulkner's notoriety at home became a match for his fame abroad, and by the end of the decade he had won the Nobel Prize. His money worries were, if not definitively over, greatly alleviated. He took on a new role as an American goodwill ambassador, involved himself in the debate about race relations during the most important social upheaval in the United States since the Civil War, acquired a second home as writer-in-residence at the University of Virginia, and became a member of a prestigious society of foxhunters, a gentleman in a pink coat who rode to hounds. It was also a period during which he suffered desperately from self-doubt, constantly worried that he was written out, and became unsure about his ability to tell good writing from bad. The problems with alcohol that eventually cut short his life continued unabated, with many more visits to clinics where he could dry out from his drinking sessions.

Many have decried the loss of imaginative energy in Faulkner's fiction written in the 1940s and 50s, accusing him of 'telling' instead of 'showing', packing his work with maxims and intruding on the fiction in unproductive ways, and preaching from a Nobel-inspired pulpit.[1] The question is a large and complicated one, and any discussion of the novels of these last decades, *Intruder in the Dust*, *Requiem for a Nun*, *A Fable*, and *The Reivers*, along with *The Town* and *The Mansion*, can hardly avoid addressing it. I have been arguing that the unevenness in works from the second half of Faulkner's career is the product of something that was there from the outset, namely the multiplicity of interests that he was always keen to pursue in a single work, and his relative lack of concern for observing certain conventions or satisfying readers' expectations. As we saw in the discussion of the Snopes trilogy, simply thinking about the plot as secondary can bring into sharper focus the more interesting things going on in Faulkner's late fiction. In all this talk of the great falling off, another thing that is sometimes forgotten is how unusual it is for a writer as obsessed with matters stylistic as Faulkner was to see into print as many books as he did. Fitzgerald published four novels during his lifetime, Hemingway six, Woolf eight, Forster five, Broch six, and so on. My interest here is in the amount of imaginative energy that Faulkner was still able to call on as he pursued his career, and this in the face of extraordinary difficulties. It seems entirely fitting that the writer who always thought of the novel as a 'sequence of discoveries'[2] should have made so many new ones in the last part of his career. This chapter focuses again on the extended meditations that are a feature of his fiction from the beginning, the style used to convey their nuances, and the tropes that link them to his work as a whole. The extent to which one sees his late fiction as informed by open-ended arguments and discussions of complex questions affects the judgements that one finally makes about it.

Although Faulkner was intrigued by mystery stories and published a whole book of them in 1949, *Knight's Gambit*, for a number of reasons his genius was not ideally suited to this genre. Plot is usually paramount in the mystery novel, whereas for Faulkner it is just another fictional device, one of many. He likes withholding certain kinds of information until the reader is ready for it, but the identity of a murderer is not one of them – *Light in August, Requiem for a Nun, The Mansion* are all organized in precisely the opposite way – and as a writer he is not partial to giving the reader all the clues necessary for solving a mystery. The guilty person works better if he/she is an integral part of the story and one of a plausible group of suspects, not just brought in at the end as a narrative convenience. Because Faulkner tends to concentrate on the consciousness of just a few characters, this can be difficult for him to arrange. Normally the hero figures out who committed the crime by using information available to all and the standard procedures of logical deduction. Faulknerian logic, particularly its premises, is sometimes idiosyncratic and hard to follow. Ambiguity works well in a mystery novel but only in certain, fairly limited ways, and clarity is normally of the essence, particularly in the details. Here, too, Faulkner has to work against his natural gifts if he is to obey the rules of the genre. Of course all these rules are made for innovative writers to break, but the conventions of the mystery novel are relatively inflexible and its adherents somewhat conservative.

Intruder in the Dust is, among other things, an attempt to add to the genre. It came out in September 1948 and sold better than any other Faulkner novel. His reputation had grown apace since the publication of Cowley's volume two years earlier. A number of his novels had been reissued by Random House, and magazines like *Life* were interested in doing a profile on this author who was becoming an important figure in the public imagination. As a murder mystery, the novel is not a success, and it does not do very well by the criteria just mentioned. It contains long pauses in which conceptual issues more or less unrelated to the 'mystery' of who killed Vinson Gowrie are taken up. The clues are dispensed in haphazard and incomplete fashion. The guilty person and the victim are almost completely unknown to us. The crime is figured out in laborious fashion by a logic that places a premium on some fairly murky suppositions and precepts, and the reasoning involved in double burying the victim is so unclear that even at the end of the story we remain uncertain about why the murderer went through it. Probably only one reader in ten can explain the reasoning and steps involved in the elaborate cover-up of the murders, and only one in ten of those believes it. The accused's refusal to drive a coach and horses through the heart of the mystery by simply telling what happened when the murderer tried to frame him begs credulity in similar fashion.

At the end of *Intruder in the Dust*, Gavin Stevens summarizes the plot of the murder mystery we have just been reading this way: Crawford Gowrie is one of the 'elect' because his crime proves what an abject species humanity is, and simultaneously proves that we have a soul. His plan that goes so badly awry, entrapping Lucas and forcing the perpetrator to swap bodies with the wrong sort of holes in them, is described as 'simple and water-tight in its biological and geographical psychology' (456), foiled only by the human link between Lucas and Chick that makes the former call on the latter for help. It would be fun to think about what phrases like 'geographical psychology' might mean, but there is something goofy about such an investigation as well, and something self-evidently absurd about calling this botched murder plan 'water-tight'. Musing about the absurdity of Dickens's melodramatic plots, Northrop Frye invites readers to think of them as absurd, 'not from incompetence or bad taste, but from a genuinely creative instinct.'[3] The plot of *Intruder in the Dust* is absurd in the Dickensian sense, and I think the part of Faulkner that loved the tall tale knew it.

The more ponderous Stevens's explanation becomes, the more comic the novel starts to seem. For these reasons, in what follows I mostly ignore the murder mystery business and concentrate on what people are thinking about other things, what is called in this novel the 'deadly reasonableness of enraged calculation, a calm sagacious and desperate rationality' (345).

At one point Faulkner posits a link between simple murder and simple speech in a way that helps explain what else he is trying to do in *Intruder in the Dust*: 'the deliberate violent blotting out obliteration of a human life was itself so simple and so final that the verbiage which surrounded it enclosed it insulated it intact into the chronicle of man had of necessity to be simple and uncomplex too, repetitive, almost monotonous even' (350). This sentence suggests that the awkwardnesses and reiterations, the unidiomatic words and expressions, the locutions that many would think of as introducing complexity are all Faulkner's way of emphasizing what he sees as simplicity. It also reminds us that he proceeds quite consciously in orchestrating, not just a series of effects with his prose, but a set of meanings that the style is supposed to stand for.

This complicated simplicity is contrasted in the novel with the simple simplicity of ordinary human speech, what is described as 'standardised meagreness not of individual vocabularies but of Vocabulary itself, by means of which even man can live in vast droves and herds even in concrete warrens in comparative amity' (343–4). This is not quite what Eliot meant by the reference to the 'dialect of the tribe' in *Four Quartets*, but the comparison is a useful one. Faulkner is making a point, not about where poetry comes from, but about where it does not. His account of this Vocabulary is a reminder that the writer's use of language, his power to make history live or point to new areas of experience, both of which are explored in *Four Quartets*, must be considered apart from how ordinary language normally functions. Wesley Morris convincingly argues that this lack in ordinary speech is a plenitude in Faulkner's mind, because these simple assertions in the Vocabulary of the mass constitute 'the very force of communal bonding.'[4] Yet Faulkner knows equally well that people who live in 'vast droves and herds' are bound together by the words used at the human equivalents of the feed trough or the stampede. Thus Vocabulary, the language used in a drunken brawl or by a mob, can work to undermine as well as facilitate 'communal bonding', and what holds the community together, the language of gossip, prejudice and innuendo, is often the thing that has the power to rip individual lives apart, as *Intruder in the Dust* shows very clearly. Even what we have been calling Faulkner's great subject, thinking itself, if it is to be 'insulated intact' into the chronicle, must be translated into words that convey all the imaginative effort involved in the process.

The ambiguity of the claims made for ordinary people and ordinary language are of a piece with Faulkner's mixed intentions in the novel, which is about resolving a mystery and about how people can thwart injustice, stop a lynching, and free an innocent man by committing themselves, simply doing something rather than theorizing about it. When correctly understood by the young man responsible for helping Lucas Beauchamp, the unjustly accused, this represents a significant moment in his coming of age. He is someone who must reconcile himself to the Southern code by rejecting it and taking sides with a black man. Instead of conveying all this as Chick Mallison registers it, Faulkner has Gavin Stevens think it through, in an autocommentary on precisely these subjects. As always, Stevens's observations are a strange mixture of lucidity and opacity, shrewd insight and facile free association, precise detail and bizarre generalization. Sorting out all these strands in his many interventions is difficult, but even if we could establish the exact nature of the claims and the authorial ironies more clearly (and Faulkner's methods militate against that), there would still be a double purpose at the centre of the novel: an elaborate plot that is a somewhat awkward vehicle for the moral lesson, and a complex verdict on the South experienced by a young man but explained by an old one. It may be disorienting, but there is no reason to suppose that it is not deliberate. It may be judged a flaw, but such dismissals lose some of their force if all they mean is that other novelists would have proceeded differently.

What makes Faulkner's take on human drama in this novel so interesting is how much of it turns around the individual and how he/she reacts to the Vocabulary of the mass. Stevens's attempt to articulate a view of the group and how it conceives itself, how it thinks as an entity, is relevant here: 'man having passed into mob passes then into mass which abolishes mob by absorption, metabolism, then having got too large even for mass becomes man again conceptible of pity and justice and conscience even if only in the recollection of his long painful aspiration toward them' (436). This is not language calculated to satisfy the freedom fighters worried about racist lynch mobs, and the proposition it makes may well seem at first blush as absurd as the plot just discussed. A mob belongs to a time and place; it has a specific goal, even if it is something as generalized as random destruction; and its anger waxes and wanes, usually over a period of hours. The mass, a word that serves as a shorthand convenience for the sociologist or political scientist, belongs to another domain altogether. No matter how much absorptive and metabolic power a mass exerts, it cannot normally do much with a mob. Yet the passage gives an accurate sense of the level of abstraction that Stevens often prefers, and it serves as the preface to an account of American history that involves an attempt to define the idea of humanity. In the process, Faulkner adds some useful information about how a Southern intellectual like Stevens looks at his country's and his culture's history.

When invoking the Civil War, Stevens claims that the principles of individual liberty so painfully affirmed at that time are precisely what is needed in the middle of the twentieth century. He contextualizes the situation of freed slaves in the American South by taking the long view, arguing that slavery is part of our species' moral education, man's 'struggle toward the stars in the stepping-stones of his expiations' (401), a characteristically evocative locution. He compliments blacks for their patience and evinces nostalgia for an agrarian America that he sees epitomized in the lot of the African American, a somewhat abstract heaven plus 'a little earth for his own sweat to fall on among his own green shoots and plants' (402). Stevens ends his account of the South in the late 1940s by arguing that blacks should be given their richly deserved civil rights and should give in their turn their former masters access to the organic links they enjoy with their environment. Critics have noted that this idea is not only racist but also long on abstraction and short on modes of implementation.[5] Besides the suspect 'biological psychology' of these claims, there is the problem that Stevens seems to have ignored some obvious real-life consequences of what he is advocating, namely that granting blacks the economic privileges which are theirs by right would make them as appreciative of and as eager for material well-being as their fellow citizens, North and South. The 'national passion for the mediocre' (401) that Stevens identifies here, the one that he sees as the fatal flaw at the heart of modern life, is contrasted with detailed accounts of man and his role as part of the natural cycle, because in his way Faulkner wants to use his character to articulate a version of Jefferson's vision of a different America. That vision is doomed, not because its proponents are naïve or Americans are excessively materialistic, but because the freedoms that the founding fathers fought so hard to defend helped to generate the country's prosperity, with all that that implied about the inevitable growth of the market economy.

Principles of individual liberty are asserted again in one of the novel's most famous passages, Stevens's claim that those in the South resemble the Germans after 1933, that they have '*no other alternative between being either a Nazi or a Jew*' (447). This sounds noble, but it is immediately qualified in an intriguing way. The Southerner can identify with the oppressed, even become 'a Jew', but he alone can do this: i.e., he cannot make common cause with others who feel as he does concerning the racial question. Not only that: no one else can even give him advice on how to handle these difficult circumstances. The appeal for universal solidarity ends up being an insistence on the parochial, on the necessity of maintaining the divide that already exists between the regions and some kind of notional federation. Rather casually, Stevens argues that the one thing on which 99.9% of Southerners are agreed is that they will take up arms to defend the Northern invader again should Federal troops be sent. This is patent nonsense of course, but Faulkner shrewdly includes it here because it is exactly the sort of thing a Southern patriot like Stevens might say when fully launched into such an analysis. Here Faulkner could even argue that Stevens has history on his side. The Civil War began the process by which the Lucas Beauchamps of the South would eventually become free and equal citizens, yet in the passage under discussion the victory of the North is said to have done '*more than even John Brown to stalemate Lucas's freedom*' (447). The point is that John Brown, a martyr to the abolitionist cause, fought the first battle of the Civil War in his raid on Harpers Ferry, thereby frightening the South, hurrying on the war, and setting back the anti-slavery cause by making the South forcibly resist the dictates of the North.[6] According to this view, the freedom won for blacks by the War, the one guaranteed in the Emancipation Proclamation, is a paper exercise, a sham, something that makes a person like Lucas a prisoner. The 80-odd years that had passed since the end of the war had not accomplished what the North had hoped. More federal laws and Northern troops were simply breaches of regional autonomy that would, at best, perpetuate the unsatisfactory status quo, at worst, lead to a new dissolution. In this as in so much else, Faulkner is a writer who reminds us that the terms of the political and cultural questions facing his generation in the twentieth century were laid down in the nineteenth.

Stevens concludes with an apocalyptic scenario: he fears Northerners will scorn the warning and vow to 'perish in the name of humanity', a claim that not many civil rights advocates would have thought of making in 1948, or at any time in their campaign for that matter. And the Southerner replies: '*When all is stricken but that nominative pronoun and that verb what price Lucas's humanity then*' (447)? The rhetorical question with its quirky grammatical specificity clearly invites us to say something like, yes, 'we perish' is all that is left if one insists on standing by such vague ideals, if the other states seek to impose their will on the

South, and the nation dies for a principle that can only exist if it does. However, another possible response is 'we perish as a people' or 'we perish as a nation that stands for certain rights', if we forget that the humanity of a single individual is important, responses that make the confidence with which Stevens puts his rhetorical question seem a little hollow. A word like 'perish' is highly charged in the context, with its slightly archaic feel, and it has all sorts of biblical resonances. In the King James version of the Bible, the disciples worry 'lest [they] perish', and the famous verse from John 3:16, 'whosoever believeth in him shall not perish', hovers in the background whenever this word is quoted. More relevant perhaps is the most famous American use of the word, and one directly related to the subject of racism so central to this novel. Gettysburg was of course one of the battles that turned the tide against the South, and Lincoln concluded his great speech there by saying that the war is being fought so that democracy 'shall not perish from the earth'. The resonance of this carefully chosen word suggests that Faulkner's attempts to make *Intruder in the Dust* part of a debate concerning questions central for an understanding of American democracy are not the ham-fisted intrusions many come to the late fiction expecting.

Faulkner wrote a short story, in 1943 about American heroism in World War Two, called 'Shall Not Perish' that is directly relevant here. It too concludes with a vision of how a single incident, the death of a soldier mourned by his family, and the small community that constitutes its setting can stand for war and the whole country's response to it. The narrator thinks of all the deeds performed in the war against Germany and Japan, but the references are all to the past, the Civil War, Bedford Forrest, a general in the Confederate army, and the heroism shown by the Southern troops 80 years earlier. Their deeds are conflated with those of ordinary people 'who lasted and endured and fought the battles and lost them and fought again because they didn't even know they had been whipped' (114). The context makes clear that Faulkner means the pioneers, the settlers, and the colonizers, 'still coming, North and South and East and West, until the name of what they did and what they died for became just one single word, louder than any thunder. It was America, and it covered all the western earth' (115). The story has been faulted for its sentimentality, but that sort of criticism is bound up, not only with an aesthetic judgement of what seems like chauvinistic excess, but also with how proud or ashamed of their nation American academics are feeling at a particular time. Things have not been very good on that front for a while now. Faulkner's interest in striking a respondent chord in his fellow citizens by articulating a passionate version of American patriotism is bound up with his sense of how heroic ordinary citizens are capable of being. According to this view, great deeds performed in the fight against one tyranny are cognate with those done against another, even if Nazis and Northerners are as different as Snopeses and Sartorises, as Faulkner knew perfectly well.

Ultimately the metaphysical/ethical question central to this novel, a much more interesting one than 'Who did it?', is something that subsumes the racial question as well, namely 'What is the nature and value of existence?' In 400 unpunctuated words near the end of *Intruder in the Dust*, Stevens concentrates fiercely on this idea: life is short ('a second or two'); individual lives are of no importance, individual rights are; we take up too much space ('room-devouring carcasses'); reducing the population would be a good thing; memory is forever ('inevictable'); memory/awareness of injustice and suffering is particularly long ('ten thousand years'); human beings are always ready to forsake principle for self-interest; and a courageous minority can be a force for good in individual cases (467). With this last, Stevens rejoins the living as it were, and Chick and he get to tease each other about what actually happened in Lucas's case. The fact that Faulkner was willing to take on such issues is hardly surprising, given the things his characters have been keen to discuss from the outset. If it was not an inflated sense of self-importance that made him include disquisitions on love, art, and the nature of evil in *Soldiers' Pay*, *Mosquitoes*, and *Sartoris*, and we read those with interest, we should be as open to whatever he is attempting 20 years on, no matter what has happened in the interim.

By the time *Requiem for a Nun* was published in October 1951, Faulkner was world famous. A critical study of his novels came out in September of that year, and nine other books on him were reportedly in the works. It represents another new departure for him, the idea of writing a play interspersed with prologues serving as interchapters that set up the drama. Like the mystery story conventions he used for the previous novel and the allegorical form he was trying to work out during these years for *A Fable*, this new structure afforded him a series of opportunities and caused him a lot of problems. Faulkner said that he needed these sections, in which the histories of Jefferson, American culture, and the entire cosmos are summarized, to serve as a counterpoint for the drama in three acts that pits Gavin Stevens, Temple Drake, and Nancy Mannigoe against the state judicial system and the moral code that informs it. As in the previous novel, Faulkner's problem involves how to organize a detailed examination of semi-abstract ideas while moving the action forward.

The result is an embarrassment of riches. As before, Stevens the Heidelberg PhD is destined to be doing a lot of talking, but in this novel Temple Drake, whose devastating silences and garrulous monologues make her such an unforgettable character in *Sanctuary*, is now entrusted with an erudition and an articulateness that make her a match for Faulkner's in-house intellectual. Others add their substantial contributions to the debate. All this talking is nothing new for Faulkner, but presenting it so baldly, without the rhetorical safety net that he often uses to develop character and fill in context, makes it different in kind. His linguistic exuberance and fascination with consciousness make him as awkward a playwright as Browning and Henry James were before him. This creates a certain stilted quality to the exchanges in what is ostensibly a highly dramatic affair, what with a baby murdered, a marriage threatened by infidelity, a sordid past covered up, and a lawyer desperate to get at the truth. The stage directions and the speeches are richly informative about what histrionic people say to each other in a somewhat unreal situation, but they are less useful for exploring the interdependence of emotion and thought that we have been tracking. The murder is supposedly everything, but it happens offstage and the victim has no novelistic reality. The difficulties involved in assessing how responsible Nancy is for the crime, or the problem of deciding the degree of guilt that can be attributed to someone like Temple for what she has done also make *Requiem for a Nun* that much more complicated, particularly because we do not have the subtly evoked complexities provided by language and pattern that have guided us to this point. The primary interest of this novel therefore lies elsewhere, namely in the commentary that continues Faulkner's musings about what it is that makes us human, how we make sense of the past, the meaning of cultural history, all the subjects that have fascinated him from the outset of his career. These are what I will be concentrating on in what follows.

Act One begins with a prologue that is all about historical documents, 'land grants and patents and transfers and deeds ... diary-like annotations of births and marriages and deaths and public hangings and land-auctions' (475), the municipal equivalent of the Sartoris's family Bible. This also takes us back to the discussion of the ledgers in *Go Down, Moses*, and *Requiem for a Nun* picks up some of the arguments about history articulated there. The prologue winds its genial way to the end, bringing the reader up to the time of the Civil War, and then fast forwards to the present day. At one point, it pauses to record one of those dramatic, destructive, cleansing fires that mark crucial moments in Faulkner's fiction and create the possibility of a range of surprising phoenixes in their aftermath. This time it is the Jefferson courthouse that is burned by federal troops in the war. The narrator feels sure that the rebuilt version will be demolished in its turn before the end of the twentieth century, just because it is old, but for as long as it exists the chiming of the hours of the courthouse's new clock tower will go on sending the sparrows and the pigeons into a frenzy:

> garrulous myriad and independent the one, the other uxorious and interminable, at once frantic and tranquil – until the clock strikes again which even after a hundred years, they still seem unable to get used to, bursting in one swirling explosion out of the belfry as though the hour, instead of merely adding one puny infinitesimal more to the long weary increment since Genesis, had shattered the virgin pristine air with the first loud dingdong of time and doom.
>
> (505)

Such images represent oblique but resonant ways of thinking about history, lyric and comic by turns. Noel Polk, the author of the most insightful study devoted to the novel, equates time here with evil and the birds with innocents who are 'unaware of the long history of anguish or suffering' that humanity has endured.[7] The reference to Genesis does evoke a paradise lost at the beginning of time; the description of the ringing of the bell suggests an eschatological dimension at the end of it. A more secular symbolic reading would leave us with a somewhat different impression of the passage in question. If the striking of the hour always provokes this wild reaction, that means that, for the birds at least, there is no past, and in effect no time. According to this view, the bells are not announcing doom because there is no doom to announce. Our anthropomorphic self-absorption makes us see the birds as human ('garrulous', 'uxorious'), and see history as characterized by significant moments, deep structures, or messages destined to illuminate humanity's plight. Evolutionary biologists are happy to remind us that randomness is the only truth that space and time have to impart. The bells' ringing, marking the passage of time, produces a lovely swirl of activity and then a lapse back into somnolence. If one insists on seeing a pattern in human life, let that be it.

The introduction to Act II puts two towns, imaginary Jefferson and the real Jackson, in their geological and historical context. Faulkner's conflation of actual and created history is as bold as his creation myth. To get things started there is a 'mother-womb', 'furious tumescence', and 'one vast incubant ejaculation already fissionating in one boiling moil of litter from the celestial experimental Work Bench' (540). That is a big bang, for sure, and its size is commensurate with the excitement caused by its offspring. The passage also anticipates the way astronomers like to characterize the hot and dense universal beginning that ensued from what they call singularity all those billions of years ago. Prehistory is described in this prologue as 'the blind and tongueless earth spinning on', and with the advent of the geological ages come the scoring of the hills and 'the first scratch of orderly recording' on the 'mid-continental page' (541). As the earth moves from silence to noisy activity, Faulkner makes it clear – well, fairly clear – that he is no logo-centrist and that the history of the planet is best construed as a written work, all those scratchings on the geological page, filling in the evolutionary past. Out of this wildness comes civilization, then the founding of the state of Mississippi and its capital. The last stage in this process entails the blunting of the extraordinarily powerful force that brought life to the planet in the beginning and the gradual eclipse of frontier/pioneer lawlessness, what Faulkner calls in another charming phrase 'the old brave innocent tumultuous eupeptic tomorrowless days' (543). Yet the same process marks a huge advance for civilization and for art, which thrive on the new, the experienced, the dyspeptic, and the consequential.

In the prologue to Act Three, Faulkner's task is to write a commentary that plays on the sorts of complication involved in the very human drama that is also his subject. Having described the jail and its evolution, he moves on to the native peoples and their dealings with the authorities, who of course eventually swindle them out of their land. The town decor changes and becomes northernized. The South, corrupted by the temptation of federal money, buys its trees from Wisconsin, its windows from Pennsylvania, and sells its soul to turbo-capitalism in the process. The passage also seems eerily prescient, in the sense that it narrates the beginning of a movement that would see traditional small-town values undermined by the very forces (e.g. politicians who support anti-union Wal Marts) put into power by voters who treasured those values. As a recent commentator puts it, the South, an area that shifted its allegiance to the Republican party less than 20 years after Faulkner died, ended up 'voting [its] own fears into reality.'[8]

The conclusion involves bringing this story up to the present day. Faulkner goes on to complain, Thoreau-like, about how fashion editors in New York dictate useless changes in style to a gullible nation, and machines displace labourers from the cotton fields and force them to retreat to Northern ghettos or fight and die in America's wars, all very topical. The phrase used throughout is 'one nation' or 'one world', but its existence seems to be – again one is struck by Faulkner's feel for the future – a sort of virtual presence, 'no longer anywhere'. The 'swirling rocket-roar' that announces the coming of the new era is not just the means by which space is explored but the permanent noise that characterizes man's new cosmos: 'the very substance in which he lives and, lacking which, he would vanish in a matter of seconds – is murmurous with his fears and terrors and disclaimers and repudiations and his aspirations and dreams and his baseless hopes, bouncing back at him in radar waves from the constellations' (639). The new America is made up of the voices that have invaded what was formerly private space inside people's heads, an invasion effected by the means of communication that have torn the old world apart by bringing a new one together. The reference to rockets and constellations is apt, because the 1950s is the decade in which humankind first launches something with the power to escape the planet's gravity. Americans felt this acutely, since it was the Russian enemy that orbited the first space vehicle in 1957. The nation that had been teaching generations of science students that God made the flowers out of sunshine had to revise its high school curricula in a hurry, particularly in the South: Mississippi was one of the states that enforced a ban on teaching evolution in the aftermath of the Scopes trial. The fears about the revenge of the machines on humanity that Faulkner explored in *Pylon* had returned with a vengeance.

All these issues raised in the prologues are not much discussed in the play itself. Gavin Stevens is busy interrogating Temple about the past and playing the role of a Greek chorus, remembering horrific events, evoking ideals, expressing his support for the law, and dramatizing in his own person the difference between the young and the old. And Temple with her articulate volubility is a problem. Where did she learn words like 'euphonious' and 'patronym', and when did she develop a taste for Dostoevsky and Hemingway, both of whom she cites? Faulkner makes a sort of an attempt to acknowledge the improbability of all this by having her mumble things like '"euphonious" is right, isn't it?' (552), but it is a superficial one. Plausibility of character has to cede to the force that is always ultimately triumphant in his work, namely the imaginative exploration of the issue he has set himself to expound. Here that issue is justice, and Temple must cease to be the brittle, self-centred vamp she was in *Sanctuary*. As a result, she becomes a psychologist, a social historian, and a person who has reflected about surface and depth, artefact, and symbol, sin, guilt, and jurisprudence. In short, she often sounds a lot like a writer, the sort who could describe convicts' hands at the bars of the jail windows as 'already shaped and easy and unanguished to the handles of the plows and axes and hoes, and the mops and brooms and the rockers of white folks' cradles, until even the steel bars fitted them too without alarm or anguish' (605).

Having gone on at such length about Faulkner's right to experiment, it would be hypocritical to get all anxious about things like coherence and continuity now. Still, the difficulty is that this new Temple makes her less convincing in the role of stoical mother capable of suffering any burden, a role that is semi-crucial for the plot of *Requiem for a Nun*. Some see the reader's knowledge of her in a previous incarnation as an advantage in this regard. Polk, for example, notes that Temple 'has been trying for years to live with the incredible guilt and anguish her experiences (recounted in *Sanctuary*) have caused her.'[9] Is it a problem that these years are hard to envision? She has borrowed a name and a history from the previous novel, but for many readers that is the extent of the link. From this point of view, trying to imagine some sort of sympathetic, plausible version of Temple functioning during the time separating the events depicted in *Sanctuary* from those in *Requiem for a Nun* is a bit like trying to think about what Falstaff was up to during the 200 years between *Henry IV Part II* and *The Merry Wives of Windsor*. If the murder of Temple's baby can be justified because her suffering is an expiation, the novel threatens to collapse into grotesque bathos; if it cannot be justified, then Faulkner spends an awfully long time misdirecting us, and Nancy has a serious credibility problem in her minimalist role as an unfeeling baby-killer.

Looking for an answer to the questions raised about the meaning of human history, one is better off turning to another character, someone who is a silent as Temple is now talkative and as memorable as Nancy is unconvincing. I am thinking of Cecilia Farmer, the young girl who appears at a crucial point in the final prologue, the one who says nothing, does nothing, just scratches her name and 16th April 1861, on a pane of glass in a window, and then watches the world go by. As the extended commentary on her goes on to make clear, this girl comes to life when the town's interest in mythologizing and the writer's imagination work together to conjure her up, even though she ultimately sits in silent judgement on those imaginings. The voice of the prologue is quite explicit about the mechanics of this process: the reader is addressed as a contemporary American male, educated, an 'outlander', accompanied by a male guide, forced to think about who this woman is, using only the faint marks on a piece of opaque glass as a prompt. A number of possibilities are cited, some more imaginative than others. A conventional, romantic fate for her is worked out in great detail but rejected, and a sterner, more symbolic destiny imagined in which she becomes all the mythical female temptresses conceived as one. This sounds like the combination of truth and dream that Faulkner likes to celebrate over humble fact, but it too is not the last word. This woman proves to be something other than a product of the overheated male imagination, a different version of *l'amorosa idea*.

In the end, she is best understood as one of those ghosts Quentin speaks of in *Absalom, Absalom!*, the ones who need to be represented in notlanguage. Cecelia Farmer is fluent in it, and history has recorded what she said, not just a date scratched on a window, but a message sent across the years. In doing that, we are told, she makes time and space 'nothing', and makes silence speak. Her name and that date say: *"'Listen, stranger; this was myself: this was I'"*(649). There are verbal echoes of 'Crossing Brooklyn Ferry' here, the poem in which Whitman succeeds in speaking to posterity by straining to see it and listening for its voices, trying to define the mystery of consciousness by insisting on the power of art over time. In this novel, Faulkner succeeds in having Cecilia Farmer achieve the same effect by doing the opposite of what Whitman describes. Where he is prolix, she is taciturn. He sweeps away time in his fervent imagining of the future; she writes a date and contents herself with living in the present. His triumphant communication is an apotheosis, her desultory dream-life a truth that exists beyond the powers of expression of the minds she sets dreaming. His poem is a clear bid for a provisional immortality; her past, future, motives, and ideas are finally as opaque for us as those of the other characters in Faulkner's walk-in closet drama. Yet the mystery of her inner being remains intact and unappropriated. Hers becomes the voice of the stranger that reveals us to ourselves, and the way Faulkner draws our attention to it is a clear sign of his extraordinary and undiminished ability as a novelist.[10]

Requiem for a Nun showed how audacious a writer Faulkner could be and how undiminished his powers of invention were. By this time he knew his strengths: creating a strong, clearish story line or lines, situating everything in or near Yoknapatawpha, exploring particular human relations characterized by strong emotions, and rendering their complexity and power by working from the inside. And so, of course, he spent a large chunk of the years between 1944 and 1954 working on a novel with a scrambled story, set in a foreign country that he had visited only a few times, about a war that he had tried to serve in but could not, centred around a quasi-supernatural manifestation of Christ during the trench warfare at Easter in 1918, complete with a cast of thousands, including a clutch of abstractions to serve as characters, and an account of the vicissitudes of racing a three-legged horse in America thrown in.

Which brings us to *A Fable*, the next novel to be considered in this chapter, and the one most often cited when the idea of Faulkner's penchant for using the medium to preach a series of lay sermons is invoked. Poets go wrong in vaguely predictable ways as they get older, but ageing novelists are full of surprises. The former often take some strain of themselves and perform a perverse, unwitting self-parody of it. *The Recluse* is a poor imitation of the gorgeous things in *The Prelude*; Tennyson's stammering account of the marriage in 'Enoch Arden' ('So these were wed and merrily rang the bells, / Merrily rang the bells and they were wed. / But never merrily beat Annie's heart'[11]) is a pedestrian echo of what was rendered so memorably in *In Memoriam*. In once great lyric poets, the falling off clearly has much to do with the loss of freshness that comes when the time gap between the intense feel of things experienced and the attempt to recapture it becomes too large. With bold and innovative novelists, things are different. Their late works are often flawed in a new, adventurous way. Thus we get the weird harangues of Tolstoy's *The Kreutzer Sonata*, the romantic clichés of Conrad's *The Rover*, the gratuitous violence of Lawrence's *The Plumed Serpent*, all of which seem somewhat unexpected. The new work is often so obviously inadequate when judged by the aesthetic criteria these novelists have established with their best that it makes their readers pause before they pronounce judgement. I agree with those who think that *A Fable* is an example of one of those ambitious late productions that is flawed in interesting ways and deserves to be judged accordingly.

This novel is in a sense an ideal text for anyone interested in Faulkner's thought, particularly on the question about the meaning of history. There are scores of passages in which he discusses conceptual issues, and lots of two-man conversations in which the ideas we have been discussing are taken up again in earnest. The problem is that, even if we proceed as if Faulkner means what he says by the title, i.e. that this is not a novel but a fable, just how to read it is not entirely clear. Not many fables run to 350+ pages or leave the reader feeling as baffled as this one does. The variety of modes used induces a kind of vertigo: great swatches of military scenes replete with tough, verisimilar dialogue, lyric accounts of swarming crowds, lengthy exchanges between self-confessed allegorical figures, tall tales, and enough allusions and symbolic parallels to keep source hunters happy for decades. Inferring from *A Fable* a set of criteria that can help determine how it should be judged and what place it deserves in Faulkner's *oeuvre* has proved almost as difficult as getting this book into print was.

The question of when the events are taking place is obviously crucial for the interrogation of human history that takes up so much of the novel. Having Christ return as a corporal in the French army to stop the most murderous encounter in human history grounds the text in a specific place and time, but often the actual historical events are sketched in very briefly because that is all a fable requires. The opening crowd scene in Paris, for example, featuring relatives coming to see the men who have refused to fight, illustrates this perfectly. It is 1918, but the reference to the soldiers who came from this very *quartier* in Napoleon's time gives the reader a sense of the same sort of historical continuity that Faulkner depends on in the Yoknapatawpha novels. Yet what is left out is just as important. There is no mention of the soldiers' role in Paris in 1848, or the way Thiers used them to murder the Communards in 1870. History is elided even as it is evoked, and we get what is essentially a mythic Paris, sketched in terms that reflect its fabled heroes and conquerors, rather than the messy Paris that, by virtue of its portable paving stones and radicalized workers, made life difficult first for Louis-Philippe and then for Louis-Napoleon. The point becomes even clearer when we are told that the crowd 'underswept the military, irresistible in that passive and invincible humility, carrying its fragile bones and flesh into the iron orbit of the hooves and sabres with an almost inattentive, a humbly and passively contemptuous disregard, like martyrs entering an arena of lions' (671). This is easier to understand if we think of the crowd as an entity like the flood from *If I Forget Thee, Jerusalem*: it speaks a symbolic language, moves in mysterious but carefully ordered ways, and does impossibly brave and uncrowd-like things, such as sliding quietly under horses' hooves while thinking of something else. For Faulkner this is simply more mythic characterization appropriate to the mode in which he is working at a given point in this multifaceted text.

One can see the same approach in regard to the ultra-courageous soldiers who contemplate violent death with equanimity. The perfect soldier is 'pastless' (684) we are told at one point, obviously because a lack of personal history makes him totally focussed on the present moment. But his pristine CV creates a problem for Faulkner: if he has no past, his creator is going to have trouble generating the requisite interest in his plight when he refuses to advance or when he is threatened with execution. Since these soldiers too are symbols of the heroic victims that are supposed to make this 'fable' resonate differently, Faulkner denies himself an opportunity to engage with the inimitable self and the concerns peculiar to it, which is of course one of his great subjects, while he wanders in more unfamiliar territory. Think Dostoevsky trying his hand at the meaning of history sections in *War and Peace*.

Peter Nicolaisen and Catherine Kodat have written convincing accounts of how *A Fable* might be read as a commentary on American democracy, American institutions, and America's Jeffersonian inheritance.[12] As always, it is the judicial branch of government, rather than the legislative or the executive, that most interests Faulkner when he thinks about his country. The presentation of the justice system in *A Fable* is arcane in its vocabulary and syntax and populist in its appeal, evocative in its search for the values of the past and contemptuous of the frailties that Americans must recognize in themselves. Again in this book, Faulkner plays on America's fascination with trials. The nation that gave us Sacco and Vanzetti, Leopold and Loeb, and O.J. Simpson has lots of famous legal processes in its literature too. They figure prominently in novels as different as *The Scarlet Letter*, *Billy Budd*, and *An American Tragedy*, and of course in Faulkner's work as well. The names of Dickens and Hugo are invoked during the judicial proceedings, no doubt for their great mob and trial scenes. The imaginations that could conjure up the riots in *Barnaby Rudge* or the trial of Esmeralda in *The Hunchback of Notre Dame* were particularly interesting for Faulkner. As public confrontations, they constitute moments in which abstract notions like justice are redefined by actuality. In *A Fable*, the mob in pursuit of the men accused of stealing a horse exists for the same reason that the mob in a Twain novel does, so that a thoughtful, haughty, courageous man like the lawyer can stand against them, which he duly does. As in Twain, an impassioned speech about human nature accompanies this confrontation, although here it is the narrative voice that does the explaining. The subject is the way war has been supplanted by trade agreements and exploitation, and servitude replaced by the right to sell one's labour for profit.

The actual courtroom scene in *A Fable*, in which the accused are compared to a long list of political and religious leaders including Christ and Napoleon, Talleyrand and Billy Sunday, imagined 'as a frieze or a tapestry' (833), is central for other reasons as well. As such language makes clear, the trial is in one sense another real-life version of the urn phenomenon, another way of arresting experience, trying to extract its essence, and pass judgement on it. Representatives from the crowd can participate in such a drama, but the crowd itself inevitably threatens to destroy the authorities' attempt to impose stillness on action. The emotions of the mob are too messy to be arrested, which explains why so

many trials in Faulkner are broken up by violence. The war and indus-
trialization become large-scale versions of the same concatenation of
forces, in which leaders like the ones mentioned in the frieze-like list try
to use the anonymous power of the mass to control it. Faulkner calls
them 'the hero-giant precentors of [humanity's] seething moil' (839).
A precentor is someone who leads a choir in singing, someone whose
job is similar to the one undertaken by the artist, but instead of turning
life's cacophony into unheard melodies, these choirmasters must be
content with whatever heard ones the mass can be taught.

Faulkner is keen to reinscribe the American story in world history and
equally interested in making American exceptionalism resonate with
the reader. This means trying to find answers to the questions asked in
Go Down, Moses and *Requiem for a Nun*: What does it mean to talk about
a virgin continent? Who owns it now? Where is it going? What is the
interplay between the energies of the early Americans and the systems
that were created to constrain them? For example, in the horse-racing
digression there is an allusion to 'the old fine strong American tradition
of rapine' (821) symbolized by John Murrell, a legendary horse thief
who worked in the area of America in which Faulkner situates his story
within a story.[13] Murrell mixed with freed slaves, had a father who was
a preacher, and created a series of legends around himself – the parallels
between him and the Christ figure in *The Fable* are obvious. Yet his career
does not so much parallel as parody the corporal's. There was a book
written about him that appeared in 1835, purporting to be his
confession, in which it was claimed among other things that Murrell
was the head of a mystic clan, the mastermind of a Negro rebellion, and
the would-be potentate of all Louisiana. This is believed by historians to
be almost totally a fabrication. In fact, there is no clear verdict on where
exactly he came from, where and when he operated, how big a gang he
had, how good they were at their profession, or what happened to him
in the end. Murrell's legend serves to remind readers that ultimately any
attempt to piece together the history of a family or a community is
bound to end in one of those infinite regresses that Faulkner so brilliantly depicts, where we go back into the past in search of the truth and
all we find is story, or rather more stories.

A series of references to an authoritarian conspiracy organized to keep
the masses comfortable in their ignorance and the soldiers fighting for
economic reasons might lead to some sort of Marxist analysis in another
writer, but Faulkner is interested in using the corporal's efforts to stop
the war as a jumping off point for a discussion of humanity's spiritual
dilemma. The reader is immediately reminded of the conversation

between the Grand Inquisitor and Christ in *The Brothers Karamazov*, a book Faulkner knew well and often cited in interviews. In this novel, Jesus returns to Europe in sixteenth-century Spain.[14] He is arrested and interrogated by the Grand Inquisitor, who informs him that promising man freedom has ended up causing him endless anguish. Happiness means living with the oppression of being controlled by an earthly power that speaks in God's name. Miracle, mystery, and authority are the means by which the church exerts its control. Earthly bread for succour instead of spiritual bread for the soul is the only way to make humanity's plight bearable. The corporal's father, an army general, plays the Grand Inquisitor's role here, looking for the Christ figure to betray his followers, save his own life, and condemn the troops to the bondage from which he misguidedly tried to free them. He exudes power and confidence, knows the future, speaks of it with authority, and predicts the imminent end of the war and the shape of the peace. Like his counterpart in Dostoevsky, he offers freedom to the specially gifted individual only, and he scoffs at any suggestion that man can cope with more than this or should want anything else. He too insists that men are not heroic. If they rebel spontaneously it is only to fall back more ignominiously.

Like the narrator in *The Town* and Gavin Stevens in *Intruder in the Dust*, the general dramatizes his point of view by doing what Gavin Stevens does in *Intruder in the Dust*, looking back and down on the lights of a town from a position that reveals the patterns of the past. He goes on to talk about what is at stake: power in the earthly realm, power to declare war, to make men fight, and to convince them that ideals like universal peace will never be realized by something as paltry and piecemeal as personal initiative. We know who is going to win the argument, in the sense of say the most words, since the dialogue becomes a monologue pretty quickly. What we do not know is how much the silence or non-participation of the corporal signifies assent. The general is a subtle persuader, and he takes aim at the very idea of martyrdom, i.e. tries to get at the corporal where he is most vulnerable, by insisting that life as an absolute good. The palpable, sensuous thisness of breathing itself is what is on offer. The general does his best to convey the attractiveness of this world, not by painting it in its gaudiest colours, or in offering his interlocutor a crude version of its riches, but in choosing the most ethereal of its denizens, a bird in full song, and pointing out how the loss of something so seemingly trivial should force the corporal to think long and hard before accepting it. Significantly, the bird is indigenous to Mississippi, not to the foul mud of a foreign country. In such passages, Faulkner marries abstract idea and idiosyncratic style most successfully.

The central speech, the one that illustrates the fundamental disagreement between father and son and hence the dualistic world view that Faulkner explores in the novel, is the general's characterization of the differences between them:

> we are two articulations self-elected possibly, anyway elected, anyway postulated, not so much to defend as to test two inimical conditions which, through no fault of ours but through the simple paucity and restrictions of the arena where they meet, must contend and – one of them – perish: I champion of the mundane earth which, whether I like it or not, is, and to which I did not ask to come, yet since I am here, not only must stop but intend to stop during my allotted while; you champion of an esoteric realm of man's baseless hopes and his infinite capacity – no: passion – for unfact.
>
> (988)

This is both confused and inaccurate. Confused, because what the general denies his behaviour asserts. He says that all this is 'through no fault of ours', and yet his argument implies at every stage that human beings including him and his son are responsible for the choices that they make. Inaccurate, because the accounts of the two opposing positions are so tendentious. The general actually argues for an ideal that is anything but earthbound. He appeals to a shared sense of honour, deplores the merely materialistic, and champions an absolute definition of freedom. And the corporal's martyrdom is inextricably bound up with earthly concerns. He recognizes and implicitly admires mankind's ability to endure, takes the stand that he is not fighting for some abstract ideal but trying to save lives, and seems utterly different from the rather contemptible figure the general dismisses for his capacity for 'unfact'. The corporal knows the facts, and that is why he keeps bringing the general back to them.

A related problem with the discussion is the link between the spiritual and the material in Faulkner's view. Are they inimical or not? In one sense obviously not, since all those thousands in the division cling to life because they crave breathing as much as the general does, but are also perfectly capable of entertaining notions that are more exalted than mere breathing, patriotic fervour, a desire to protect one's loved ones, and so on. In Faulkner's work, a passion for the world and a recognition of the ideals that it engenders, ideals about which one can be just as passionate, routinely exist side by side. Nor is it clear why man's hopes should be 'baseless'. *A Fable* offers many examples of those hopes, and makes it clear that what makes the people who harbour them so worthy of compassion is that they represent something undying in the struggle for freedom that Faulkner has chosen to chronicle.

Towards the end of the discussion between the two men, the attention shifts to the threat that made Faulkner write *The Fable* in the first place, not the menace of another war, but the spectre of robotic man working as a slave to his own base desires – for money, for self-aggrandizement – in a mechanical peace. From his privileged vantage point, the general does a proleptic tour of the 1950s, with its air-conditioned cars, asphalt expanses, denuded suburbia, mod cons, and a panoply of armaments that make things like soldiers anachronistic. Why die for a lost cause now, he says, when this history awaits the species in whose name such a sacrifice is undertaken? The argument is fleshed out with two particularly impressive flourishes. First there is a sci-fi vision of man's future in which 'he will crawl shivering out of his cooling burrow to crouch among the delicate stalks of his dead antennae like a fairy geometry, beneath a clangorous rain of dials and meters and switches and bloodless fragments of metal epidermis' (994), to watch the monsters he has created duke it out. On the strength of this account, Faulkner could have kept his job as a scriptwriter in twenty-first-century Hollywood. The other set of details brought forward to support the general's argument is a paraphrase of Faulkner's Nobel acceptance speech inserted in the text at this crucial juncture. The noble Nobel sentiments that so stirred the world in the mouth of the cynical realist? Yes, but the general argues that pride rather than compassion is what will make man prevail. However we read that, the corporal, man's heroic defender, ends up without a lot of room to argue for his constituency. His answer, or rather non-answer, to this proposition that man will prevail precisely because of his self-destructiveness and pride, resembles Christ's reply to the Grand Inquisitor as well, although instead of a silent kiss the general gets a simple refusal and a goodbye. The effect of this version of notlanguage in Dostoevsky is ambiguous: the inquisitor is 'answered' by Christ's gesture of love, and all his compelling arguments relegated to the area where only arguments matter. Yet Ivan Karamazov insists that the old man keeps his idea. The effect in Faulkner is similarly unclear: the old man keeps his idea, although the priest he sends to take up the argument again shows how determined the father is to save his son.

Between the priest and the corporal, the question of earthly versus spiritual bread comes up yet again, and the priest, like the inquisitor, opts for the earthly solution. Faulkner even has the priest take the reader on a quick tour of Christian history. Christ's intercession, according to the priest, had an egalitarian impulse at its heart: his sacrifice exempted mortal man from 'suzerainty over human fate and destiny' (1002), effectively freeing him of taking responsibility for his freedom. Faulkner likes this word 'suzerainty' (it comes up in related contexts in *Go Down, Moses* and at the end of *The Town*), and he uses it twice here to conflate the notions of political power and the control of personal destiny, an important subject in all the novels under consideration in this chapter thus far. The priest mocks Christ's plan to build his church 'on this rock', i.e. on his disciple Peter, a man with high ideals, and suggests Paul with his shrewd sense of the strength of human weakness would have been a better choice. Facing up to the shortcomings of the species discourages those tempted to indulge in grand reflections on humanity's fate.

The debate concludes, the corporal dies, the people mourn, his followers cannot stand up to the instruments of temporal power. But all this is inconclusive, as of course it must be, given Faulkner's refusal to countenance an apocalyptic ending, his recognition that humans have a lot of enduring to do before they can even think about prevailing. The flaw in *A Fable*, such as it is, is perhaps the thing that kept Faulkner at it for such a long time, his belief that it could ever be finished. Raising such far-reaching religious and political questions condemned him to producing an open-ended text. The last sound we hear on the last page is human laughter, the voice of the English message runner, a man maimed and mistreated, too crippled even to be a poor forked animal, laughing as if to acknowledge the ironic gap between noble aims and actual results. Seeking to rally the ordinary citizens, he has turned them into his bitter enemies. His attempt to tell them the truth about the war has left them convinced he is a traitor. His laughter locates the world of *A Fable* as equidistant 'between the bizarre and the terrible', between comedy and tragedy. But he too insists, despite all his bitterness, that the story is not over.

In the 1950s, intellectuals' interest in constructing plausible alternatives to the ideals of Western democracy was still undiminished, so Faulkner's willingness to take on in a single book the will to power and the will to believe might well have seemed less audacious to his contemporaries than it does to us. Having to invent the form in which to try such a thing merely exacerbated the difficulties. It may have been a gamble that did not quite pay off, but it won him a Pulitzer Prize, not as a lifetime achievement award, or as the result of a conspiracy to honour a cold warrior, or for having supplied Americans with a dull treatise stuffed full of homilies, but as a tribute to a writer willing to try to extend the possibilities of the novel form by using it to assess the spiritual status of Western culture.

Three things stand out when one thinks about the appropriateness of *The Reivers* as a conclusion to Faulkner's career. The first is that sympathetic reviewers immediately compared it to *The Adventures of Huckleberry Finn*, while unsympathetic ones said it was no such thing. If more proof were needed that this is a writer judged by special criteria, surely this is it. Faulkner's 19th novel either was on the level of something universally acknowledged to be a world classic, or it was not. In the end, readers decided that it was not, quite, but – and this is the second thing that stands out – Faulkner was rightly credited for doing something that he had never attempted before, namely having written a novel in which the author arrogates to himself the right to set a new, more relaxed tone, impose a happy ending, and banish the terrible from his purview. Finally, the idea of writing a reminiscence, working with yet another new form, makes Faulkner four for four in so far as innovation in the novels under consideration here is concerned. It is a Twainlike reminiscence of sorts. Faulkner's hero Lucius Priest certainly resembles Huck Finn, with his hypertrophied sense of responsibility, innocent eagerness to defend women from insult, ability to dupe adults at will and adapt plans to circumstances, and general likeability. But their situations are a little different. Huck is fleeing civilization, Lucius is learning to live with it. Twain's hero holds a man's life in his hands and makes a decision that commits him to the idea of equality that he has slowly internalized. Faulkner's is a rich man's son who does not have to function in Huck's world yet, and the lessons he learns involve a code that only adults can articulate.

The Reivers constitutes an interesting coda to the books we have been looking at in this chapter. The nation's historical trajectory is still the topic. Faulkner's narrator is worried about a mechanized, impersonal, over-developed America, but speaks of it in a lower key. He complains at one point that there are too many cars and too many people generally:

> humanity will destroy itself not by fission but by another beginning with f which is a verb-active also as well as a conditional state; I wont see it but you may: a law compelled and enforced by dire and frantic social – not economic: social – desperation permitting a woman but one child as she is now permitted but one husband.
>
> (193)

This is reminiscent of but more temperate than Gavin Stevens's inveighing in *Intruder in the Dust* against the American male's sexual obsession with his automobile. It is the good-natured grumpiness of the aged, and conveys how in a book as firmly situated in the land of wish fulfillment as this one, where the whores have hearts of gold, and boys extricate themselves from impossibly complex predicaments with amazingly clever ploys, the irretrievable past looks much more attractive than the gloomy future.

The narrator's mature voice wanders into that past to recall some family legends, including a story about a mule. Faulkner is intrigued by these creatures because he associates their slow, repetitive movements with the dreamy side of human consciousness and with humanity's capacity for endurance. The mule is identified with the stupefaction induced by mindless routine in *Soldiers' Pay*, assigned the task of transporting a sensuous woman in a dream vision in Faulkner's unfinished novel 'Elmer', and praised in *Sartoris* as a symbol of the patient resistance of the South after the war. There it is said to stand for absence of desire, utter isolation, and malign misanthropy, its nature misunderstood, its labour unremarked, and its passing unmourned. This creature makes a farewell appearance in one of the most successful comic scenes in *The Reivers*, the one in which Lucius, Boon, and Ned get their stolen car stuck in the mud and have to pay to have it pulled out. The scene gives Faulkner a last chance to dramatize another sleepy encounter between a timeless realm and one where people are in a hurry, 'the peacefully swish and stamping at the teeming infinitesimal invisible myriad life' of the mule's world compared to 'the expensive useless mechanical' (794) movement, or rather non-movement of the machine.

There are other links worth exploring, but *The Reivers* is finally quite different from its predecessors, in the sense that Faulkner keeps the serious reflection to a minimum here. The section in which Lucius ranks animals according to intelligence contains a disquisition on 'the anguishes of mortality – famine, plague, war, injustice, folly, greed – in a word, civilised government', but not a lot is made of these things, and the indictment of contemporary America is again good-humoured. The bad things in *The Reivers* are all outside, in the person of a couple of handy villains, not inside tearing characters apart. Revealingly, the definition of intelligence offered in the text is 'to accept environment yet still retain at least something of personal liberty' (823). It is a compromise announcement, entirely in keeping with the mood and action of a nostalgic reverie. Given the fascinating struggles in all the novels in which the characters refuse to be intelligent in this sense, and the imaginative energy Faulkner invested in recreating them, he had earned the right to take his mind off the darker side of 'civilised government' for a while and to let the comic forces for good make the appropriate accommodations.

The multifaceted and open-ended fiction of this period in Faulkner's career would seem to militate against grand conclusions, and I shall avoid them here. By choosing such large and varied subjects and using such a range of new forms to fit them, he made his task difficult during his last two decades, but that is par for the course. Obviously not all the new things he tried were equally successful, but the temptation to characterize late he as undigested moralizing and gloomy proof of waning powers generally should be resisted. The crowning moment of his literary career, the Nobel acceptance speech in which he does opt for the homiletic and the hortatory, is instructive in this regard.

At the Nobel Banquet in the Stockholm City Hall on 10 December 1950, having already received their awards at the official ceremony held earlier that day, Faulkner and eight other winners made speeches at a dinner for a thousand people. As recollected by Dr Philip Hench, a winner of the prize in medicine that year for his discovery of cortisone, it was a daunting affair. During and after dinner, trumpets would sound announcing the next speaker, a name would be read out, and the recipient would 'rise from the head table, walk up eleven marble steps to a rostrum on the first landing, then turn and face the awesome assemblage'. Dr Hench quotes Faulkner as having quipped on the occasion: 'They make you earn the prize all over again.'[15] Bertrand Russell, the 1950 winner for Literature, spoke first; Faulkner, chosen for the 1949 prize that had not been awarded, spoke last. Russell's speech was entitled 'What Desires are Politically Important?'. After a brief assessment of the most significant ones, acquisitiveness, rivalry, vanity, thirst for power, and love of excitement, Russell summarized the problems caused by these all too human traits. He insisted that humanity's mental makeup was 'suited to a life of very severe physical labour', and lamented the sedentary quality of modern existence, speculating that if people were to walk 25 miles a day, they would be less likely to 'assemble in Trafalgar Square to cheer to the echo an announcement that the government has decided to have them killed.'[16] Russell concluded his speech on what he offered as an optimistic note, suggesting that because so many of the problems he raised had to do with intelligence, we can place our hope in our system of education and build a world that keeps us safe from the worst consequences of our desires.

Faulkner never recorded his impressions of this speech, but it must have struck him as curiously relevant to his own reflections and as somewhat naïve. His view of mankind's predicament as expressed in his Nobel address is superficially similar to Russell's: we have got ourselves into a mess that threatens the annihilation of the entire planet, he begins, and we must do something to get ourselves out of it. Faulkner's optimism is based, not on his faith in the existence of our basic intelligence, or on his belief in a species capable of reason that needs educating, or on a plan for keeping the world safe, but on our capacity for feeling that includes compassion. His characters make active use of their ratiocinative abilities in all those impassioned discussions about who they are and where they have come from, and those abilities reveal a lot about the hidden springs of their behaviour and their individual and collective pasts. But it is the other ways of knowing, the ones based on 'the truths of the human heart', that Faulkner emphasizes here. For the purposes of the occasion, and to make it easier for himself to end on an upbeat note by celebrating the immortality of the species as he saw it, Faulkner left out egoism, jealousy, fear, despair, and so on, the truths of the heart that he had so often studied in his work. Nonetheless, his was and is a timely message. In light of what has happened in the years since 1950, we can hardly pretend that the secrets of that particular organ have yielded themselves up to our dispassionate analysis. They give every sign of being, in all their antirational complexity, as difficult to understand as consciousness itself. Faulkner's willingness to contemplate that particular truth and to say such interesting things about it is what earned him the invitation to Stockholm in the first place.

Since he made his famous speech, few twentieth-century novelists have enjoyed such an extensive and diverse readership. The successive generations that have interested themselves in Faulkner's work are as dedicated to reading for pleasure as they are to exploring the issues that have made it the centre of critical attention for so long. With so many stimulating questions still hovering around his novels, it seems foolhardy to try to predict the next stage of Faulkner's career. All the 'fierce and rigid concentration' that characterizes them is a sign of his extraordinary and multifaceted ability, and of his fascination, not only with the life of the mind as he understood it, but also with the plurality of possibilities that reveal themselves when one makes it an object of study. Readers willing to conjure with all this and to approach his work with the requisite patience and humility should ensure him a very long literary life indeed.

Notes

1 Introduction

1. Northrop Frye articulates and develops this idea in *Fables of Identity* (New York: Harcourt Brace and World, 1963), p. 222.
2. *Selected Letters of William Faulkner*, ed. Joseph Blotner (New York: Random House, 1977), p. 185.
3. *Faulkner in the University*, eds. Frederick L. Gwynn and Joseph Blotner (Charlottesville: University Press of Virginia, 1977), p. 53.
4. *Letters*, p. 166.
5. 'In Memory of W.B. Yeats', *Collected Shorter Poems: 1927–1957* (London: Faber and Faber, 1966), p. 141.
6. See Lawrence Schwartz, *Creating Faulkner's Reputation: The Politics of Modern Literary Criticism* (Knoxville: University of Tennessee Press, 1988).
7. *Letters*, p. 285.
8. *Lion in the Garden: Interviews with William Faulkner 1926–1962*, eds. James B. Meriwether and Michael Millgate (New York: Random House, 1968), p. 238.
9. At the height of his fame in 1955, when he agreed to visit Japan at the request of the State Department to attend a seminar on English and American literature, he hoped that any reference to his being a writer would be avoided and that he could go as simply a 'private individual'. See Joseph Blotner, *Faulkner: A Biography* (New York: Random House, 1984), p. 600. This book is still an indispensable guide for those interested in Faulkner's life and I have drawn extensively on it.
10. *Letters*, pp. 382, 185; *Faulkner in the University*, p. 39. See Frederick Crews, 'The Strange Fate of William Faulkner', *The New York Review of Books*, 38, 5 (7 March 1991), pp. 47–52 for a detailed summary of various issues at stake in Faulkner criticism.
11. Vladimir Nabokov, *Strong Opinions* (New York: McGraw-Hill, 1973), p. 155.
12. *Lion in the Garden*, p. 250.
13. *Letters*, pp. 215–6.
14. *Love and Death in the American Novel* (New York: Criterion Books, 1960), p. 309.
15. 'Where was that Bird? Thinking America Through Faulkner', *Faulkner in America* (Jackson: University Press of Mississippi), pp. 98–115, p. 104.
16. *The Ink of Melancholy: Faulkner's Novels from 'The Sound and the Fury' to 'Light in August'* (Bloomington and Indianapolis: Indiana University Press, 1990), p. 355. I am greatly indebted to this book.
17. *Faulkner in the University*, p. 117.
18. *Lion in the Garden*, p. 255.
19. *Mythologies* (New York: Macmillan, 1959), p. 336.
20. Unless otherwise noted, all references are to the Library of America edition of Faulkner's novels and included parenthetically in the text.
21. 'The Soul of Man Under Socialism', *Complete Works of Oscar Wilde* (London and Glasgow: Collins, 1948), p. 1049.

2 Early Faulkner

1. 'Books and Things: Joseph Hergesheimer', *William Faulkner: Early Prose and Poetry*, ed. Carvel Collins (Boston and Toronto: Little, Brown, 1962), p. 102.
2. *I Canti*, ed. Luigi Rosso (Florence: G.C. Sansoni, 1974), p. 335. There is a slight misquotation in Faulkner's version: the last noun needs no definite article.
3. *Linda Condon* (Toronto: S.B. Gundy, 1919), pp. 31–4.
4. *Faulkner in the University*, p. 207.
5. *The Marble Faun and A Green Bough* (New York: Random House, 1960).
6. Vladimir Nabokov, *Pale Fire* (New York: Vintage, 1989), p. 202.
7. *William Faulkner: His Life and Work* (Baltimore: Johns Hopkins University Press, 1980), p. 36.
8. Judith Sensibar, 'Introduction' to *Vision in Spring* (Austin: University of Texas Press, 1984), ix.
9. *Charles Dickens* (New York: Schocken Books, 1965), p. 68.
10. *The Origins of Faulkner's Art* (Austin: University of Texas Press, 1984), p. 166. Sensibar is arguing against Cleanth Brooks's dismissive description of the poem, *William Faulkner: Toward Yoknapatawpha and Beyond* (New Haven and London: Yale University Press, 1978), p. 13.
11. *Early Prose and Poetry*, pp. 90–2.
12. 'Matthew Arnold's New Poems', Vol. 5 (Prose Works), p. 117, and 'An Autumn Vision', Vol. 6 (Poetical Works), p. 96, *The Complete Works of Algernon Charles Swinburne*, eds. Edmund Gosse and Thomas James Wise (New York: Russell and Russell, 1925), pp. 115, 96.
13. *Uncollected Stories*, ed. Joseph Blotner (New York: Random House, 1979).
14. *The Achievement of William Faulkner* (New York: Random House, 1966), p. 65. This book is still one of the most useful ever published on Faulkner.
15. *Origins of Faulkner's Art*, p. 36.
16. Duane J. MacMillan, '"Carry on, Cadet": Mores and Morality in *Soldiers' Pay*', in ed. Glenn O. Carey, *Faulkner: The Unappeased Imagination* (Troy, NY: Whitston Publishing, 1980), pp. 39–58, p. 48, and Daniel Singal, *William Faulkner: The Making of a Modernist* (Chapel Hill: University of North Carolina Press, 1997), p. 65.
17. Ralph Waldo Emerson, 'Nature', *Essays and Lectures* (New York: Library of America, 1983), p. 10.
18. *One Matchless Time: A Life of William Faulkner* (New York: HarperCollins, 2004), p. 100.
19. 'A Portrait of the Artist', eds. Richard M. Kain and Robert E. Scholes, *Yale Review*, 49 (Spring 1960), pp. 360–6, p. 360.
20. *A Portrait of the Artist as a Young Man* (New York: Viking, 1965), p. 214.
21. John S. Duvall, 'Faulkner's Crying Game: Male Homosexual Panic', *Faulkner and Gender*, eds. Donald M. Kartiganer and Ann J. Abadie (Jackson: University Press of Mississippi, 1996), pp. 48–72, p. 55, sees the aerial battle in psychosexual terms: 'Each time a German dives on the decoy plane, Bayard responds. To do what? To meet the German in a much mythologized but seldom enacted face-to-face dogfight? No, to penetrate him from the rear.'
22. 'A Valediction: Forbidding Mourning', *John Donne's Poetry*, ed. Arthur L. Clements (New York and London: W.W. Norton, 1997), p. 31.

23. Just before Bayard dies, there is a scene in which blacks congregate 'in shadowy beds among the dry whispering cane-stalks' where 'youths and girls murmured and giggled' (781). For a comprehensive discussion of Faulkner's stereotypical depiction of blacks, see the exchange in successive issues of *Connotations*: Arthur F. Kinney, 'Faulkner and Racism', *Connotations*, 3.3 (1993–4), pp. 265–78; Pamela Knights, 'Faulkner's Racism: A Response to Arthur F. Kinney', *Connotations*, 4.3 (1994–5), pp. 283–99; John Cooley, 'Faulkner, Race, Fidelity', *Connotations*, 4.3 (1994–5), pp. 300–12; Philip Cohen, 'Faulkner and Racism: A Commentary on Arthur F. Kinney's "Faulkner and Racism"', *Connotations*, 5.1 (1995–6), pp. 108–18; Arthur F. Kinney, 'Author's Commentary', *Connotations*, 5.1 (1995–6), pp. 119–24; Arthur F. Kinney, 'Faulkner and Racial Mythology', *Connotations*, 5.2–3 (1995–6), pp. 259–75.
24. *John Keats*, ed. Elizabeth Cook (New York: Oxford University Press, 1990), p. 288.
25. *Lion in the Garden*, p. 255.

3 Major Achievement I

1. See, for example, David Lodge, 'The Language of Modernist Fiction: Metaphor and Metonymy', *Modernism 1890–1930*, eds. Malcolm Bradbury and James McFarlane (Harmondsworth: Penguin, 1976), pp. 481–98.
2. *Contingency, Irony, and Solidarity* (Cambridge: Cambridge University Press, 1989), p. 36. Freud's idea that civilizations develop like individuals and can become neurotic, that the links between unreason and waking rationality are important, and that with a lot of therapeutic work we can trade recurrent plunges into extreme human misery for ordinary, everyday unhappiness all suggest useful ways of engaging with Faulkner's novels.
3. *The Complete Poems and Plays, 1909–1950* (New York: Harcourt, Brace, 1952), p. 58.
4. Bergson claims that tragedians avoid references to their hero's body so as not to lose the tragic effect. He adds that Napoleon saw that 'the transition from tragedy to comedy is effected simply by sitting down', *Laughter: An Essay on the Meaning of the Comic*, trans. Cloudesley Brereton and Fred Rothwell (New York: Macmillan, 1937), pp. 51–2.
5. *Dostoevsky's 'Crime and Punishment': Murder as Philosophic Experiment* (Edinburgh: Scottish Academic Press for Sussex University Press, 1978), p. 120.
6. In revising the ms., Faulkner added in a number of places 'Father said' to make the exchange clearer for the reader.
7. For a fascinating account of the links between Quentin's idea of incest and American nativist culture in the 1920s, see Walter Benn Michaels, *Our America: Nativism, Modernism, and Pluralism* (Durham and London: Duke University Press, 1995), pp. 1–16. Michaels argues that nativism and modernism are both 'efforts to work out the meaning of the commitment to identity – linguistic, national, cultural, racial' (p. 3).
8. *The Bodley Head G.K. Chesterton*, ed. P. J. Kavanagh (London: The Bodley Head, 1985), p. 275.

9. 'Experience', *Essays*, p. 473.
10. If one chooses to read these conversations as in part imaginary, then Quentin himself becomes responsible for masochistically torturing himself here. Faulkner said that Quentin and his father never discussed incest, but that still leaves a number of questions about this exchange unanswered. For a closely argued, much harsher view of Quentin, see Bleikasten, *Ink of Melancholy*, pp. 71ff. He concludes by dismissing Quentin as a 'moral moron' (p. 123).
11. 'An Introduction to *The Sound and the Fury*', *Mississippi Quarterly*, 26 (1973), pp. 410–5, p. 414, and quoted in James B. Meriwether, 'The Textual History of *The Sound and the Fury*', *Merrill Studies in 'The Sound and the Fury'* (Columbus, Ohio: Charles E. Merrill, 1970), p. 5.
12. *Macbeth* 5.5.21, in *The Riverside Shakespeare* (Boston: Houghton Mifflin, 1974), p. 1337.
13. For a different view of Dilsey see Deborah Clarke, *Robbing the Mother: Women in Faulkner* (Jackson: University Press of Mississippi, 994), pp. 34–5: 'Dilsey's idealized status as a madonna/mammy denies her both subjectivity and sexuality, and thus robs her of the mother's pervasive power, her control over being and language.'
14. Bleikasten, *Ink of Melancholy*, p. 155. Eric Sundquist argues that 'the form of *As I Lay Dying* ... astutely challenges [the assumption of] a narrative consciousness formed by a supposed union between the author and his language, a union formalized and made conventional by the standard device of omniscient or at least partly omniscient, narration, which the novel explicitly discards and disavows', *Faulkner: The House Divided* (Baltimore and London: Johns Hopkins University Press, 1983), p. 29. In a book about the disjunction between self and identity, this narrative disjunction is thematically appropriate.
15. 'Anthony Trollope', *The Art of Fiction and Other Essays* (New York: Oxford University Press, 1948), p. 60.
16. *Roland Barthes par Roland Barthes* (Paris: Seuil, 1975), p. 178.
17. See Panthea Reid Broughton, 'The Cubist Novel: Toward Defining the Genre', *'A Cosmos of My Own'*, eds. Doreen Fowler and Ann J. Abadie (Jackson: University Press of Mississippi, 1981), pp. 36–58.
18. Bleikasten, *Ink of Melancholy*, p. 194.

4 Major Achievement II

1. Bleikasten, *Ink of Melancholy*, p. 215.
2. Rebecca West, Review of *Sanctuary*, in *Faulkner: The Critical Heritage*, ed. John Earl Bassett (Boston and London: Routledge and Kegan Paul, 1975), p. 117.
3. Albert Guerard, *The Triumph of the Novel: Dickens, Dostoevsky, Faulkner* (New York: Oxford University Press), p. 131, describes this passage as one of the number of 'momentary extravagances', and deplores the inclusion of Horace's hyper-literary monologues as well. He notes that, generally speaking, 'the educated consciousness in Faulkner is at a disadvantage ... as against the earthy or laconic talk of the blacks and Ratliff', but it is unclear from the context whether he means that it causes such figures to lose stature with the reader or lose confrontations with their interlocutors.
4. 'Circles', *Essays*, p. 401.

5. *Letters*, p. 17.
6. *Moral Literacy: or, How to do the Right Thing* (London: Duckworth, 1992), p. 16.
7. Gerald Langford, *Faulkner's Revision of 'Sanctuary': A Collation of the Unrevised Galleys and the Published Book* (Austin and London: University of Texas Press, 1972), p. 22, calls this 'a loose end that is vaguely irritating.'
8. *Shelley: Poetical Works*, ed. Thomas Hutchinson (London: Oxford University Press, 1968), p. 670.
9. In 'Human Universals, Literary Representation, and the Biology of Mind', *New Literary History* 31.3 (2000), pp. 553–72, Alan Richardson offers a historical explanation of the fact that the Romantics idealized brother–sister incest, but arranged tragic ends for those who transgressed this taboo. See also John T. Irwin, 'Horace Benbow and the Myth of Narcissa', *American Literature*, 64, 3 (Sept 1992), pp. 543–66.
10. *Faulkner in the University*, p. 74.
11. *Lion in the Garden*, p. 221.
12. Edmond Volpe, *A Reader's Guide to William Faulkner* (New York: Farrar, Straus and Giroux, 1964), p. 168n, notes that Joe may be older by this point. See Singal, *Making of a Modernist*, p. 238, for a much more sympathetic view of this character: 'by the final stage of life [Joe Christmas] verged on becoming a black Christ capable of showing the South a path to possible redemption through the integration of racial identities he had achieved within his own being.'
13. See David Williams, *Faulkner's Women: The Myth and the Muse* (Montreal and London: McGill-Queen's University Press, 1977), p. 162; and Bleikasten, *Ink of Melancholy*, pp. 286–90.
14. Fredric Jameson, *Postmodernism, or The Cultural Logic of Late Capitalism* (Durham: Duke University Press, 1991), p. 133, argues in this regard that 'Faulkner's style took the situation of memory itself as its formal precondition: the violent action or gesture in the past; a vision that fascinates and obsesses storytellers who cannot but commemorate it in the present and yet who must project it as a complete tableau – "motionless" as well as "furious", "breathless" in the stillness of its agitation, and compelling "stupor" and "amazement" in the viewer.'
15. Laura Doyle, 'The Body against Itself in Faulkner's Phenomenology of Race', *American Literature*, 73, 2 (2001), pp. 339–64, p. 361, reads the passage as 'an uncloseable moment', a 'prayer, enmeshed in the tragic sublime of the body that provokes and escapes our names for it.'
16. *John Keats*, p. 289.
17. A further conflation confirms this, as the language makes clear that Hightower and Christmas, the priest and the pagan, the compassionate and the compassionless, are also to be identified with each other. 'I wanted so little', Hightower says, echoing the man whose death he tried unsuccessfully to prevent, and as he says it we read of a 'final flood which had rushed out of him, leaving his body empty and lighter than a forgotten leaf' (431), just as Joe disappears in the bloodletting that accompanies his ending.
18. *These 13* sold well. These days the going price for a copy of the first edition is $2500. Jonathan Cape provided it with a front cover blurb by Arnold Bennett: 'An American who writes like an angel.'
19. All references to Faulkner's short fiction are to his *Collected Stories* (New York: Random House, 1950).

20. See Millgate, *Achievement*, pp. 263–4.
21. 'Desire and Dismemberment: Faulkner and the Ideology of Penetration' in *Faulkner and Ideology*, eds. Donald M. Kartiganer and Ann J. Abadie (Jackson: University Press of Mississippi, 1995), pp. 129–71, p. 141. Claiming that 'Ideology is about words, representations, naming', Jones sees McLendon as 'a victim of Southern ideology too'. By lashing out violently at his wife, just as Mayes does against his attackers, 'in the register of gender, he fails to control both consent and coercion, ideology and force', and we leave him naked and sweating, 'pressed not against his wife (which within the ideology would be a sign of success) but, impotent, against a dusty screen on a dark porch' (142–3). The pairing is a bold one, but it seems risky to equate the desperate violence of a man about to be murdered with that of someone turning on his wife for some imagined dereliction of duty. Calling both men victims of an ideology suggests a real equivalence, which may compel us to ignore the moral choices coded in the text.

5 Two Views of History

1. John Duvall, *Faulkner's Marginal Couple: Invisible, Outlaw, and Unspeakable Communities* (Austin: University of Texas Press, 1990), p. 82; Reynolds Price, *Pylon, Awake and Sing!,* and the Apocalyptic Imagination', *Criticism*, 13 (1971), pp. 131–41, p. 138; Richard Pearce, Introduction to *Pylon* (New York: Signet, 1968), vi.
2. *The Education of Henry Adams: An Autobiography* (Boston: Houghton Mifflin, 1946), p. 382.
3. 'Test Pilot', *Essays, Speeches and Public Letters*, ed. James B. Meriwether (New York: Random House, 1966), pp. 188–92. When he tries to imagine the pilots of tomorrow, he sees them as sexless, 'not game chicken but capons' (p. 191). This is curious, because he refers briefly to Francesco Agello, who set a record of 711 km/h on an Italian seaplane in 1934, a record that still stands for piston-engined seaplanes. He and his fellow pilots were a breed apart in a sense, but their macho courage was their most distinguishing characteristic, particularly in view of the almost certain death that awaited test pilots and racers in this era. Faulkner usually writes admiringly about male heroism, and the testosterone-inspired kind as much as any. The comment about 'capons' suggests an important qualification in his feelings for the new pilots, a sense that he is writing against a part of himself, and that he is trying to imagine a different sort of being altogether.
4. For those like J.M. Coetzee who think that Faulkner's alcoholism is *the* mystery that none of his biographers has ever explained satisfactorily, such a sentence must be tantalizing. Blotner is, as always, very sensible and helpful on the subject. See *Faulkner*, pp. 225–9. Doreen Fowler speculates that Faulkner's 'epic drunkennesses, when read for their symbolic significance, ... reveal a desire to return [to the mother]', '"I want to go home": Faulkner, Gender, and Death', *Faulkner and Gender*, pp. 3–19, p. 12.
5. Hugh Ruppersburg notes that the epithets create 'an hallucinatory atmosphere which seems to shimmer and change, stripping familiar objects and

scenes of their familiarity, puzzling the reader with the source and meaning of their foreignness', 'Image as Structure in Faulkner's *Pylon*', *South Atlantic Review*, 47, 1 (1982), pp. 74–87, p. 76.
6. *John Keats*, p. 288.
7. *Education of Henry Adams*, p. 381.
8. '*Pylon*, Joyce, and Faulkner's Imagination', *Faulkner and the Artist*, eds. Donald M. Kartiganer and Ann J. Abadie (Jackson: University Press of Mississippi, 1996), pp. 181–207, p. 188.
9. *The Complete Poems and Plays of T.S. Eliot* (London: Faber and Faber, 1969), p. 21.
10. 'Against Narrativity', *Ratio*, 17.4 (2004), pp. 428–52. Strawson's claim has stimulated a great deal of discussion. See, for example, Walter L. Reed and Marshall P. Duke, 'Personalities as Dramatis Personae: An Interdisciplinary Examination of the Self as Author', *Common Knowledge*, 11, 3 (2005), pp. 502–13; James Phelan, 'Who's Here? Thoughts on Narrative Identity and Narrative Imperialism', *Narrative* 13, 3 (2005), pp. 205–10; and James Battersby, 'Narrativity, Self, and Self-Representation', *Narrative*, 14, 1 (2006), pp. 27–44.
11. 'Against Narrativity', pp. 437–43.
12. See John T. Irwin, *Doubling and Incest/Repetition and Revenge: A Speculative Reading of Faulkner* (Baltimore and London: Johns Hopkins University Press, 1975), pp. 148–51, for a suggestive and detailed reading of the biblical parallels with the novel.
13. The domination of male voices in the novel has been much discussed. See Minrose Gwin, *The Feminine and Faulkner: Reading (Beyond) Sexual Difference* (Knoxville: University of Tennessee Press, 1990), pp. 104–5, who argues that 'these voices encode the sexual politics of patriarchy by silencing women as speaking subjects within its narrative of mastery', but holds out the hope we can hear 'the mad voice of Faulkner's own text' that '*speaks out of* a feminine silence which men created but which men cannot control.'
14. Noting the oddity of Faulkner's using 'fault' as an adjective, John T. Matthews, *The Play of Faulkner's Language* (Ithaca: Cornell University Press, 1982), p. 15, observes that 'Faulkner arrests us at the site of a misusage or neologism – kindly violences performed by the writer on the common tongue – in order to accent the exercise of invention that the passage endorses.'
15. 'Ideology and Topography in *Absalom, Absalom!*', *Faulkner and Ideology*, pp. 253–76, p. 275. For a quite different view of the relation between Quentin and Shreve, see Irwin, *Doubling and Incest*, p. 120: 'For Quentin realizes that by taking revenge against his father though a substitute, by assuming the role of active teller (father) and making Shreve be the passive listener (son), he thereby passes on to Shreve the affront of sonship, the affront of dependency.'
16. For an insightful account of how national myths can affect our understanding of history, see Sacvan Bercovitch, *The Rites of Assent: Transformations in the Symbolic Construction of America* (New York and London: Routledge, 1993), pp. 1–9.
17. *Prophets of Extremity* (Berkeley: University of California Press, 1985), p. 346. Rorty has some suggestive things to say on the subject of life's necessary incompleteness and attempting to generalize with the vocabulary of self-creation. See *Contingency*, pp. 118–20.

6 More Experiments with the Novel

1. *Achievement*, p. 169.
2. Patricia Yeager, 'Faulkner's "Greek Amphora Priestess": Verbena and Violence in *The Unvanquished*', *Faulkner and Gender*, pp. 197–227, pp. 207, 211, notes that this makes Drusilla 'a vessel ritualizing and containing regional trauma' and 'a site of transference for the most clichéd and intractable of her society's desires ... a somatic battlefield for the race and class struggles that mark Faulkner's understanding of the postbellum South'. She therefore reads the prose in this scene as 'mesmerizing', the hyperbole as parodic, and the characterization as something that becomes more and more compelling while the plot becomes more absurd.
3. *Munera Pulveris* (Chicago and New York: Bedford, Clarke, n.d.), p. 23.
4. *Faulkner in the University*, p. 42.
5. *William Faulkner's 'The Wild Palms': A Study* (Jackson: University Press of Mississippi, 1975), pp. 27–32.
6. McHaney, *'The Wild Palms'*, p. 103, suggests that the 'fluxive Yes' here is 'simply that affirmation of life expressed in the process of generation', yet Harry sees this affirmation in purely solipsistic terms.
7. Those who have read parts of Harry's story as autobiographical make a particularly compelling case. See, for example, Richard Gray, *The Life of William Faulkner* (Oxford: Blackwell, 1994), pp. 248–53; and James G. Watson, *William Faulkner: Self-Presentation and Performance* (Austin: University of Texas Press, 2000), pp. 158–71.
8. See Cedric Watts, *A Preface to Conrad*, 2nd edn. (London and New York: Longman, 1993), pp. 115–6.
9. See, for example, Cleanth Brooks, *First Encounters* (New Haven: Yale University Press, 1983), pp. 160–74; Matthews, *Faulkner's Language*; and the most comprehensive study of the novel to date, Arthur F. Kinney, *Go Down, Moses: The Miscegenation of Time* (New York: Twayne, 1996).
10. *Achievement*, p. 214.
11. *Robert Frost: Poetry and Prose*, eds. Edward Lathem and Lawrance Thompson (New York: Holt, Rinehart and Winston, 1972), p. 145.
12. *John Keats*, pp. 288–9. For a detailed commentary on 'Ode on a Grecian Urn', to which I am indebted here, see Cedric Watts, *A Preface to Keats* (London and New York: Longman, 1985), pp. 132–7.
13. See Bertrand Russell, *A History of Western Philosophy* (New York: Simon and Schuster, 1947), pp. 691–2.
14. See John Johns, *Wonders of the Stereoscope* (London: Cape, 1976).
15. See Bleikasten, *Ink of Melancholy*, pp. 280–2, for a different reading of the urn's message in relation to the allusions in *Light in August*.

7 The Snopes Trilogy

1. *Lectures on Russian Literature*, ed. Fredson Bowers (New York and London: Harcourt Brace Jovanovich, 1981), p. 238.
2. See Urgo, 'Where was that Bird?', *Faulkner and America*, p. 114, n. 12, for more on the subject of the significance of birdsong in Faulkner.

3. See Martin Kreiswirth, '"Paradoxical and Outrageous Discrepancy": Transgression, Auto-Intertextuality, and Faulkner's Yoknapatawpha', *Faulkner and the Artist*, pp. 161–80, for a stimulating discussion of the implications of Faulkner's flouting of convention.
4. *Selected Essays* (New York: Harcourt, Brace, and World, 1950), p. 380.
5. *Parodies: An Anthology from Chaucer to Beerbohm – and After*, ed. Dwight Macdonald (London: Faber and Faber, 1960), pp. 465, 467, 469.
6. *Heart in Conflict: Faulkner's Struggles with Vocation* (Athens: Georgia University Press, 1987), pp. 3–34. John Duvall, 'Faulkner's Crying Game', *Faulkner and Gender*, p. 69, suggests that 'Afternoon of a Cow' 'does not simply reproduce hegemonic stereotypes or reactionary images of women and effeminate men; the story also recognizes that masculinity is always inescapably an enactment, whether it is inflected in terms of the hegemonic norm (Farmer Faulkner) or of queer alternatives (Ernest V. Trueblood).'
7. See, for example, the brilliant spoof by Sam Apple, 'The Administration and the Fury', the winner of the 2005 Faux Faulkner contest, at http://www.slate.com/id/2113927/
8. *Faulkner in the University*, pp. 139–40.
9. James Boswell, *Life of Johnson*, ed. R.W. Chapman (London: Oxford University Press, 1966), p. 440.
10. Faulkner slightly misquotes Housman here. The actual lines are:

> Oh, when I was in love with you,
> Then I was clean and brave,
> And miles around the wonder grew
> How well did I behave.
>
> And now the fancy passes by,
> And nothing will remain,
> And miles around they'll say that I
> Am quite myself again.

It is poem XVIII from *A Shropshire Lad*, *The Poems of A.E. Housman*, ed. Archie Burnett (Oxford: Clarendon Press, 1997), pp. 19–20.
11. *The Picture of Dorian Gray*, p. 32.
12. Rorty speaks of 'Freud's claim that every human life is the working out of a sophisticated idiosyncratic fantasy', noting that 'no such working out gets completed before death interrupts. It cannot get completed because there is nothing to complete, there is only a web of relations to be rewoven, a web which time lengthens every day', *Contingency*, pp. 42–3.
13. Noel Polk, 'Faulkner: The Artist as Cuckold', *Faulkner and Gender*, pp. 20–47, p. 46, points out: 'In his late career, Faulkner seems to understand that men cannot claim their own histories until women can claim theirs, too, and tell their stories themselves: if they choose and in their own voices, their own language, without yielding to the cultural narrative that binds us all to a singular story too often reducible to sexual pathology.'
14. Millgate, *Achievement*, p. 247.

15. William Cullen Bryant, *Complete Works* (New York: AMS Press, 1969), p. 23.
16. The phrase 'democracy of the dead' is Chesterton's definition of tradition, *Chesterton*, p. 256.

8 Late Faulkner

1. For example, Singal describes Faulkner in 1941 as 'about to enjoy a long reign banging out his preachy messages at the keyboard', *Making of a Modernist*, p. 261.
2. The phrase is Milan Kundera's from *The Art of the Novel*, trans. Linda Asher (New York: Grove Press, 1986), p. 14.
3. *The Stubborn Structure: Essays on Criticism and Society* (London: Methuen, 1970), p. 220.
4. *Reading Faulkner* (Madison: University of Wisconsin Press, 1989), p. 224.
5. Patrick Samway, S.J., '*Intruder in the Dust*: A Re-evaluation', *Gathering of Evidence: Essays on William Faulkner's 'Intruder in the Dust'*, eds. Michel Gresset & Patrick Samway (Philadelphia: St. Joseph's University Press and New York: Fordham University Press, 2004), pp. 189–223, pp. 196–7.
6. Polk has ably traced the twists and turns in Faulkner's 1950s commentary on the race question in 'Man in the Middle: Faulkner and the Southern White Moderate', in *Children of the Dark House: Text and Context in Faulkner* (Jackson: University Press of Mississippi), pp. 218–41. Faulkner's defence of moderation, refusal to identify with Gavin Stevens, temptation to identify with Gavin Stevens, resistance to stereotyping, belief in the equality of blacks, belief in the inferiority of blacks, courageous espousal of contempt for violence, and reluctant admission that Southern whites might have to resort to violence are all lucidly dealt with in Polk's even-handed analysis. See also Thadious M. Davis, *Faulkner's 'Negro': Art and the Southern Context* (New Orleans: Louisiana State University Press, 1983), and Theresa Towner, *Faulkner on the Color Line* (Jackson: University Press of Mississippi, 2000).
7. *Faulkner's 'Requiem for a Nun': A Critical Study* (Bloomington: Indiana University Press, 1981), p. 52.
8. Timothy Snyder, 'The Old Country', *Times Literary Supplement*, 5 March 2005, p. 32. In the 2006 mid-term elections, only 25% of Mississippians bothered to vote, the lowest turnout in the country. As early as *Soldiers' Pay*, Faulkner expressed his concerns about rampant consumerism. In a note added to the typescript, he glossed a line about acquiring 'unnecessary things' with the comment: 'And that is already the curse of our civilization – Things. Possessions, to which we are slaves', *William Faulkner Manuscripts 3*, Vol II, Ribbon Typescript (New York and London: Garland, 1987), p. 79.
9. *Faulkner's 'Requiem for a Nun'*, p. 62.
10. See E. O. Hawkins, Jr, 'Jane Cook and Cecilia Farmer', *Mississippi Quarterly*, 18 (Fall 1965), pp. 248–51; and Polk, '*Requiem for a Nun*', pp. 264–5, n. 7.
11. *Tennyson's Poetry*, ed. Robert W. Hill, Jr (New York: W.W. Norton, 1971), p. 262.
12. Peter Nicolaisen, 'William Faulkner's Dialogue with Thomas Jefferson', and Catherine Gunther Kodat, 'Writing *A Fable* for America', *Faulkner in America*, pp. 64–81 and 82–97.

13. See James L. Penick, *The Great Western Land Pirate: John A. Murrell in Legend and History* (Columbia: University of Missouri Press, 1982).
14. Philip Blair Rice, 'Faulkner's Crucifixion', *William Faulkner: Three Decades of Criticism*, eds. Frederick J. Hoffman and Olga W. Vickery (New York: Harcourt, Brace and World, 1960), pp. 373–81, p. 379, contains a useful commentary on the parallel with Dostoevsky. In the same volume, see also Heinrich Strauman, 'An American Interpretation of Existence: Faulkner's *A Fable*', pp. 349–72.
15. http://nobelprize.org/award_ceremonies/ceremony_sthlm/eyewitness/hench/index.html
16. *Human Society in Ethics and Politics* (London: George Allen and Unwin, 1954), p. 167.

Further Reading

All of Faulkner's novels are now available in the five-volume, corrected text Library of America edition (1985–2006), eds. Joseph Blotner and Noel Polk. *Collected Stories*, first published by Random House in 1950, was reissued as a Vintage paperback in 1995, ed. Erroll McDonald. *Uncollected Stories* was published by Random House in 1979 and by Vintage in1997, ed. Joseph Blotner. The 44-volume set *William Faulkner Manuscripts* (1984–87) was produced by Garland, eds. Joseph Blotner, Thomas L. McHaney, Michael Millgate, and Noel Polk. Faulkner's poetry, screenplays, essays, speeches, interviews, and letters are widely available. The largest collection of Faulkner's papers, manuscripts, typescripts, and letters is housed at the University of Virginia. Archives and Special Collections at the University of Mississippi Libraries has a superb collection of Faulkner books and many valuable early manuscripts. Other important Faulkner materials can be found at the Brodsky Faulkner collection at Southeast Missouri State University's Kent Library, the University of Texas in Austin's Harry Ransom Humanities Research Center, the Special Collections department in Tulane University's Howard-Tilton Library, and the William Faulkner Collection at the University of Michigan.

Important books on Faulkner's life and work include the following (I have omitted studies of individual novels):

Atkinson, Ted. *Faulkner and the Great Depression: Aesthetics, Ideology, and Cultural Politics*. Athens: University of Georgia Press, 2006.
Bauer, Margaret. *William Faulkner's Legacy: 'What Shadow, What Stain, What Mark'*. Gainesville: University Press of Florida, 2005.
Beck, Warren. *Faulkner: Essays*. Madison: University of Wisconsin Press, 1976.
Bleikasten, André. *The Ink of Melancholy: Faulkner's Novels from 'The Sound and the Fury to 'Light in August'*. Bloomington: Indiana University Press, 1990.
Blotner, Joseph. *Faulkner: A Biography*. New York: Random House, 1974; rev. ed. 1984.
Bockting, Ineke. *Character and Personality in the Novels of William Faulkner: A Study in Psychostylistics*. Lanham, MD: University Press of America, 1995.
Brodsky, Louis Daniel. *William Faulkner: Life Glimpses*. Austin: University of Texas Press, 1990.
Brooks, Cleanth. *William Faulkner: First Encounters*. New Haven: Yale University Press, 1983.
———. *William Faulkner: The Yoknapatawpha Country*. New Haven: Yale University Press, 1963.
———. *William Faulkner: Toward Yoknapatawpha and Beyond*. New Haven: Yale University Press, 1978.
Carothers, James B. *William Faulkner's Short Stories*. Ann Arbor: UMI Research Press, 1985.
Claridge, Henry, ed. *William Faulkner: Critical Assessments*. Robertsbridge: Helm Information, 1999.

Clarke, Deborah. *Robbing the Mother: Women in Faulkner.* Jackson: University Press of Mississippi, 1994.

Cox, Leland H. *William Faulkner: Biographical and Reference Guide.* Detroit: Gale Research, 1982.

Davis, Thadious M. *Faulkner's 'Negro': Art and the Southern Context.* Baton Rouge: Louisiana State University Press, 1983.

Dowling, David. *William Faulkner.* New York: St. Martin's Press, 1989.

Doyle, Don H. *Faulkner's County: The Historical Roots of Yoknapatawpha.* Chapel Hill: University of North Carolina Press, 2001.

Duvall, John N. *Faulkner's Marginal Couple: Invisible, Outlaw, and Unspeakable Communities.* Austin: University of Texas Press, 1990.

Fargnoli, A. Nicholas and Michael Golay. *William Faulkner A to Z: The Essential Reference to His Life and Work.* New York: Checkmark Books, 2002.

Fowler, Doreen. *Faulkner: The Return of the Repressed.* Charlottesville: University Press of Virginia, 1997.

Godden, Richard. *Fictions of Labor: William Faulkner and the South's Long Revolution.* Cambridge: Cambridge University Press, 1997.

Gray, Richard J. *The Life of William Faulkner: A Critical Biography.* Cambridge, MA: Blackwell Publishers, 1994.

Gresset, Michael. *A Faulkner Chronology,* trans. Arthur B. Scharff. Jackson: University Press of Mississippi, 1985.

Grimwood, Michael. *Heart in Conflict: Faulkner's Struggles with Vocation.* Athens: University of Georgia Press, 1987.

Gwin, Minrose C. *The Feminine and Faulkner: Reading Beyond Sexual Difference.* Knoxville: University of Tennessee Press, 1990.

Hahn, Stephen and Robert A. Hamblin, eds. *Teaching Faulkner: Approaches and Methods.* Westport, CT: Greenwood Press, 2000.

Hamblin, Robert W. and Charles A. Peek, eds. *A William Faulkner Encyclopaedia* Westport, CT: Greenwood Press, 1999.

Harrington, Gary. *Faulkner's Fables of Creativity: The Non-Yoknapatawpha Novels.* Athens: University of Georgia Press, 1990.

Hlavsa, Virginia V. James. *Faulkner and the Thoroughly Modern Novel.* Charlottesville: University Press of Virginia, 1991.

Hoffman, Daniel. *Faulkner's Country Matters: Folklore and Fable in Yoknapatawpha.* Baton Rouge: Louisiana State University Press, 1989.

Hönnighausen, Lothar. *Faulkner: Masks and Metaphors.* Jackson: University Press of Mississippi, 1997.

Howe, Irving. *William Faulkner: A Critical Study.* New York: Random House, 1952.

Inge, M. Thomas, ed. *William Faulkner: The Contemporary Reviews.* Cambridge: Cambridge University Press, 1995.

Irwin, John T. *Doubling and Incest/Repetition and Revenge: A Speculative Reading of Faulkner.* Baltimore: Johns Hopkins University Press, 1975.

Jehlen, Myra. *Class and Character in Faulkner's South.* New York: Columbia University Press, 1976.

Karl, Frederick R. *William Faulkner: American Writer.* New York: Weidenfeld and Nicolson, 1989.

Kartiganer, Donald M. *The Fragile Thread: The Meaning of Form in Faulkner's Novels* Amherst: University of Massachusetts Press, 1979.

Kinney, Arthur F. *Faulkner's Narrative Poetics: Style as Vision.* Amherst: University of Massachusetts Press, 1978.

Kreisworth, Martin. *William Faulkner: The Making of a Novelist.* Athens: University of Georgia Press, 1983.

Labatt, Blair. *Faulkner the Storyteller.* Tuscaloosa: University of Alabama Press, 2005.

LaLonde, Christopher A. *William Faulkner and the Rites of Passage.* Macon: Mercer University Press, 1995.

Matthews, John T. *The Play of Faulkner's Language.* Ithaca and London: Cornell University Press, 1982.

McHaney, Thomas L. *William Faulkner: A Reference Guide.* Boston: G.K. Hall, 1976.

Millgate, Michael. *Faulkner's Place.* Athens: University of Georgia Press, 1997.

——. *The Achievement of William Faulkner.* New York: Random House, 1966.

Minter, David. *William Faulkner: His Life and Work.* Baltimore: Johns Hopkins University Press, 1980.

Moreland, Richard C. *Faulkner and Modernism: Rereading and Rewriting.* Madison: University of Wisconsin Press, 1990.

Morris, Wesley and Barbara Alverson Morris. *Reading Faulkner.* Madison: University of Wisconsin Press, 1989.

Mortimer, Gail L. *Faulkner's Rhetoric of Loss: A Study in Perception and Meaning.* Austin: University of Texas Press, 1983.

Oates, Stephen B. *William Faulkner: The Man and the Artist.* New York: HarperCollins, 1987.

Parker, Robert Dale. *Faulkner and the Novelistic Imagination.* Urbana: University of Illinois Press, 1985.

Parini, Jay. *One Matchless Time: A Life of William Faulkner.* New York: HarperCollins, 2004.

Peck, Charles A. and Robert W. Hamblin, eds. *A Companion to Faulkner Studies.* Westport, CT: Greenwood Press, 2004.

Polk, Noel. *Children of the Dark House: Text and Context in Faulkner.* Jackson: University Press of Mississippi, 1996.

Railey, Kevin. *Natural Aristocracy: History, Ideology, and the Production of William Faulkner.* Tuscaloosa: University of Alabama Press, 1999.

Roberts, Diane. *Faulkner and Southern Womanhood.* Athens: University of Georgia Press, 1994.

Rollyson, Carl E. Jr. *Uses of the Past in the Novels of William Faulkner.* Ann Arbor: International Scholars Publications, 1984.

Ross, Stephen M. *Fiction's Inexhaustible Voice: Speech and Writing in Faulkner.* Athens University of Georgia Press, 1989.

Ruppersburg, Hugh M. *Voice and Eye in Faulkner's Fiction.* Athens: University of Georgia Press, 1983.

Schwartz, Lawrence H. *Creating Faulkner's Reputation: The Politics of Modern Literary Criticism.* Knoxville: University of Tennessee Press, 1988.

Singal, Daniel J. *William Faulkner: The Making of a Modernist.* Chapel Hill: University of North Carolina Press, 1997.

Skei, Hans Hanssen. *William Faulkner: The Novelist as Short Story Writer.* Oslo: Universitetsforlaget, 1985.

Slatoff, Walter J. *Quest for Failure: A Study of William Faulkner*. Ithaca and London: Cornell University Press, 1960.

Stonum, Gary Lee. *Faulkner's Career: An Internal Literary History*. Ithaca and London: Cornell University Press, 1979.

Sundquist, Eric J. *Faulkner: The House Divided*. Baltimore: Johns Hopkins University Press, 1983.

Taylor, Walter. *Faulkner's Search for a South*. Urbana: University of Illinois Press, 1983.

Towner, Theresa M. *Faulkner on the Color Line: The Later Novels*. Jackson: University Press of Mississippi, 2000.

Vickery, Olga W. *The Novels of William Faulkner: A Critical Interpretation*. Baton Rouge: Louisiana State University Press, 1964.

Volpe, Edmond L. *A Reader's Guide to William Faulkner*. New York: Farrar, Straus, & Giroux, 1964.

Wadlington, Warwick. *Reading Faulknerian Tragedy*. Ithaca and London: Cornell University Press, 1987.

Watson, James Gray. *William Faulkner: Letters and Fictions*. Austin: University of Texas Press, 1987.

——. *William Faulkner: Self-Presentation and Performance*. Austin: University of Texas Press, 2000.

Weinstein, Philip M. *Faulkner's Subject: A Cosmos No One Owns*. Cambridge: Cambridge University Press, 1992.

——, ed. *The Cambridge Companion to William Faulkner*. Cambridge: Cambridge University Press, 1992.

Williams, David. *Faulkner's Women: The Myth and the Muse*. Montreal and London: McGill-Queen's University Press, 1977.

Williamson, Joel. *William Faulkner and Southern History*. Oxford: Oxford University Press, 1993.

Wittenberg, Judith. *Faulkner: The Transfiguration of Biography*. Lincoln: University of Nebraska Press, 1979.

Zender, Karl F. *Faulkner and the Politics of Reading*. Baton Rouge: Louisiana State University Press, 2002.

——. *The Crossing of the Ways: William Faulkner, the South, and the Modern World*. New Brunswick: Rutgers University Press, 1989.

There is the 'Annotations to the Novels' series, published by Garland (New York). Titles include:

Annotations to William Faulkner's 'A Fable' (ed. Nancy Butterworth, 1989).

Annotations to William Faulkner's 'Mosquitoes' (ed. Edwin T. Arnold, 1989).

Annotations to William Faulkner's 'Pylon' (ed. Susie Paul Johnson, 1989).

Annotations to William Faulkner's 'Sanctuary' (ed. Melinda McLeod Rousselle, 1989).

Annotations to William Faulkner's 'As I Lay Dying' (ed. Dianne C. Luce, 1990).

Annotations to William Faulkner's 'Soldiers' Pay' (ed. Margaret J. Yonce, 1990).

Annotations to William Faulkner's 'Absalom, Absalom!' (ed. David Paul Ragan, 1991).

Annotations to William Faulkner's 'Go Down, Moses' (ed. Nancy Drew Taylor, 1994).

Annotations to William Faulkner's 'The Hamlet' (ed. Catherine D. Holmes, 1996).

Annotations to William Faulkner's 'The Town' (ed. Merrill Horton, 1996).

The 'Reading Faulkner' series, published by the University Press of Mississippi (Jackson). Titles include:

Reading Faulkner: 'Light in August' (ed. Hugh Ruppersburg, 1994).
Reading Faulkner: 'The Unvanquished' (eds. James Hinkle and Robert McCoy, 1995).
Reading Faulkner: 'Sanctuary' (eds. Edwin T. Arnold and Dawn Trouard, 1996).
Reading Faulkner: 'The Sound and the Fury' (eds. Stephen M. Ross and Noel Polk, 1996).
Reading Faulkner: 'Collected Stories' (eds. Teresa M. Towner and James B. Carothers, 2006).

The 'Critical Essays on American Literature' series, published by G.K. Hall (Boston), ed. Arthur F. Kinney. Titles include:

Critical Essays on William Faulkner: The Compson Family (1982).
Critical Essays on William Faulkner: The Sartoris Family (1985).
Critical Essays on William Faulkner: The McCaslin Family (1990).
Critical Essays on William Faulkner: The Sutpen Family (1996).

The conference proceedings of the Faulkner and Yoknapatawpha conference, the most important annual gathering of Faulkner scholars, have been published annually by University Press of Mississippi (Jackson) since 1974. Conference topics include:

'Faulkner and Women' (1985).
'Faulkner and Race' (1986).
'Faulkner and the Craft of Fiction' (1987).
'Faulkner and Popular Culture' (1988).
'Faulkner and Religion' (1989).
'Faulkner and the Short Story' (1990).
'Faulkner and Psychology' (1991).
'Faulkner and Ideology' (1992).
'Faulkner and the Artist' (1993).
'Faulkner and Gender' (1994).
'Faulkner in Cultural Context' (1995).
'Faulkner and the Natural World' (1996).
'Faulkner at 100: Retrospect and Prospect' (1997).
'Faulkner in America' (1998).
'Faulkner and Postmodernism' (1999).
'Faulkner in the 21st Century' (2000).
'Faulkner and War' (2001).
'Faulkner and His Contemporaries' (2002).
'Faulkner and the Ecology of the South' (2003).
'Faulkner and Material Culture' (2004).
'Faulkner's Inheritance' (2005).
'Global Faulkner' (2006).
'Faulkner's Sexualities' (2007).
'Faulkner: The Returns of the Text' (2008).

There is also the American Novel series (Cambridge University Press), the Modern Critical Interpretations series, edited by Harold Bloom (Chelsea House),

Twayne's Masterworks series (Twayne Publishers), and the Twentieth Century Interpretations series (Prentice Hall), all of which contain multiple volumes on Faulkner.

Faulkner's work is massively present on the Internet as well. John B. Padgett's extraordinarily comprehensive 'William Faulkner on the Web' is the best place to begin: http://www.mcsr.olemiss.edu/~egjbp/faulkner/faulkner.html

This site contains information on every aspect of Faulkner's life and art, as well as many other links. These include:

The Mississippi Writers Page: William Faulkner (University of Mississippi Department of English): http://www.olemiss.edu/mwp/dir/faulkner_william/

The William Faulkner Foundation (Rennes University, Rennes, France): http://www.uhb.fr/faulkner/wf/index.htm

The Center for Faulkner Studies (Southeast Missouri State University): http://www.semo.edu/cfs/ (includes online exhibits from the Brodsky Faulkner Collection: http://www6.semo.edu/cfs/brodsky_collection.htm and the Teaching Faulkner Newsletter: http://www6.semo.edu/cfs/teaching_faulkner.htm)

The William Faulkner Society: http://www.olemiss.edu/depts/english/faulkner//

The William Faulkner Society of Japan: http://www.isc.senshu-u.ac.jp/~thb0559/faulkner.htm (includes the online *Faulkner Journal of Japan*: http://www.isc.senshu-u.ac.jp/~thb0559/fjournal.htm)

The Faulkner Journal (The University of Central Florida): http://www.english.ucf.edu/faulkner/

The Faulkner Email Discussion: md@listserv.olemiss.edu

Faulkner and Yoknapatawpha Conference: http://www.outreach.olemiss.edu/events/faulkner/

The William Faulkner Collections (Special Collections at University of Virginia Library): http://www.lib.virginia.edu/small/collections/faulkner/

The William Faulkner Collection/Rowan Oak Papers (Special Collections at University of Mississippi Library): http://www.olemiss.edu/depts/general_library/files/archives/guides/faulknerlink/faulklink.html

Elizabeth Getz's 'A Faulkner Pathfinder' is also excellent: http://www.unc.edu/~egetz/faulkner.html#Bibliographies

Its annotations of a range of secondary material and web resources are particularly useful.

There is a hypertext version of *The Sound and the Fury* available at http://www.usask.ca/english/faulkner/

Index